13 11313

BLAKE'S PRELUDE

BLAKE'S PRELUDE

Poetical Sketches

ROBERT F. GLECKNER

THE JOHNS HOPKINS UNIVERSITY PRESS
BALTIMORE AND LONDON

The Johns Hopkins University Press, Baltimore, Maryland 21218
The Johns Hopkins Press Ltd., London

Library of Congress Cataloging in Publication Data
Gleckner, Robert F.
Blake's prelude.
Includes bibliographical references and index.
1. Blake, William, 1757-1827. Poetical
sketches. I. Title.
PR4144.P63G5 1982   821'.7   82-47976
ISBN 0-8018-2850-3   AACR2

Title page illustration: engraving from
William Blake's *For Children: The
Gates of Paradise,* 1793.

For Karran and Kristen
and Joseph Michael

CONTENTS

ACKNOWLEDGMENTS

THE RESEARCH FOR, and writing of, this book have been supported by a summer stipend from the National Endowment for the Humanities, a grant-in-aid from the American Council of Learned Societies, and several research grants from the Duke University Research Council. The latter stages of the manuscript's revision were completed during an extra-ordinary year's sabbatical leave awarded me by Duke University, a more-than-welcome time when I also enjoyed the generous support of a National Endowment for the Humanities Research Fellowship. It is difficult for me to estimate when this book might have seen the light of day had I been without such largesse. But it is those other debts, to colleagues and friends, simple acknowledgment of which on a page such as this seems always so inadequate, so baldly routine. "How wide the Gulf & Unpassable between Simplicity & Insipidity," as Blake said. I hope so, for I turn here to the sort of simple thanks that, one hopes, will carry the burden of the deep heart's core: for more than they may know, to Joseph Anthony Wittreich, Stuart Curran, David V. Erdman, Morton Paley, Morris Eaves, David Wagenknecht, Leigh DeNeef, Wallace Jackson, Mary Lynn Grant, Robert N. Essick, Neil Fraistat, Jim Springer Borck—and to my most valued life-long colleagues and cheerleaders, Stanley N. Stewart and Hugo Rodríguez-Alcalá. And to Earl R. Wasserman, who will never know. My typists, Deborah Gilliland and Josephine Ellis, I could not have asked more of; and my wife, Glenda, already knows that there would be no book without her.

Early versions of two of my chapters, reshaped, revised, and amplified, appeared previously as "Blake's Seasons," *Studies in English Literature* 5 (1965): 533-51, and "Antithetical Structure in Blake's *Poetical Sketches*," *Studies in Romanticism* 20 (1981): 143-62.

BLAKE'S PRELUDE

INTRODUCTION

In 1783, when *Poetical Sketches* was printed in circumstances now well detailed by Michael Phillips,[1] Blake was neither a youth nor untutored, the volume's "Advertisement" to the contrary notwithstanding. He had completed a seven-year apprenticeship to James Basire, engraver to the London Society of Antiquaries, had studied at the Royal Academy under G. M. Moser, had assiduously followed the progress of the American Revolution (as Erdman has shown us in impressive detail), and had married. Even more important, he was well on the way to a single-mindedly dedicated artistic career which, despite our present lack of "proof," must have included steady attention to, and practice in, poetic, as well as his better documented graphic, enterprises. Similarly, it is inconceivable that, having written the poems we now know as *Poetical Sketches* (the latest of which, on scanty evidence, have been assumed to date from about 1778-79[2]), he would have ceased his pursuit of verbal art until 1785-89, the period in which, if we can so interpret the appearance in *An Island in the Moon* of three early versions, the *Songs of Innocence* were most likely composed. His early interest and wide reading in the English poetic tradition is abundantly evident in the *Poetical Sketches* volume, as well as in his own brief later comments on his early mentors: "Milton lov'd me in childhood and shew'd me his face. / Ezra came with Isaiah the Prophet, but Shakespeare in riper years gave me his hand"; further, "terrors appear'd in the Heavens above / And in Hell beneath, & a mystery & awful change threatened the Earth. / The American war began. All its dark horrors passed before my face / Across the Atlantic. . . ."[3]

Although this thumbnail autobiography has often been alluded to, its implications for Blake's early poetic career have not been taken as fully into account as they might. That Milton was in his consciousness and imagination "from the beginning" has become a commonplace, and Blake's word "childhood" here, governing as it does both Milton and the biblical prophets, serves as a powerful antidote to the fawning preface to *Poetical Sketches*. We all know what Isaiah is about, but we tend to forget that the book of Ezra opens with the God-given charge to Cyrus to build God's house in Jerusalem. And, Ezra adds,

> Who is there among you of all his people? his God be with him, and let him go up to Jerusalem, which is in Judah, and build the house of the LORD God of Israel, (he is the God,) which is in Jerusalem. (1:3)

This house, Ezra further tells us, is the one "builded these many years ago" by Solomon.[4] Such building, or rebuilding, of the ancient house of the Lord we have come to associate, properly, with Blake's prophecies—as, indeed, he himself has taught us. In the justly celebrated prefatory poem to *Milton,* England is the ancient site of Jerusalem, its "mountains green" and "pleasant pastures" the place of "the holy Lamb of God." Blake's task as prophet is the "Mental Fight" that will destroy the "dark Satanic Mills" constructed on the ruins of the house of the Lord, and build "Jerusalem / In Englands green & pleasant Land."[5]

To apply this mature expression of Blake's prophetic mission to *Poetical Sketches* seems on the surface an absurd and vain enterprise, especially given the apparent derivativeness of that volume's contents: the Thomsonian seasons poems, the Spenserian diurnal poems, the Percyan Gothic ballad *Fair Elenor,* the Elizabethan songs, the Chattertonian *Gwin, King of Norway,* the eighteenth-century Spenser imitation, the Shakespearean *King Edward the Third,* the Ossianic prose poems, and the Miltonic *Samson.* Add to these the distinct evidence of Collins, Gray, Akenside, the Wartons, Beattie, and of course the Bible, and we have what Eliot called, setting the tone and direction of all further commentary on the *Sketches,* "what the poems of a boy of genius ought to show, immense power of assimilation . . . , quite mature and successful attempts to do something small."[6] While Eliot has often been misinterpreted here as saying that Blake in the *Sketches* was imitative rather than assimilative, he is nevertheless quite wrong about Blake's attempting something "small." In an otherwise strained and unsatisfactory discussion of the volume, John Ehrstine is more nearly correct in saying that Blake was attempting "to do something very large."[7] If that view has gained further credence through the work of McGowan, Tolley, and Phillips, not to mention Erdman's more specialized political approach,[8] the anticipative fallacy inherent in these respective studies, while not as ardently pursued as in Ehrstine, nevertheless still clouds the status of the *Poetical Sketches* as our only indication of Blake's poetic achievement circa 1777-83 without respect to what he produced after that.

The temptation to look forward to Blake's "maturer" works is virtually irresistible, as it is perhaps in any reading of a major poet's juvenilia or early "phase." Although Margaret Lowery over forty years ago opened the "windows of the morning" for us with a studious objectivity and avoidance of hindsight,[9] Frye's more influential *Fearful Symmetry* encouraged virtually all of his successors to find the four zoas, the female will, the covering cherub and other aspects of Blake's later myth at least embryonically present in the *Sketches*. Similarly, for all its excellence Erdman's analysis of the volume against the "background" of Blake's later *America*, in its very illumination of the intensity of Blake's awareness of and response to the politics of his age, often obscures the fundamental "completeness" of Blake's total poetic vision in 1777-83 as that incorporates, rather than being dominated by, the insistent ironies inherent in his political, economic, and social awareness. At the same time Erdman demonstrates conclusively the quite extraordinary maturity and complexity of Blake's handling of political themes, just as Tolley later establishes that "from the first, Blake's vision of an English spring is apocalyptic, that time when the holy feet again visit our clime"[10]—a vision found in and richly supported by his obviously assiduous and remarkably retentive reading of the Bible. To such poetry "assimilative" is but a poor—and seriously misleading—word to apply.

In the wake of Eliot's branding Blake a "boy" when he wrote *Poetical Sketches*, we have forgotten that however youthful he may have been, he was writing these poems at precisely the same time that he was a working apprentice to James Basire—or so we must assume if we accept Benjamin Heath Malkin's testimony as absolutely accurate.[11] According to Malkin, between the ages of ten and fourteen, when Blake was a student at Pars's drawing-school, he was given money by his father to buy prints either from print-dealers or at auctions.

> Langford called him his little connoisseur; and often knocked down to him a cheap lot, with friendly precipitation. He copied Raphael and Michael Angelo, Martin Hemskerck [i.e., van Heemskerk] and Albert Durer, Julio Romano, and the rest of the historic class, neglecting to buy any other prints, however celebrated. (P. 422)

Malkin goes on to point out that Blake was often ridiculed "by his youthful companions" for his unfashionable taste (ibid.). In his later advertisement of *A Descriptive Catalogue of Blake's Exhibition*, written in 1809 when Blake was fifty-two years old, he announced the return to England of "real Art, as it was left us by *Raphael* and *Albert Durer, Michael Angelo*, and *Julio Romano*"—that art, of course, his own "Poetical and Historical Inventions" in "the Ancient Method of Fresco Painting Restored."[12] The recurrence of these names like a refrain throughout Blake's writings about art is less remarkable, however, than the implicit conclusion one may draw from Malkin's assertion that even before he was fourteen Blake had embraced what, to him, these painters stood for—or, at the very least, stood against: an eighteenth-century worship of the art of classical antiquity. Those "other prints, however celebrated," that Blake refused to buy must surely have included products of that worship—as well as perhaps the "blots and blurs" and "Ignorances" of Rubens, Rembrandt, Titian, and Correggio.[13]

We must not, however, leap too fast, and imagine the fourteen-year-old Blake maturely conceptualizing a theory of art. Malkin reminds us that at the same time he was copying Raphael, Michelangelo, Dürer, and Romano he was also at Pars's "drawing from casts in plaster of the various antiques" (p. 422)—that is, Greek and Roman art. This apparent incompatibility of styles, however, is only apparent, for as Bindman remarks, it was the "Neoclassical artists and theorists in the 1770s and 1780s [who] were the first to rescue the Italian 'Primitives' from oblivion."[14] Yet there may be some significance in the fact that while Pars was setting him to the routine copying tasks standard in eighteenth-century drawing schools, and while Blake's father (again if we can credit Malkin's account) "bought for him the Gladiator, the Hercules, the Venus of Medicis, and various [no doubt classical] heads, hands and feet" (p. 422), Blake's own taste led him away from such "standards" in the auction rooms and printshops. Similarly his early reading, Malkin tells us, subordinated contemporary poets and their "elegance and delicacy" to "Shakespeare's Venus and Adonis, Tarquin and Lucrece, and his Sonnets," "Johnson's Underwoods and Miscellanies," "the book of Revelation," Milton, and "the devotional pieces of the Hebrew bards."[15] As a result his earliest poetry Malkin pronounces as assimilating "more with the bold and careless freedom, peculiar to our writers at the latter end of the sixteenth, and former part of the seventeenth century, than with the polished phraseology, and just, but subdued thought of the eighteenth" (p. 425).

Malkin's list is incomplete, of course, especially so when we recognize that he is talking about not only Blake's *Poetical Sketches* but *Songs of Innocence and of Experience* as well; and, if we read Malkin's account carefully, we see that his inclusion of Jonson is but a guess. Nevertheless, the collocation of Shakespeare, Milton, and the prophetic books of the Bible is as maturely "Blakean" as his copying of Michelangelo, Raphael, and Dürer. At fourteen, having joined Basire's shop, Blake obviously persisted in these offbeat interests, happily finding in his new master a "taste . . . like his own" (Malkin, p. 422). If that taste included literary works we have no way of knowing, but Basire did apparently recognize in his apprentice an already developed aesthetic sense unshared by the two other apprentices who joined his shop two years later. Thus, at sixteen Blake was set to drawing old buildings and monuments in which he apparently found corroboration for his artistic as well as perhaps his literary tastes. To the artists and poets already mentioned, then, we must now add Gothic architecture and ornament—the beginnings of Blake's lifelong championing of Gothic as true art, antipodal to the false art of the classics.

There have been a number of attempts, especially in recent years, to understand what Blake *really* saw in Gothic art that permitted him to blur its principles and contours into an aesthetic that embraced Milton, Spenser, and the Bible as well. While all these attempts do not quite agree in their particulars, at the core of each is consensus: Gothic was, in Bindman's words, characterized "by simplicity and purity of style" as well as, in the painter Romney's words, "strength of character and expression."[16] E. J. Rose says that to Blake the "Gothic revealed spiritual energy" in its embodiment of mental forms, an antinaturalistic art unlike that of Flemish or Venetian artists[17] — and, one might add, unlike the mathematical neatness of classical form with its verisimilitudinous imitation of nature. Gothic was also, Blake surely saw, a-temporal as well as a-spatial, an art of simultaneity that disrupted, if it did not destroy, the perspicuous temporal linearity of "modern" artistic practice and its classical precedents. In Burke's terminology (and Blake says that he read *The Sublime and Beautiful* early in his life) it was the art of the sublime standing over and against the orderliness of beauty. While this is not the place to discuss the intricacies of Blake's conception of the sublime and the beautiful (a subject, by the way, that deserves a good deal more study than it has received), his enthusiastic embracing of Michelangelo's giant forms, Shakespeare's "wildness" (to use the standard Enlightenment description), Spenser's "fairy way of writing," Milton's daring graces beyond the reach of art, and the biblical prophets' grandeur — however "conventional" such an embrace may be in terms of the developing aesthetics of the latter eighteenth century — is a strikingly mature development in the aesthetic life and thought of the youthful Blake.

There is little doubt that Thomas Warton's *Observations on the Fairy Queen of Spenser* and perhaps Hurd's *Letters on Chivalry and Romance,* not to mention other influential critical pronouncements of the time, had some bearing on the firmness of Blake's initial aesthetic convictions; but I find it difficult to believe that Blake was reading such things at fourteen to sixteen years of age. Committed early to the practice of literature as well as art, he was a doer rather than a conceptualizer — although it would be foolish to assume that the ideas expressed most fully later in his *Descriptive Catalogue* were not at least nascent in the context of that doing. For example, he surely knew that standard neoclassical decorum led to branding the Gothic as grotesque and unnatural, the same criterion indeed that underlies even the champion Malkin's chiding of Blake for his unrestraint in some of his verse, for being "not unfrequently betrayed . . . into so wild a pursuit of fancy, as to leave harmony unregarded, and to pass the line prescribed by criticism to the career of imagination" (p. 431).

The nature of that "career" is rather remarkably adumbrated by one of his first engravings, the *Joseph of Arimathea among The Rocks of Albion,* executed, he says, "when I was a beginner at Basires from a drawing by Salviati after Michael Angelo" (E660). Based on Michelangelo's fresco of the *Crucifixion of St. Peter* in the Pauline chapel, the *Joseph* displays the now familiar yoking of the great Renaissance painter-sculptor with the Bible, both of which Blake, in a later version of the engraving, fuses with the Gothic and true art in the legend he added: "This is One of the Gothic Artists who Built the Cathedrals in what we call the Dark Ages Wandering about in sheep skins & goat skins of whom the World was not worthy such were the Christians [i.e., the true artists] in all Ages."[18] Whenever this inscription was made (Keynes guesses "twenty years later, or more" — that is, about 1793[19]), the eighteenth-century conventionalized Druidism of the giant form of Joseph is substantial evidence of Blake's early conviction about the spiritual agency of history. Such spiritual agency was at the core of the nontemporal truth of Michelangelo, Milton (perhaps he had read the *History of Britain* already), and the Bible as manifest in the mythological art that was the product of his own "Gothicised imagination," as Malkin characterized it (p. 423).

Nevertheless 1773, when the *Joseph of Arimathea* was first executed, is far too early to credit Blake at sixteen with his later notion of the ancient originals of true art, of which the classics were mere (and inadequate) copies. But his experience at Basire's and with the Society of Antiquaries, whose commissions Basire's shop executed, did seem to lead him to consider "Gothic" as less a historical period or even a style than a perceptual mode, a state of mind so to speak, untrammeled by worldly facts and thus capable of seeing the infinite in all things — as Michelangelo, Milton, and the biblical prophets did. Although evidence for attributing such a belief to Blake at this time is sketchy at best, it seems to me insufficient to say, as Bindman does, that "Blake accepted the widespread eighteenth-century assumptions of the supremacy of Greek art" up into the 1790s.[20] While there is no doubt that Blake continued throughout his life "to make explicit references to classical and other formulae," indeed deliberately attempted to emulate those precious remains of antiquity, these formulae were to him but part of "the language of art."[21] The spirit, however, was in his head, with the result that however formula-laden his graphic work may seem to be — even in the early Gothic drawings and engravings — his fundamental iconoclasm as well as his imaginative power quickly led him to transform this received language into his own, even to the point of pitting that language against itself to reveal the truth that was hid. In his youthful poetic endeavors the same artistic processes are in evidence, Blake learning the language that he may better expose its inadequacies and false vision, and even turn it to ends as foreign to most of his models as Gothicism was to Michelangelo or Raphael or Dürer.[22] The effectual agencies of such transformations are what he later called the bright originals of Los's halls, the biblical prophets and — purged of his temporal husk — Milton, Gothic artists all.

By 1777, when Malkin tells us the poems we now know as *Poetical Sketches* were complete, Blake was twenty, an accomplished engraver and steadily practicing poet, far more widely read than we tend to remember and at least as widely acquainted with the history of art. If he was a beginner at Pars's or even in his early years with Basire, by the time *Poetical Sketches* was published (1783) he was, I think, much farther beyond that stage than most have allowed. To assume that he plied his studies, both graphic and poetic, with some sort of blind imitative spirit is totally to misconceive the man. Even the bits and pieces we do know of his early life up through his marriage to Catherine argue eloquently for a pulsing originality of thought, an ingrained suspicion of entrenched authority of whatever sort, and a principled con-tentiousness that led him, for example, never (so far as we know) to read a book without engaging it in vigorous mental warfare in the margins. One can even imagine, deliciously, his annotated Bible—annotations, whether apocryphal or not in that as yet undiscovered treasure, that emanate in his later graphic commentaries on biblical subjects. In one important sense *Poetical Sketches* may be seen as his earliest efforts at such "commentary," one text allusively challenging another before he hit upon the notion of graphically commenting upon his own words in *There Is No Natural Religion* and *All Religions Are One.*

Before I turn to the nature of that literary allusiveness, however, I should like to say something about another of Blake's earliest graphic works, *Glad Day* as it was once prettily known, *Albion Rose* as Erdman has taught us to see it. In his splendid *Angel of Apocalypse,* Wittreich adjudged this design as "among the most enigmatic of Blake's creations" as well as "among the most complicated and profound of his pictorial statements"[23]—a quite extraordi-nary estimate of a work that Blake first executed in pencil when he was but twenty-three years old, three years before the publication of *Poetical Sketches.* Acknowledging the comprehensive and exacting nature of Erdman's analysis of *Albion Rose,* Wittreich nevertheless proceeds to construct a complex—and to me persuasive—interpretation based upon the elaborate allusiveness of the design:

> When the literary echoes of Blake's design and inscription are perceived, it becomes evident that the artist is juxtaposing the defeated Samson of the inscription [to the line-engraved version] with the seemingly triumphant Samson of Milton's tragedy and of his own design, or so it would appear until we take account of one fact: Blake is not content with simple juxtaposition and thus insists that we scrutinize the nature of that triumph that Samson-Albion achieves.[24]

Although Wittreich is here speaking of the later line engraving, he speculates that the pencil sketches (there are two), containing only the figure of Albion without background and iconographical detail, suggest "another pencil sketch dating from 1780, that, carrying the full design, accounts for Blake's wish to identify his engraving of the 1790's with a conception he had arrived at a full decade before." And since, as Erdman notes, until 1795 Albion is a land rather than a person in Blake's works, the pencil drawings (including the speculative third) Wittreich proposes as contrasting with, not merely replicating, "a conception arrived at much later, when the figure of Albion became fixed in Blake's mythological system."[25]

If this is so, the pencil sketches of circa 1780 obviously lend themselves to the theory, originated by Mona Wilson and elaborated by Robert Essick, that the figure is Blake himself, emancipated now from the "slavery" of Basire's shop and ready to engage in the mental warfare and "redemptive energies of eternal art."[26] Although Wittreich finds fault with this interpretation, his attack on Essick particularly is for the latter's reading of the line-engraved version in these terms—a version Wittreich regards as "less a celebration of revolution than a critique of it . . . tied closely to *Samson Agonistes*": "In *Samson Agonistes*, Milton presents the tragedy that accompanies energy divorced from prophecy and that marks the failure to distinguish corporeal from mental warfare. The same tragedy is the subject of Blake's line engraving."[27] It is impossible, however, to read the pencil sketches so darkly; the obvious energy of the sketched figure is unqualified by the later iconographical punctuation that fills out the line engraving. It is equally impossible to deny that the pencil sketches represent *some* combination of Blake, the risen Christ (now liberated, though cruciform), Apollo, and almost certainly Milton's Samson, about whom Blake had recently written in *Poetical Sketches*. The figure also seems to be a quotation from one or more illustrations of the proportions of the human figure, but it may very well derive, indirectly at least, from Michelangelo and Dürer and thus signal what Phillips claims for Blake's prose poem *Samson*, his "acceptance and willingness to take up the mantle of the last poet-prophet of England."[28] Cast in the Gothic spirit of Michelangelo and Dürer, that acceptance would overthrow in the name of Christ the Apollo of Milton's *On the Morning of Christ's Nativity*, who, we recall, "Can no more divine" and "With hollow shriek [leaves] the steep of Delphos." Moreover, although Blake's pencil sketches include no nimbus around the figure's head as the subsequent line engraving and color print do, it is at least possible in light of these later versions that even the pencil figure of "Heaven's new-born heir" is intended to be the "greater Sun" that causes the natural sun to hide

> his head for shame,
> As his inferior flame
> The new-enlightened world no more should need.

Be that as it may, Blake's 1780 pictorial conception of himself is achieved in large part through a singular allusiveness *in posse* that bears abundant fruit in his later reworking of the pencil sketches. And at the center of the allusiveness, poetically, are the biblical prophets and Milton, no longer now merely emulatable exemplars of the language of art but the embodiments of true art—as Michelangelo, Raphael, Dürer, Giulio Romano, and the "Gothic" were graphically. Since we have only Malkin's word about the compositional dates of the poems in *Poetical Sketches,* can we say, then, with any real certainty that none were composed as late as 1780 or even 1783? For what it is worth, I think not; but even more important, Blake's artistic enterprises and study during his Basire years and immediately after, and his demonstrably wide reading in the English poetic tradition before and during the writing of the *Poetical Sketches,* combine to discredit the notion that in that volume Blake was merely dabbling, or "trying his hand at" various poetic forms and modes, or amusing himself while single-mindedly pursuing his engraving and drawing studies. He knew, I think, exactly what he was doing in those poems — or, more accurately, what he was trying to do. That they are not uniformly successful, that a few even seem so absurdly jejune that one wonders why they were saved by a poet of his self-critical abilities, that the volume is often more audacious than technically accomplished — all this should not blind us to what is in many ways a stunning achievement. Swinburne was essentially right, if embarrassingly fulsome: it was "not simply better than any man could do then; better than all except the greatest have done since: better too than some still ranked among the greatest ever managed to do." Simpler and more incisive is Vivian de Sola Pinto's judgment: *Poetical Sketches* is "one of the most amazing first volumes of poetry in the history of literature."[29]

What I intend in the following pages is, I suppose, a kind of "justification" of Pinto's adjective without succumbing to the inevitable temptation, when dealing with a great poet's earliest works, to claim at least emergent greatness for all and sundry. "Amazing" is just right — certainly more right than the condescension of the preface (no doubt at least partly tuned to the current rage for discovering "original geniuses" and "untutored bards" and to the cautionary presentation of their work to the public), or triumphant critical revelations of the later Blake buried amid the debris of derivativeness. Richly allusive as *Poetical Sketches* undoubtedly is, it is also, paradoxically, the least derivative "juvenilia" I have ever read — except, of course, that of poets who aspire so desperately to rise above their memory of illustrious, and less-than-illustrious, poetical predecessors that their "innovations" are "monstrosities"[30] or mere claptrap. There is no such innovative claptrap in *Poetical Sketches* — nor is there anxiety, sensitivity to the burden of the past, or a sense of the embarrassments of poetic tradition. If anything, there is instead a kind of brash confidence unsullied by bravado or rashness or cultivated self-conscious newness. Imaginative originality, as always with Blake, emerges out of his literary encounters, out of what he will later call "Mental Fight." "Without tradition," Wittreich has written, perhaps a bit excessively, "Blake would have been speechless; and without a knowledge of multiple traditions and of the ways Blake altered them we, too, are speechless, especially when it comes to defining the nature of his artistic statement and the breadth and subtlety with which it is invested." "Blake moves," he continues, "decidedly beyond a poetry of allusion, creating instead a poetry of contexts."[31] I could not agree more—though I prefer, for reasons that I hope will become clear, to call his early poetry, at least, the poetry of significant allusion; of contexts, yes, but only insofar as they are energized by the richness of minutely particularized word and phrase.[32] If English was later to be for Blake's Los the "rough basement" of visionary art, for Blake himself the English poetic tradition was that basement upon which he would endeavor to build, not the palace of art, but Jerusalem in England's green and pleasant land. *Poetical Sketches* is the cornerstone of that building.

Any effort to identify precisely the quarry from which such cornerstones are mined and carved is inevitably vulnerable to the charge of "over-reading," of teasing out "allusive intricacies . . . at the risk of losing the flow of the passages as a piece of verse writing,"[33] of obscuring the forest entirely in microscopically examining the trees. With respect to *Poetical Sketches* it also risks imposing on the efforts of "untutored youth," if not the full panoply of the prophetic-mythologizing Blake of later years, then the mature conceptualizing power and shrewd critical capacities of the proven artist-thinker. Although earlier pages of this introduction are intended, at least in part, to forestall, if not to preclude, such charges, probing into Blake's language and insistent allusiveness does lead on occasion to a kind of critical elaborateness—but one without, I trust, mere windiness or irresponsible extrapolation. That the language of the *Sketches* for the most part is not that of the mature Blake goes without saying. At the same time one can show, without undue difficulty, that much of the phrasing and imagery of the *Sketches* reappears time after time in later contexts, a habitual self-quotation and intracanonical allusiveness that one comes to perceive quickly as a staple of Blake's mythopoeic method, as indeed a kind of "concise shorthand for some complicated train of thought and imagery."[34] Before that mythopoesis is possible, however, there must be a rough basement upon which to construct it, a linguistic and imagistic substratum to which he may allude and on which he can capitalize and elaborate. To change the metaphor for a moment, into the reservoir of even Blake's youthful imagination streamed an astonishing variety of poetic languages and images sprung from his voluminous early reading, each carrying with it the remnants of received mythologies, traditions, and conventions along with the flotsam and jetsam of parochial and historical qualifications and obscurity. Acutely sensitive to his age's growing suspicion of the adequacy of prevailing world views and their poetic enactments, and committed early to the truth of the biblical prophets and their latter-day reincarnation in Milton, Blake sought to develop a poetic "composite art" whereby the latter could expose the nature of the former's inadequacies—or, in some cases, whereby the "false" or unsatisfactory "public enactments" could be manipulated so as to militate against the validity of their own received and incorporated notions: a "Striving with Systems to deliver Individuals from those Systems" (*Jerusalem* 11:5, E153).[35]

Although this last seems to demand a technique identifiable with satire, for whatever reasons Blake generally eschewed such a mode, at least in its conventional formulations[36] — perhaps, indeed, because of his distrust of the received truths upon which satire perforce must lean, systems of shared belief against which his mind seemed as instinctively to war as his taste in art and poetry ran counter to that of his youthful companions at Pars's and Basire's. While it would be rash to assume that at eighteen or twenty, perhaps even twenty-six, he said to himself, as Los will say later, "I must Create a System, or be enslav'd by another Mans," it was surely the spirit of that self-admonition that provoked his early and serious questioning of the conceptual bases of the poetry he had been reading in the same way that his dissatisfaction with current aesthetic norms exfoliated into what Bindman calls, somewhat severely but not without admiration, "one of the most bizarre artistic theories in the history of art"[37] — the "truth" of Michelangelo, Raphael, Dürer, Giulio Romano, and the Gothic.

To question, however, meant also to use, to ex-pose; that is, to imitate. Petrarch once said (as Young did much later in his *Conjectures on Original Composition*, which Blake along with everyone else in his day surely knew), "we should make use of another man's inner quality and tone, but avoid his words. For the one kind of similarity is hidden and the other protrudes; the one creates poets, the other apes."[38] Blake said, "Ideas cannot be Given but in their minutely Appropriate Words" (*Public Address*, E565). In *Poetical Sketches*, he will thus play the ape, allow the similarity to protrude, in order to provide a context within which he may engage "another man's inner quality and tone" in the mental warfare that resurrects the crucified truth. His own weapons, of course, are also words, "well contrived words, firm fixing, never forgotten," like those that are part of the building of Golgonooza, the city of art, in *Jerusalem* (12:35) — Revelation's sword out of the mouth.[39] Such a linguistic antagonism runs the serious risk of obscurity, for the prevailing mode of imitation in Blake's day tended to accommodate itself to the reader's normal expectations, and thus any subtle allusiveness to contrary, or at least different, contexts as they are invoked by a word or phrase or image would be buried in the familiarity of the dominant context. To use Saussure's terminology, the *parole*, however individual, would be subsumed in the larger framework of the *langue*. The demands upon the reader that Blake's sort of allusive "doubling" makes are extraordinary. He clearly expected his reader to know the Bible and Milton as well as he did, for his business was not to reason and compare but to create — and especially to create out of verbal and contextual (later combined with graphic) contrariety. Without contraries is no progression, *The Marriage of Heaven and Hell* tells us; and in the same spirit, Blake will subvert his ostensible apishness by a contrary or antithetical vision inspired and articulated by true art, the source and language of which he found in the biblical prophets and in Milton. Their works provide what one might call Blake's protomyth, the contexts of a vision he would later amplify into his own "private" mythology. Thus, what Wittreich says of that later mythology, that it "offers a context for any allusions Blake makes to it,"[40] may be understood in *Poetical Sketches* as a biblical-Miltonic protomythology (salted with, particularly, Spenser's related formulations) that offers a context not merely for allusions to it but for providing a vision of truth in many ways antithetical to those that inhere in the contexts Blake imitates. The result, when it is successful, is not merely a poem but a mental event whose significance, and whose recognizableness, depend upon the reader's knowledge of both contexts—a craftily manipulated transformation, in other words, of narration or plot into imaginative experience.

To claim that all of the poems in *Poetical Sketches* achieve this end is as absurd as settling comfortably for the relative excellence of their imitative, emulative, or assimilative values. I make no such claim. Rather I wish to examine what might be called the contours of the volume as they are defined largely by Blake's manipulative and allusive technique, by his imaginative exploitation of the verbal and imagistic traditions he inherited—on occasion irrespective of the technical excellence or mediocrity or even failure of the poetry as poetry.

To separate the two absolutely is of course finally impossible; but my efforts will be directed toward discovering *what* is happening *in* the poems, why I think *that* is happening rather than something else—and trying to account, therefore, for the poem's existence (or Blake's preservation of it) at all. Any judgments made follow from this.[41] Blake never set himself an easy row to hoe. Perhaps he remembered Upton's remark at the end of his commentary on Book I of *The Faerie Queene*, the edition Blake may very well have owned or read: "where therefore the moral allusion cannot be made apparent, we must seek (as I imagine) for an historical allusion; and always we must look for more than meets the eye or ear; the words carrying one meaning with them, and the secret sense another."[42] Blake's imitativeness carries one meaning; his significant allusions, contextualized, constitute the "secret sense." The idea is ubiquitous in his writings. "That which can be made Explicit to the Idiot is not worth my care," he wrote in 1799 to Trusler, who had apparently taken him to task for his "method of Study" (E676). And in *A Descriptive Catalogue*, speaking of the "wonderful originals" of true art seen in his visions, Blake says they all contained "mythological and recondite meaning, where more is meant than meets the eye" (E522). But he did not need to go to Upton or Spenser for the idea, of course. The nature of biblical prophecy was sufficient justification for his own reconditeness: "These things saith he which hath the sharp sword with two edges" (Revelation 2:12); only the spiritual ear can "hear what the Spirit saith," the imaginative or spiritual eye see what God reveals (2:29 and elsewhere as well). John of Patmos *eats* the Book; he does not read it. His tongue thus becomes the two-edged sword that separates truth from falsity. In *Poetical Sketches* it is Blake's tongue (and pen) that strive to separate imitative error (the product of the Muses of Memory) from allusive truth (the product of the Muses of Imagination). If too often for our comfort his "lucent words" are insufficient to illuminate fully his "darkling verses" for our purblind eyes, such are the fortunes of criticism with all its "laws . . . to keep fair play." This last phrase I have appropriated from Blake's *Blind-Man's Buff* hoping to import some of its tongue-in-cheekness there; for "the explanations available for inconsistencies in a poem are endless"[43]—as are, we might add, the opportunities for misinterpretation, especially of poems which, for whatever reasons we might adduce or "sense," are not fully "realized" (read "clear"). And Blake does not always help us—even in his maturer works. He is not interested in fair play, for he knew from the beginning that he was dealing, in the words of *King Edward the Third*, with minds that are fettered. Even Milton's—and certainly ours. As Damrosch has put it most recently, Blake refuses to be bound by the ordinary contract between author and reader; instead he "campaigns energetically against our normal tendency to be guided by language without seeing how it imposes the rules of a game." Thus he "plays a language-game in which he constantly reinvents the rules."[44] To be a "true Poet" demanded what Eliot shrewdly called a peculiarly terrifying honesty that brooked no compromise with fashion or received opinion,[45] and if we are to learn his rules, we must do no brooking either. Prudence, the proverb says in *The Marriage of Heaven and Hell*, "is a rich ugly old maid courted by Incapacity" and "No bird soars too high, if he soars with his own wings" (E35). The eagle does not learn from crows but

> scorns the tow'ry fence
> Of Alpine hills round his high aery,
> And searches thro' the corners of the sky,
> > Sports in the clouds to hear the thunder's sound,
> And see the winged lightnings as they fly,
> > Then, bosom'd in an amber cloud, around
> Plumes his wide wings, and seeks Sol's palace high.

With an amazing dexterity, to again borrow Pinto's adjective, Blake in *Poetical Sketches* searches through the corners of his teeming brain, stored with the poetic resources and resonances of his "apprenticeship" reading, and "bosom'd" with outrageous confidence in his own version of the amber cloud (not yet become a chariot of fire) demands that we fly with him on his plumed wide wings to the realms of truth. If indeed, as many claim, the Spenser imitation from which the above-quoted passage comes is one of Blake's earliest poetic efforts, his allusion in the penultimate line is all the more indicative of the direction, fundamental intent, and *modus operandi* of the *Poetical Sketches* to come: "Unmuffle, ye faint stars," says the Elder Brother separated from the Lady in Milton's *Comus,*

<blockquote>
and thou, fair moon,
That wont'st to love the traveler's benison,
Stoop thy pale visage through an amber cloud
And disinherit Chaos, that reigns here
In double night of darkness and of shades;
Or if your influence be quite dammed up
With black usurping mists, some gentle taper,
Though a rush-candle from the wicker hole
Of some clay habitation, visit us
With thy long leveled rule of streaming light,
And thou shalt be our star of Arcady,
Or Tyrian Cynosure.   (Ll. 331-42)
</blockquote>

If the full appropriateness of the allusion to Blake's poem may be in doubt, there is no doubt that he revered such stars himself. In any case, in the following pages I propose to follow this star, even as it dims on occasion to a rush-candle, to try to illuminate by its light the beginnings of vision amid the darkness and shades Blake perceived early as obscuring his poetic universe. I would hope that what I find will be more than, as Eliot's Magi put it, "you might say, satisfactory."

One final word by way of introduction. As I have already noted, Malkin's account notwithstanding, we know almost nothing of the dates of composition of the several "poetical sketches," and we know less about the reasons, if any, for the arrangement of the poems in the volume. Based on his research into the history of the printing of the *Poetical Sketches,* Phillips concluded that "there is good reason to believe that the responsibility of arranging for the printing of the poems was in the hands of John Flaxman," whom Blake had met sometime earlier at the salon of the Reverend and Mrs. A. S. Mathew.[46] Furthermore the three copies that we know Flaxman or his wife gave away as gifts all contained careful handwritten emendations by Blake, suggesting a closeness between the young poet and his more famous artist contemporary, even if that closeness seems related only to the publication of the *Sketches.* Other than these facts, there is no evidence that Blake himself had any hand in the printing, reviewing the proofsheets (if any), or the arranging of the poems in the volume. Despite this paucity of information, and thanks no doubt to over-earnest extrapolations from Malkin's slim account, the few Blake critics who have addressed the problem of the "sequence" of poems in the *Sketches* also "solve" it in one or more of the following ways: (1) the poems are chronologically arranged (largely discredited now); (2) the poems are arranged as a kind of spiritual autobiography, a "record of self in relation to its increasing sense of poetic vocation" as well as to Blake's sequential embracing of classical myth, Spenserian "prophecy," Shakespeare (especially *King Lear*), Milton's Hebraism, and finally biblical prophecy;[47] (3) the poems represent a movement from "calm and confident lyric artistry, cosmic in scope (the seasons), to the uncertainties of increasing involvement with the secular world (the love songs), to the terrors of political chaos during a time of war and of the responsibility to be a public artist (the political pieces). Such a movement is clearly represented in the ordering of the sketches as they appear in the printed volume";[48] (4) more simply, Blake progresses from lyric to dramatic to an essentially Hebraic idiom;[49] and (5) an arrangement "on the basis of complexity and growing thematic awareness in Blake"—though, to be fair, this critic acknowledges that his arrangement is "simply a way of talking about" the poems, "of seeing themes and techniques as they emerged in Blake's mind."[50]

Of these, the first four err in the same way and degree as other critics do in finding the four zoas in the seasons poems, the spectre in *Mad Song*, *America* in *King Edward the Third*, and *Milton* in *Samson*. Nevertheless each of the four recognizes the superficial contours, as I have called them, of the volume, revealing in ways heretofore ignored, the fundamental seriousness, depth, and daring of these "productions of untutored youth." Rather than theirs, I prefer other risks, as I have suggested above; and I shall not speculate, except en passant and then without pursuit, about the possible order of the poems' composition. Perhaps, indeed, we should be warned away from such speculation in any case, given the apparently insoluble problem of the ordering of the later *Songs of Innocence and of Experience*. The fifth approach listed above, then, is mine, though I trust that my lesser interest in "themes" will preclude the unsatisfactory results of that commentator's analysis of the volume.

THE MUSES
OF MEMORY

THE LEAST accomplished, and per-
haps the most "un-Blakean," poems in *Poetical Sketches* are *An Imitation of
Spencer, Fair Elenor,* and *Blind-Man's Buff.* Almost certainly among the earliest
he wrote, they show Blake at his worst technically, and two of them demonstrate just how imitative he could be before he recognized true imitation to
be an act of criticism. Yet, for my purposes the poems do have an interest
beyond the nature of their youthful inadequacies, for they reveal a curious
insensitivity to the implications of the poetic languages (not to say modes)
he chose to imitate—an insensitivity he outgrew in remarkably short order
to advance toward the varied accomplishments, however uneven, of the rest
of the *Sketches.*

At first glance what strikes us, aside from the radical variety of verse
forms, is the range of poetic languages employed: from the inflated rhetorical formalities of the Spenser imitation to the exclamatory Gothic of *Fair
Elenor* to the singsong colloquialism of *Blind-Man's Buff.* A similar various-
ness of verse form and language obtains in other poems of the *Sketches* as
well, but in most of those Blake's appropriation of a "traditional" poetic
diction tends to become a means of stripping that diction of the dress of
poetic respectability or conventional expectation; he will punctuate (and
puncture) it with a wide range of allusions, cast it into forms that militate
against the reader's easy acquiescence in the canons of the tradition from
which both the forms and the language have been derived—or otherwise
"use" his sources in bold, even perverse (sometimes cryptic or obscure),
ways. Few of these iconoclastic manipulations seem to me to occur in the
three poems I have gathered together here. I think we need to try to
see why.

Youthful inexperience is the obvious critical refuge and it would be
foolish not to admit such a predictable cause of ineptness. Yet by itself I find
such a reason (or excuse) insufficient to explain, for example, why Blake
preserved the poems at all or, more important, precisely what his youth and
inexperience led him to do *in* the poems that might have some bearing on

the ultimate shape of the volume in which they appear. *Fair Elenor* recalls any number of ballads in Percy's *Reliques*, but the rough grace and music of that ancient song are lost in the cacophony of Blake's Walpolean Gothicism. The *Reliques* appeared in 1765, and some sections of Blake's own copy of this three-volume first edition, sections given over largely to ballads, Lowery testifies as having "had very hard usage."[1] The general contemporary response to Percy's work, particularly by practicing poets, was predictable: most were unable to free their poetic psyches from the trammels of prevailing Bysshean prescriptive codes and produced, in Albert Friedman's words, "ballad-and-water" imitations.[2] Blake's *Fair Elenor* is one of these. It exhibits little of what Blake learned shortly thereafter, probably through his reading of Chatterton, about "the spirit and style of the old poetry," as Ostriker puts it.[3] All the same it is likely that Blake, even in his teens, perceived in the Gothic ballad and its ancient bardic authors a genuineness he obviously found absent from the sentimental drivel that passed for balladic poetry among his contemporaries—a perception corroborated by Percy himself who pronounces his "minstrels . . . the genuine successors of the ancient Bards."[4] Perhaps in his zeal to embrace that genuineness, a zeal akin to that which led him to the Westminster tombs, Blake's effort is excessively orchestrated with, paradoxically, a notable poverty in the language despite its moments in a line or two.[5] After the poem's opening line, whose simplicity of diction and movement largely redeems an essential triteness, simplicity collapses into banality:

> fair Elenor
> Walk'd by the castle gate, and looked in.

The second stanza is clogged with sibilants that all but bury Blake's effort to establish portents of Elenor's husband's death. Indeed portent becomes comically—in the hands of a better poet it would have been satirically—most unportentous as Elenor shrieks "aloud" (despite Spenser's example in *The Faerie Queene* IV,viii, how else?) and clumsily "sunk upon the steps / On the cold stone her pale cheek." Somehow "Walking, feeling," her "Fancy returns" despite our having just been given a signal exercise of her fancy—and, in near-parodic graveyard-school fashion, "now she thinks of bones." The specious mysteriousness of the next stanza (5) is echoed in the ungrammaticalness of

> A rushing sound, and the feet
> Of one that fled, approaches—

at which Elenor redundantly, "Like a dumb statue, froze to stone with fear." Stanzas 6-8 (dealing with the crucial encounter of the poem) reverberate with the clamor and confusion of cries and howls and rushings about, climaxed by a Peter-Sellers-like maneuver:

> the wretch,
> Howling, leap'd o'er the wall into the moat,
> Stifling in mud.

And so on, throughout the rest of the poem to the, by then, ludicrous speaking of her husband's severed head—telling Elenor what, as the previous stanzas indicate (especially stanza 10), she already knows.

Even the narrative itself stutters uncertainly from the castle gate to some steps somewhere, to "narrow passages" and "the outer gate," to the moat, to the bridge, then abruptly to "the pathless plain," Elenor's house, and bed. Why she was so far from there in the first place, at one o'clock in the morning, is never explained (presumably she was seeking her husband, who with equal mysteriousness was sleeping "on the stones of yonder tower" when he was murdered). All of this is exacerbated by a plethora of obligatory formulaic phrase and Blake's clumsy handling of the balladic stanza unit. To be sure, Percy's ballads tended to encourage various irregularities, but despite Blake's interesting avoidance of rhyme (sanctioned probably by the Wartons and Collins rather than Percy), his have all the indications of technical incapacity. One need look only at Percy's *Lord Thomas and Fair Ellinor*, from which Blake may have borrowed his title, to see the difference. What we have, then, in *Fair Elenor* is not, I think, an illustration of "the curious refinements that a thorough knowledge of old ballads made of the cruder substance prevalent as 'Gothic' poetry and fiction,"[6] but an imitation that has all the earmarks of the neophyte trying to outdo his models. In short, the poem emerges as a kind of fraud. It would be pleasant to find evidence of satiric or deliberately parodic intent here, but I find none; and the surrender to fashion remains unredeemed[7] by the mechanicalness of its few allusions beyond the Gothic.

Damon long ago[8] noted Blake's adaptation in his ninth stanza of Psalm 91:5-6:

> Thou shalt not be afraid for the terror by night, nor for the arrow that flieth by day;
> Nor for the pestilence that walketh in darkness; nor for the destruction that wasteth at noonday.

Blake's version is flattened by the flew-fly-flies-fled verb sequence that culminates in the prosaic, if inverted, last phrase of the stanza. The allusion is thus inert, nongenerating, not surprisingly dissipating immediately in the frantic exclamations of the following stanza. The other allusion is also biblical, to The Song of Solomon, chapter 5:

> I opened to my beloved; but my beloved had withdrawn himself, and was gone: my soul failed when he spake: I sought him but I could not find him; I called him, but he gave me no answer.

> The watchmen that went about the city found me, they smote me, they wounded me; the keepers of the walls took away my veil from me.

Verses 10-16 then go on to catalog the graces of her beloved that make him "more than another beloved." While the specifics of the comparisons in Elenor's similar speech (lines 41-48) are different, the "plot" of Blake's poem and his use of these biblical formulae make possible this otherwise seemingly absurd suggestion. The inappropriateness of the allusion is, curiously, instructive, for it is perhaps Blake's first effort to make "use" of a source, to bend the allusion to his own context or to qualify his context through allusionary "punctuation." That it doesn't work here is due to the excessiveness of the Gothic-balladic frame and language which throw into absurd relief the marginally better verse and diction of Elenor's speech—itself framed firmly by the requisite wailing exclamations. Schorer optimistically suggests that in *Fair Elenor* Blake's "apocalyptic imagery takes its start and with that, his images of a convulsive universe."[9] Such a development, I submit, could only eventuate when Blake realized, as he did shortly, that mere Gothicism with its melodramatic gnashings, shriekings, and howlings was but rhetorical bombast to disguise a vacuous imagination. Fancy was not enough to body forth a mythology, much less to engage us in its fiction.

If there is anything of real interest in the poem it is, aside from their biblical origins, stanzas 11-13. *Fair Elenor* is a night poem and, its simplistic requirement as the setting for a Gothic tale aside, Blake very early was intent on mythologizing night beyond both the obvious and the trivial.[10] In these stanzas we have the rudiments of the sort of antithetical structure I shall discuss in the next chapter. Elenor's "lord was like a flower upon the brows / Of lusty May," "like a star, in highest heav'n," "like the opening eyes of day" and "the breath of heaven dwelt among his leaves." The spring-morning-star imagery, though heavily freighted with overuse, nevertheless does contrast sharply with the prevailing visual climate of the rest of the poem—and most particularly with Blake's reworking of the psalm in lines 34-35. That he recognized at least the possibilities inherent in the contrast is evidenced by the Jekyll-Hyde antithesis of her lord's being figured as a flower on May's brows, which death's "cruel hand" plucks off to deck his own "horrid temples." But Blake seems incapable of capitalizing on this beginning, for the next stanza lapses into the vagueness of "spells" and the moral conventionality of "wickedness," drawing Elenor's starlike lord "down to earth." Similarly, the (in this poem) unusually graceful concluding lines of stanza 12 give way to the tumbled confusions of dark, summer's noon, cloud, a fallen or "cut down" tree, the breath of heaven, and a hand-wringing concluding line. The contrast thus remains just that, in its curious prominence and near-genuineness of emotion serving but to accentuate the poem's essential lack of structural integrity. In the "Songs" of the *Sketches*, as we

shall see, Blake will intensify such constrast and elevate it to energetic
antithesis.

Yet somehow *Fair Elenor* was memorable to Blake himself. Some thirty
years later he used the kernel of its story and one of its few powerful lines to
pillory Hayley's friendship in a Notebook epigram:

> When H— —y finds out what you cannot do
> That is the very thing hell set you to
> If you break not your Neck tis not his fault
> But pecks of poison are not pecks of salt
> And when he could not act upon my wife
> Hired a Villain to bereave my Life[11]

The searing visceral anger of these last two lines, if we set them against their
"source," is perhaps the best indication we have of what is at the heart of *Fair
Elenor*'s failure. Blake is simply not there, not even behind his own lines.
He had not yet discovered that the true art he sought emanated from his
own powerful feelings, convictions, desires, "elevated" or not beyond the
merely personal or local (or fashionable) to mythopoeic truth. Or, to put
that another way, the poem is an example of his absorption of ideas, phrases,
and a manner he liked without regard to their contexts or the felt reality to
which (at least "originally") they belonged. It is a product, as it were, of his
first days at Pars's, not his last days at Basire's.

The *Imitation of Spencer* is not much better than *Fair Elenor*, although
recently it has received a better press.[12] It too is a "fraud"—eighteenth-
century Spenserianism decked in the bravery of its title. Aside from a word
or phrase here and there, the poem almost suggests that Blake as yet had not
read Spenser at all.[13] When he did, or rather when he imaginatively absorbed
what he had read, he could write *To Morning* and *To the Evening Star*. If
comparing these accomplished poems with the Spenser imitation smacks a
bit too much of apples and oranges to be amenable to equitable critical
judgment, a closer look at the opening of Blake's *Imitation* set alongside his
related introduction to *Samson* will get us to the heart of the matter. The
Spenser begins with:

> Golden Apollo, that thro' heaven wide
> Scatter'st the rays of light, and truth's beams!
> In lucent words my darkling verses dight,
> And wash my earthy mind in thy clear streams,
> That wisdom may descend in fairy dreams:
> All while the jocund hours in thy train
> Scatter their fancies at thy poet's feet;
> And when thou yields to night thy wide domain,
> Let rays of truth enlight his sleeping brain.

This is Warton's and Hurd's Spenser, the purveyor of fairy fancies and dreams in which may be more wit and wisdom than in the "tinkling rhymes, and elegances terse" of the neoclassical establishment.[14] Such verse, like Orpheus's, is "nervous":[15] it "can charm to harmony with potent spell," "dispel / Envy and Hate, that thirst for human gore," and fly eagle-winged to the very palace of the sun. Spenser's invocation to Book I of *The Faerie Queene* comes to mind:

> O Goddesse heauenly bright,
> Mirrour of grace and Maiestie diuine,
> Great Lady of the greatest Isle, whose light
> Like *Phoebus* lampe throughout the world doth shine,
> Shed thy faire beames into my feeble eyne,
> And raise my thoughts too humble and too vile,
> To think of that true glorious type of thine,
> The argument of mine afflicted stile.

Whether or not Blake remembered the passage, the absence of Spenser's "holy Virgin chiefe of nine" and Elizabeth in favor of Apollo and the "jocund hours" in his train scattering "their fancies" at the poet's feet speaks to Blake's neoclassic reductionism rather than a Spenserian heroic-epic intent or the passionate loftiness of the four hymns whose invocations are similar. Such a diminution is underscored by the absence of Milton's influence here (except for scattered Augustan versions of his diction). Indeed, despite his own testimony in the Flaxman letter noted in chapter 1, one wonders whether Blake had read much Milton either by the time of his writing of the *Imitation;* or, if he had, he was not yet listening to his predecessor's attack on "fancies" as

> vain deluding Joys,
> The brood of Folly without father bred,

that "fill the fixèd mind with . . . toys" and

> Dwell in some idle brain,
> And fancies fond with gaudy shapes possess,
> As thick and numberless
> As the gay motes that people the sunbeams,
> Or likest hovering dreams,
> The fickle pensioners of Morpheus' train. (*Il Penseroso*, ll. 1-10)

While it is perhaps unwarranted to expect Milton to assert himself in Blake's imagination when that is engaged in a redaction of neo-Spenserianism, as we shall see elsewhere in *Poetical Sketches* such assertion quickly becomes the mark of Blake's transformational genius working on the dross of imitated manner; and that transformation will have nothing to do with the charming to harmony, "sweet Eloquence," and "sense" invoked in the *Imitation.*

If we turn now to the invocation to *Samson,* my point, I trust, will become clearer. There Blake deliberately and self-consciously dons the mantle of true prophecy and, as if to point up the contrast with his *Imitation*, forges his language out of the untempered ore of the earlier poem:

> O Truth, that shinest with propitious beams, turning our earthly night to heavenly day, from presence of the Almighty Father! thou visitest our darkling world with blessed feet, bringing good news of Sin and Death destroyed!

The abandonment of a moribund classicism and polytheism in favor of a vibrant Miltonic Hebraism is so obvious as to require no comment, but the language of the change also signals a moribund Spenserianism being abjured in favor of genuine wisdom and truth. Now it is Truth itself that shines with propitious beams rather than an un-Blakean Apollo scattering "rays of light." The effete and affected "lucent words" and "darkling verses" harden into "words of truth" inscribed with iron pen on lofty rocks to enlighten not the "sleeping brain" of the speaker but a darkened world. Instead of Mercury entering "Heav'n's halls . . . with holy feet," Truth "visitest our darkling world with blessed feet," bringing not the mistaken wisdom of an outmoded pantheon but "good news of Sin and Death destroyed."[16] In this striking simplification of language that Blake himself stresses by modulating Spenserian "poesy" into cadenced prose, at once direct and elevated, one might find a clue to the connection, however seemingly farfetched, between the Gothicism of *Fair Elenor* and the Hurd-Warton Spenserianism of the *Imitation*.[17] As I indicated previously, it is doubtful that Blake read Hurd very early, if at all, but his own youthful experiments in Spenser-imitation and Gothic horror (at what I believe was approximately the same time) place him solidly in the mainstream of critical and poetic developments in the third quarter of the eighteenth century.

Schorer long ago suggested that Blake's main interest in the Spenser imitation was in "verbal effects,"[18] the "lucent words" he calls upon to "dight" his darkling verses—the last phrase a totally uncharacteristic self-humbling. But we should also be aware that the Renaissance poet was also valued highly for his moral allegory, for his uniting of the *utile* with the *dulce* in true Homeric and Virgilian fashion—despite his deplorable, but correctable, lapses in architectonic harmony. In the very context of Blake's rather surprising surrender, however young he was, to the critical canons of his day, it is thus possible to credit the *Imitation* as a kind of genuine self-awakening to his task as a poet. In this sense it is a search poem, a fumbling sort of *Prelude* casting about for a muse to "assist" the poet's "lab'ring sense." One wonders, however, about the terms by which this "task" is defined. Like a good 1770s aspirant to the temple of fame, he wishes to be endowed with the language, good sense, eloquence, and wisdom to purge from "sweet society" envy, hate, and the vileness of "savage minds." At the same time he longs to plume his wings and soar like the eagle to "Sol's palace high," to walk the "solemn grove" with Contemplation and Wisdom, to fly o'er "the burning field" and "waves of battle," and view with "soft piteous eyes" the "weary wanderer" roving "thro' the desert" and the "afflicted man." In other words, he will embrace the fairy dreams and fancies of Warton's Spenser and transform them, like a good Augustan imitator, into satire, moralized song, the wisdom of eloquence, the rural walk in "solemn gloom," Rule Britannias, and the sympathetic tear of benevolence. Such a program is clearly inauspicious (though it suspiciously suggests the contents of *Poetical Sketches*).[19] In its imitation of imitations, imagination remains "unenlighted" in the poet's "sleeping brain." If, according to Malkin, *How Sweet I Roam'd* was written by Blake before he was fourteen, the Spenser appears to have been written before he was twelve.

Blind-Man's Buff may be an imitation too, though I must confess that any model for it that may be extant has eluded me. There is no question, however, about its being both an enigma and an embarrassment to Blake scholars, most of whom pass over it quickly with a suitably pejorative adjective or pretend that it really isn't there—though even the finicky Rossetti included it in the selections from *Poetical Sketches* that he reprinted in Gilchrist's *Life of William Blake: 'Pictor Ignotus.'* It has been suggested that the inception of the poem was stimulated by Chatterton's *Antiquity of Christmas Games,* which appeared in the December 1769 issue of the *Town & Country Magazine:*

> The ancient Christmas gambols were, in my opinion, superior to our modern spectacles and amusements: wrestling, hurling the ball, and dancing in the woodlands, were pleasures for men: it is true, the conversation of the hearthside was the tales of superstition: the fairies, Robin Goodfellow, and hobgoblins, never failed to make the trembling audience mutter an Ave Maria, and cross their chins; but the laughable exercises of blindman's buff, riddling, and question and command, sufficiently compensated for the few sudden starts of terror.[20]

The general manner of Blake's poem, however, oddly reminds one more of Ambrose Philips's "namby-pambyness." In any case, hint or no from Chatterton, Blake's conception seems to me to derive from a passage from Thomson's *Winter,* replete with moral lesson:

> Meantime the village rouses up the fire;
> . . . .
> . . . frequent in the sounding hall they wake
> The rural gambol. Rustic mirth goes round—
> The simple joke that takes the shepherd's heart,
> Easily pleased; the long loud laugh sincere;
> The kiss, snatched hasty from the sidelong maid
> On purpose guardless, or pretending sleep;
> The leap, the slap, the haul . . .
> (Ll. 617-27)

And one from Milton's *L'Allegro:*

> Then to the spicy nut-brown ale,
> With stories told of many a feat,
> How fairy Mab the junkets eat;
> She was pinched and pulled, she said —

the "she" one of the assembled story-tellers.[21] Once again, it is tempting, especially in light of Chatterton's contrast between modern "dissipation and joyless festivity" and "the amusements of the days of old,"[22] to regard Blake's intent here as satiric; but he seems, rather, totally taken up with the fortunes and misfortunes of "the game," which, like life, must be governed by "wholesome laws . . . to keep fair play."[23] Otherwise the "best of hopes, how soon they fail," and man, stumbling his way through life blindfolded, is brought rudely down by another's lying in his way. Alternatively, he can cheat his way through the vicissitudes of worldly play, but since that leads to other "mischief" he must go "surer bound" through the game.

Pasteboard figures enact the charade, each replete with bathetic Homeric epithet: "hob-nail Dick" whose rustic tag is signally irrelevant, "blear-ey'd Will," "Peggy Pout," "titt'ring Kate," "Kitty, pert," and so on. The "game," we should note, however, is not merely blindman's buff but the post-"chat" mischief as well:

> The lasses prick the lads with pins;
> Roger from Dolly twitch'd the stool,
> She falling, kiss'd the ground, poor fool!
> She blush'd so red, with side-long glance
> At hob-nail Dick, who griev'd the chance.

There is a muted violence here despite the aura of jollity ushered in by the opening ten lines of the poem, and it is perhaps worth noting that once the blindman's game begins, "laughter stops" or, like "titt'ring Kate," is "pen'd up in the corner strait." From this point on the scene is filled with pushing and dodging, tripping and falling, trickery and cheating, all leading to the excessively portentous "With crimson drops he stains the ground." Vulnerable to all this is the blindman, the victim of "hood-wink'd chance"; and it is he who bleeds as his "best of hopes" are dashed. There are, one suspects (or hopes), the seeds of something here, a subversion of Thomson's happy evening idyll insulated from winter's rages outside, a perversion of Milton's innocent mirth, an attack through trivialization on the fortunes of life. Clearly, one must be skilled in one's art to play one's appointed role properly, by the rules of fair play "surer bound" from the excesses of "liberty" that otherwise become dangerous mischief. "There is," as Cowper says in *The Task,* "a public mischief in your mirth" (I,769).

But Cowper's poem is a model of the genre, and Blake's comes off, finally, neither as sportive farce laced with moral exhortation nor as parable or fable.[24] And if it confutes the idyllicism of Thomson's snug cottages, it advances an equally specious history of mankind and "sweet society." The ethic espoused is one of self-restraint, playing one's part, regimentation, and eye-for-an-eye justice so totally foreign to Blake even in *Poetical Sketches* that one may be justifiably puzzled why he saved this piece from the "hearth so red" with which it begins. The only reason I can suggest—and I confess to the desperateness of the reach—is inherent in the last line of the Spenser imitation. Is *Blind-Man's Buff* one example of Minerva-inspired wisdom whose bosom is moved by "the afflicted man"? Perhaps. But even if that were so, the game itself clearly emerged out of the same bag of fancies the jocund hours scattered at his feet in the Spenser imitation—one that he would try to play once more, with greater élan, inspired by the farces and burlettas of the late-eighteenth-century London stage, in *An Island in the Moon*. The essential difference between the two works lies in the latter's wit, farcicality, and nonsense, that transform "sweet society," particularly the intelligentsia, into a vehicle for sometimes incisive, but always surprising and lively, commentary on various forms of imaginative blindness and, as we say today, the games people play. In *Blind-Man's Buff* wit is usurped by authorial moral taglines, and the narrow earnestness of the game-players precludes the broadness of equally earnest, but more imaginatively significant, nonsense and idiocy. Or, to put it another way, the "blindness" of the characters in *An Island in the Moon* needs no blindfold to flag the reader into recognition.

These three early poems, then, are variously inept, so much so that even the wide spectrum of poetic "languages" essayed is all but unnoticeable amid the general mawkishness. The few allusions (including the oft-noted Shakespearean opening of *Blind-Man's Buff*) are unable to penetrate the poeticized façades.[25] Further, the language limps uncertainly through straitened paces, displaying little of the "nervousness" advanced in the Spenser imitation as a desideratum. Although Blake's later prophetic fourteeners (and variations thereon) are hardly noted for their restraint, the furious wars of the mind will obviously demand a pen different from the ones used here—just as the delicacies (and the ferocity) of his *Songs of Innocence and of Experience* will claim no ancestry in the swains and maids of *Blind-Man's Buff* or the "ancient simplicity" of *Fair Elenor*.

Earlier I suggested that despite their being otherwise forgettable, these three early efforts are nevertheless of some interest as abortive births. Each in its own way claims a "muse" the progress of whose "genius" has demonstrably reached the shores of England to claim the allegiance of any poet who wishes to be among her cloudy trophies hung. Cloudy indeed, as we have seen. But the almost quantum leap from imitation, even from assimilation, to most of the rest of *Poetical Sketches* is so extraordinary a development that my little fun at Blake's expense may be, if not salutary and medicinal, at least pardonable. For he demonstrates in virtually all other poems in the volume that his own, perhaps instinctive, drive is not toward assimilation but dissimilation, the wrenching of an astonishing range of traditions out of their appropriately comfortable modes (as well as their later adaptations) into an evolving vision of the nonprogress of poetry. What is attacked thereby is the prostitution of the "Poetic Genius" in the "cause" of a dead, not merely moribund, traditionalism. The question for Blake was not how to be different but how to expose the folly and emptiness of sameness—of Spenserianism, Shakespeareanism, Miltonism, Gothicism, Elizabethanism, Petrarchism—in short of imitationism. These are, as he says later in the margins of Reynolds's *Discourses,* the result of finding only "Patches. Paint. / Bracelets & Stays & Powderd Hair" rather than seeing "the sweet Outlines / And beauteous Forms that Love [that is, artist and man] does wear" (E627). The former are the deplorable consequences of the "Greeks Caling the Muses Daughters of Memory" (E632). The isms produced by such reflexivity and misperception were a spurious art, avatars not only of the nonprogress of poetry but of the "fact" that the poetic genius was long dead and buried. "If Art was Progressive," Blake writes in his copy of Reynolds, "We should have had Mich Angelo's & Rafaels to Succeed & to Improve upon each other But it is not so. Genius dies with its Possessor & comes not again till Another is Born with It" (E645).

One might draw an analogy between Blake's later composite art of text and design (a battleground of verbal and pictorial modes upon which is fought the only warfare that yields the truth of vision—mental warfare) and his earlier allusionary mode, wherein texts fight with texts, contexts with contexts, in similar imaginative fight. It is not that Blake saw himself as "right" and the other poets "wrong" (though he seems often to legitimize such a simplistic charge), but that the others have become, through time and the ceremony of history, the agents of dogma, closed books spawning idolatrous imitation which obscure the genius and truth of their inception. Like the interanimation of text and design in the more familiar Blake, the interanimation of text and text is an attempt to re-reveal and reinterpret the verbal hieroglyphs of ancient wisdom, in more prosaic terms to illuminate what has become obscure or debased through overuse and to counteract the mental blindness familiarity inevitably breeds. His own kind of imitation, then, as he insists, is criticism, a reading of texts in their "infernal sense" to recover what was hid—and *is* hid; it is an imitation of his allusionary text's "original meaning"—that is, its eternal truth else lost forever beneath "apparent surfaces." Frye once said that the Spenserian stanza "has a role rather similar to the engraved design in Blake: it deliberately arrests the

narrative and forces the reader to concentrate on something else."[26] Exactly
so. Blake's significant allusions do the same thing, frustrating that easy continuousness which seems to have "an inevitable affinity" with "the unreflecting."[27]

To be sure, Blake did write what he announced, in the spirit of his age, as
an *Imitation of Spencer,* just as elsewhere in the *Sketches* he wrote other
"imitations"—of the Elizabethan lyric, Shakespearean drama, Ossianic prose
poetry, Gothic ballad, and so on. But, as I trust has become clearer in the
above discussion, there are imitations and then there are imitations. To
assume from what I have said that Blake's idea of imitation as criticism
sprang full-grown and armed from his infant brain is obviously absurd.
Indeed one useful way to "read" the *Poetical Sketches* is not so much as a
psychic history of Blake's discovering his prophetic calling as a series of
struggles, in the poetry itself, with the *idea* of imitation; not as essays in
definition (Blake was rarely a definer) but as imaginative engagements with
an idea that held dominion over his times. Moreover it was an engagement
(in the sense of battle now) that needed continual waging, as we see from the
Reynolds annotations; and it is to them that we must turn once again to try
to understand much of what Blake is about in *Poetical Sketches.* "No one can
ever Design," Blake wrote in Discourse II, "till he has learnd the Language
of Art by making many Finishd Copies both of Nature & Art & of whatever
comes in his way from Earliest Childhood" (E634). Indeed "Servile Copying
is the Great Merit of Copying" (E634), for in such servility is both the birth
of discovery as well as the acquiring of a "Facility in Composing" that "is the
Greatest Power of Art & Belongs to None but the Greatest Artists i.e. the
Most Minutely Discriminating & Determinate" (E632). Merely to be different, to innovate in a vacuum, was to perform the "Labours of Ignorance"
(E625). The "Vehicle of Genius" is propelled by "Mechanical Excellence"
which is earned only "by an infinite number of acts,"[28] explorations (precisely in Keats's sense in the Chapman's Homer sonnet) of the range of
adaptive languages the Poetic Genius has been reduced to in its accommoda-
tion to the "weaknesses of every individual" age (*All Religions Are One,* E2).
The discovery, then, is of *the* language of art, disentangled from its adaptations—an unveiling, so to speak, in Spenser, Shakespeare, Milton, the Elizabethan lyricists, Thomson, Gray, Collins, of the abiding core of the poetic
genius. "As all men are alike in outward form, So (and with the same infinite variety) all are alike in the Poetic Genius" (*All Religions Are One,* E2).
To "copy" them, therefore, is to give wheels to the chariot of one's own
genius; and to "imitate" is to reaffirm the eternal presence and power of the
poetic genius shackled or muted or lost in the critical canons of time.

But Blake also quickly came to realize (as he demonstrates in all but a few
of the *Poetical Sketches*) that criticism, if it was to be something more than
angry marginalia, must assume the garments of its quarry so that they may

be exhibited as the visible capitulations to fashion consequent upon the "weaknesses of the individual" artist. The three poems I have discussed in this chapter are, then, "learning experiences," as educationists unfortunately have taught us to say, soundings of the poetic tradition without (to change the metaphor) the fledged shoulders Keats posited as necessary to his achievement:

> The difference of high Sensations with and without knowledge appears to me this—in the latter case we are falling continually ten thousand fathoms deep and being blown up again without wings and with all [the] horror of a bare shoulderd Creature—in the former case, our shoulders are fledge[d], and we go thro' the same air and space without fear. (Ltr. to John Hamilton Reynolds, 3 May 1818)

The analogy is inexact, of course, but it is useful here. In the *Imitation, Fair Elenor,* and *Blind-Man's Buff* Blake was, as we say, trying his wings. It is inconceivable, to me at least, that he did not discover almost immediately that those wings were like Icarus's, not his own; and if in the rest of his first volume of flights his shoulders *are* fledged—sometimes skimpily, sometimes in astonishing fullness—it is doubtful that all fear was conquered much before, say, 1777-83, when the last of the *Sketches* were probably written. In any case, if even the "Jewish & Christian Testaments," which "are An original derivation from the Poetic Genius," were inadequate "from the confined nature of bodily sensation" (*All Religions Are One,* E3), the overlay of ages of adaptations that the eighteenth century presented to him as evidences of the poetic genius's survival required greater corrosives than Blake had at hand when he essayed these three early poems. They are the poetic versions of the "rather mechanical style" Bindman and others find characteristic of Blake's graphic work at least through his early apprentice days, despite that graphic work's "turning upside-down of the accepted views of the Society of Antiquaries"—that is, the conventions of history and historical art.[29] The Westminster tombs that he copied, Sir Richard Gough's *Sepulchral Monuments in Great Britain,* and his other models (most particularly Jacob Bryant's *A New System, or An Analysis of Ancient Mythology,* 1774-76, engraved by Basire's shop and surely read by Blake) enabled him with remarkable speed to reject historical truth in favor of his own series of designs of the "real" (that is, mythological) history of Britain. Concurrently out of the textbook mechanicalness of his earlier style gradually emerged a pictorial language of imaginative vision and power. Like its more slowly evolving verbal counterpart, that language is his greatest discovery.

The best illustration of my point here, in addition to the several versions of *Albion Rose* discussed earlier, may be the two versions of *Joseph of Arimathea,* the first bearing the date 1773, the later one (c. 1810) in his most mature engraving style. Analogically the latter is to the former as *To the*

Evening Star and *To Morning* (or the seasons poems) are to the *Imitation of Spencer, Fair Elenor,* and *Blind-Man's Buff.* Mediating between these two groups of poems, and almost certainly composed sometime in that interim, is a quite extraordinary poetic confession of the falseness of his earlier imitations that has no counterpart among his earlier designs but does lie only barely beneath the surface of the later *Public Address*'s attack on journeyman engravers and the commercial preference for smooth imitations. That confession is *To the Muses.*

The poem has been justly praised. Blake's touch is as restrainedly sure here as it was tentative, flat, or heavy-handed in the three other poems dealt with in this chapter. Such a comparison smacks of unfairness until one recognizes the fundamental Augustan conventionality of the diction of *To the Muses.* Yet in its quiet elegance, simplicity, and subtle music it owes virtually nothing to any poetic model and achieves a bold complexity belied by its limpid surface. In my view there is no other song in *Poetical Sketches* that so approaches the unobtrusive density of *Songs of Innocence,* well over a decade away. It does have "models" of a sort however: the "progress poem" of the eighteenth century which, as Hartman observes, embodies "one of the few genuinely visionary themes" of that century.[30] Typically, as in Gray's most famous example of the genre, the poetical spirit is portrayed as migrating from Greece to Rome and thence to England, East to West, though more often than not England as its final resting place is a fond, if not desperate, hope belied by the absence of a worthy successor to Milton (Gray stops with Dryden, for example).

Blake's even more insistent elegiac note, however, harks back to Spenser's equally youthful and far more shrill *The Teares of the Muses,* wherein each of the "sacred Sisters nine" in turn bewails the wretched world's iniquity and ignorance, folly and barbarism, error and corruption, and "from [their] owne natiue heritage exilde" they "their learned instruments did breake" (lines 1, 341, 599). Although it is possible to read the whole of *Poetical Sketches* as Blake's testament to the truth in his own time of Spenser's too-sweeping condemnation of the death of the arts in *his* time, *The Teares* more particularly may have been in the back of Blake's mind when he wrote his *Imitation of Spencer.* There, ignoring the impotent muses, Blake turns uncharacteristically (and one might add, un-Spenser-like) to an odd mixture of Greek and Roman gods for inspiration. This invoking of a classical pantheon (one that he attacked willy-nilly throughout the rest of his life as "dishumanizd terrors" and "the Gods of Ulro dark," whose continued influence, even in a neoclassical age, led poets to be false to their own imagination),[31] not to mention the unassimilated neo-Spenserianism I have already commented upon, confesses not only the poet's youth but an uncritical acceptance of the inspirational power and effectiveness of what he later called "the rattle traps of Mythology" (*Public Address,* E568). Of greater interest, perhaps, in light of *The Teares of the Muses* is the Renaissance-like attack in the *Imitation* on ignorance and its resultant poetry of "sound without sense." Spenser's version is as follows:

> Heapes of huge words vphoorded hideously,
> With horrid sound though hauing little sence,
> They thinke to be chiefe praise of Poetry;
> And thereby wanting due intelligence,
> Haue mard the face of goodly Poesie,
> And made a monster of their fantasie.   (Ll. 553-58)

Spenser's "brutish Ignorance" and "rudeness foule" Blake translates into "brutish Pan" whom, in his "rude affray" with reason and sense, Midas crowns the victor. His "vulgar sort," in Spenser's words,

>   now pipe and sing,
> And make them merrie with their fooleries,
> They cherelie chaunt and rymes at random fling,
> The fruitfull spawne of their ranke fantasies:
> They feede the eares of fooles with flattery,
> And good men blame, and losels magnify.   (Ll. 319-24)

Imbued with Apollo's "rays of truth" and Mercury's "golden rod" and "potent spell," Blake will be able, he says, to banish ignorance, folly, envy, and hate from "sweet society," "round the circle of the world" flying like the eagle of genius. But despite the bravura performance of the first five stanzas of the *Imitation,* the poem ends with a series of questions attendant upon the ambiguity of Pallas Athena as the operative muse. While her presence in the poem continues the theme of Apollo's wisdom, it also reinvokes the "thirst for human gore" that was presumably to be dispelled by Mercury-inspired "sweet Eloquence." Minerva is armed not with wisdom but "the terrors of Almighty Jove"; a "warrior, maid invincible" and "terrible," her guardianship of "rays of truth" is called into serious doubt by her apparent indifference to "the weary wanderer" roving through the desert and the "afflicted man."

Left with these negatively rhetorical questions, the reader must find it difficult, if not impossible, to credit the efficacy of Blake's prayer. If his "lab'ring sense" *would* fly round the circle of the world shedding (presumably) benign influence, no such flight takes place in the poem. Instead "the weary wanderer" and "afflicted man" of the closing lines blur into Spenser's muses, who

> wander . . . all carefull comfortlesse,
> Yet none doth care to comfort vs at all;
> So seeke we helpe our sorrow to redresse,
> Yet none vouchsafes to answere to our call:

> Therefore we mourn and pittilesse complaine,
> Because none liuing pittieth our paine.   (Ll. 349-54)

Blake does, however — in *To the Muses;* that plaintive elegy is *his* "mournfull tune" at the cessation of "their sweete instruments" which erstwhile had caused "all their groues . . . with the heauenly noyses" to sound (*Teares,* lines 12, 19-20).

Despite Spenser's (largely unwarranted) pessimism about the progress of the arts, he himself, not unselfconsciously, bore the mantle of the westering genius of poetry virtually to the birth of its seventeenth-century inheritor, Milton — and it is this point in literary history that constitutes the watershed of the progress myth and the operative context into which Blake fits his poem. For while Milton alone among the moderns, in Collins's adaptation of Spenser's Florimel story in *Ode on the Poetical Character,* was able to gird his "blest prophetic loins" with "the magic girdle" or the "cest of amplest power," Milton clearly regarded himself, for all of his Spenserian heritage, as a latter-day biblical prophet.[32] Thus in *Paradise Regained* Christ responds to Satan's championing of Homer as the source of

> the secret power
> Of harmony in tones and number hit
> By voice or hand

with the assertion that Greece derived these arts from Hebrew psalm and hymn. Moreover, Greece

> Ill imitated, while they loudest sing
> The vices of their deities, and their own,
> In fable, hymn, or song, so personating
> Their gods ridiculous, and themselves past shame.[33]

Similarly, for all his adulation of Milton, Blake does not accept him as merely a modern acculturation of the steadily westering poetic genius. Indeed it is such acculturation that for Blake finally necessitates his re-generative poem, *Milton,* to reveal beneath the veneer of historical mediation the ahistorical true poet, true man, true prophet, *the* Genius of the "an-cients" — the same ones Christ cites to Satan. Such an "Eastering," as Hartman calls it, is in reality nondirectional and nonspatial, as well as nontemporal. "Blake will not localize the poetic genius," he says more correctly later on in the same essay, for its "source" is no land but the "true Man"; and, even more succinctly, "the East is wherever poetry is."[34] That is why Albion is Jerusalem is England.

For the eighteenth century, however, the genius loci was crucial: the "parting Genius" of Milton's *Nativity Ode* is restored through Lycidas's be-coming the "Genius of the shore," "an English genius for an English place" as Hartman says.[35] Newton may have demanded the muse, but England as a whole demanded it more: "a new poetry might be founded, peculiarly English, both great and enlightened, enchanting and rational."[36] Unfortunately (not, I think, tragically) for most of the many progress-of-poetry writers, again in Collins's words, "With many a vow from hope's aspiring tongue," their "trembling feet" Milton's "guiding steps pursue: / In vain . . ." (*Ode on the Poetical Character*, lines 70-72). In *The Passions. An Ode for Music* the message is the same:

> O Music, sphere-descended maid,
> Friend of pleasure, Wisdom's aid,
> Why, goddess, why to us denied?
> Lay'st thou thy ancient lyre aside?
> . . . .
> O bid our vain endeavors cease,
> Revive the just designs of Greece,
> Return in all thy simple state!
> Confirm the tales her sons relate![37]

This is as crucial a confession of the alienation of poetic power in late eighteenth-century Britain as Collins's settling at the end of his *Ode to Evening* for Fancy, Friendship, Science, and Peace as tutelary deities of England's green and pleasant land. If they are "civilizing" influences "expressive of the ideals of polite society," as Hartman calls them, they are, despite his making this connection, no Blakean giant forms to "compel our imagination."[38] There were, of course, assorted self-appointed candidates for the "magic girdle"—all, so far as I know, having the good grace to advance themselves with considerable trepidation, protestations of modesty, and, more often than not, final confessions of inadequacy. In the words of the most famous of the eighteenth century's progress poems, Gray's *The Progress of Poesy*, they each may "mount and keep his distant way / Beyond the limits of a vulgar fate"; but without "the pride [or] ample pinion" that bore

> the Theban eagle . . .
> Sailing with supreme dominion
> Through the azure deep of air,

none may aspire to more than being far beneath the good, if far above the worldly great (lines 121-22, 114-17, 123).

Gray, we recall, moves the poetic spirit as far as Dryden—though even his "car" is "less presumptuous" than Milton's; but since Dryden's hands did explore the lyre to produce "Thoughts that breathe and words that burn," Gray must confess that even such music is "heard no more" (lines 103-11). In *To the Muses*, if we may now return to that poem, Blake obviously agrees, but the terms of his agreement diverge sharply from the conviction, however frustrated, of the progress-poem writers that it is meet and right that a British bard be crowned—indeed *will* be crowned. His poem invokes no place, but rather absence from place; wherever you are, he sings to the Muses, you have forsaken poetry. It is not England that cries out here, or even a British bard, but rather the poet whose universe (for that is his province) no longer sings as it did of yore. The "ninefold harmony" of the spheres is not merely silent, but the belief that animated the metaphor is dead: and where'er Blake's muses are (Spenser at least knew *where* his were), their only unforced sounds are those of Milton's "parting Genius" and the "nymphs" in the *Nativity Ode:*

> The lonely mountains o'er,
> And the resounding shore,
> A voice of weeping heard, and loud lament;
> From haunted spring and dale
> Edged with poplar pale,
> The parting Genius is with sighing sent;
> With flow'r-inwoven tresses torn
> The nymphs in twilight shade of tangled thickets mourn.
>
> (Stanza XX)

Blake's emphasis, like Milton's, is on time, not place: now as against then; and, most important, Blake's "then" is ancient times, his poets "bards of old," his song "antient melody." That ancientness Blake associates with the Bible and with the Hebraic Milton. The grammatical structure of Blake's poem, however, a long single sentence, mimics not that of the *Nativity Ode* but that of a passage from *Lycidas,* itself of course an elegy on the death of poetry:

> Ay me! whilst thee the shores and sounding seas
> Wash far away, where'er thy bones are hurled,
> Whether beyond the stormy Hebrides,
> Where thou perhaps under the whelming tide
> Visit'st the bottom of the monstrous world;
> Or whether thou, to our moist vows denied,
> Sleep'st by the fable of Bellerus old,
> Where the great Vision of the guarded mount
> Looks toward Namancos and Bayona's hold:
> Look homeward, Angel, now, and melt with ruth.   (Ll. 154-64)

If Blake has radically gentled Milton's stormier lines, his implicit identification of his muses with Lycidas and Milton himself is corroborated by two other passages in the elegy:

> Begin then, Sisters of the sacred well
> That from beneath the seat of Jove doth spring,

> Begin, and somewhat loudly sweep the string.
> Hence with denial vain, and coy excuse. (Ll. 15-18)

These absent and recalcitrant muses Blake conflates with Milton's angry berating of Nature's nymphs:

> Where were ye, Nymphs, when the remorseless deep
> Closed o'er the head of your loved Lycidas?
> For neither were ye playing on the steep
> Where your old bards, the famous Druids, lie,
> Nor on the shaggy top of Mona high,
> Nor yet where Deva spreads her wizard stream. (Ll. 50-55)

But, Milton realizes, what could they have done even if they had been there? "The Muse herself" was powerless when her "enchanting son," Orpheus, was torn to pieces by the Thracian Bacchantes (lines 57-63).

Against this powerlessness of Nature and the Muse alike, Milton hymns the triumph of poetry "Through the dear might of him that walked the waves" (line 173); and, as Blake's muses may be wandering "beneath the bosom of the sea," forever lost, Lycidas shall be "the Genius of the shore," in his "large recompense . . . good / To all that wander in that perilous flood" (lines 183-85). Here, then, is Milton's British Bard, the Poetic Genius, just as a Hebraic Lycidas-Milton is Blake's. *They* have not left "the antient love / That bards of old enjoyed" in the spirit of poetry; their strings move sweepingly beyond those of the "Sisters of the sacred well"; their sounds are not from "forced fingers rude"; their notes rise abundantly to join the "solemn troops and sweet societies / That sing, and singing in their glory move."[39] Blake's truncated elegy, of course, stops short of such a triumph, but the triumph seems to me to inhere in the voice of the singer, whose lyre is functioning very well indeed—albeit without the muses. "Antient melody" revives phoenix-like, Lycidas-like, from the ashes of its debasement, the day-star rising from its "ocean bed" to flame "in the forehead of the morning sky" (*Lycidas,* lines 168, 171).

In his *At a Vacation Exercise in the College* Milton salutes his native language, wherewith he will essay "some graver subject," and then envisions his muse visiting the sources of exalted poetry: it

> may soar
> Above the wheeling poles, and at heav'n's door
> Look in, and see each blissful deity
> How he before the thunderous throne doth lie,
> Listening to what unshorn Apollo sings
> To the touch of golden wires, while Hebe brings
> Immortal nectar to her kingly sire. (Ll. 33-39)

In Blake's Spenser imitation, as we have seen, having invoked Apollo as his muse, he will be further inspired by Mercury who "dost mount aloft," "thro' Heav'n's halls" enters "to where on high / Jove weighs the counsel of futurity," and soars beyond where the "thunders sound" to "Sol's palace high." Similarly, as Milton's muse will then descend to "tell at length how green-eyed Neptune raves" (line 43), so Blake's Mercury will "go / Down" and "o'er the surface of the silent deep dost fly." Milton closes this passage with a gentle chiding:

> But fie, my wand'ring Muse, how thou dost stray!
> Expectance calls thee now another way.   (Ll. 53-54)

That "expectance" and "call" Blake translates into *To the Muses*, where indeed the wandering muses stray—"in Heav'n," to "the green corners of the earth," in "the blue regions of the air" (Milton's "misty regions of wide air"), "on chrystal rocks," and "Beneath the bosom of the sea." The "antient love / That bards of old enjoy'd in you" may be Blake's redaction of Demodocus's "solemn songs at king Alcinous' feast,"

> While sad Ulysses' soul and all the rest
> Are held with his melodious harmony
> In willing chains and sweet captivity.   (Ll. 49-52)

One final note on this remarkable poem. Curiously inappropriate to the above conceptions, *To the Muses* is suffused with the language of *Comus:* "shady brows" (*Comus,* line 38), the sun's "chamber of the east" (line 101), the earth's "green shops" and "corners" (lines 716, 717), "the green earth's end" and "corners of the moon" (lines 1014, 1017), "regions mild of calm and serene air" (line 4), "diamond rocks" (line 881; cf. the "crystal wall" of mountains in *PL* VII,293), the "bosom of the deep" (line 23), the "coral-paven bed" of the sun (line 886; cf. "groves / Of coral" in *PL* VII,404-5). Although much of this diction was commonplace in the poetic realm Blake was nurtured in, its collective occurrence in *Comus* and *To the Muses* argues against mere coincidence. Yet the borrowings seem indiscriminate, patternless, without corroborative power or contextual significance, out of tune so to speak with Blake's elegiac music. Milton's poem Blake must have recognized, however, as his most sustained essay on the power of music, the very music so lamentably absent from the speaker's universe in *To the Muses*. As Angus Fletcher observes, "the triumph of the song is the main thing that happens in *Comus*"[40]—from the Orphic voice of the Attendant Spirit-Thyrsus

> Who with his soft pipe and smooth-dittied song
> Well knows to still the wild winds when they roar,
> And hush the waving woods   (ll. 86-88)

to his incantational summoning of the "muse" Sabrina (lines 859-89), to his musical return to precisely those regions in which Blake's muses seem forever lost:

> I can fly, or I can run
> Quickly to the green earth's end,
> Where the bowed welkin slow doth bend,
> And from thence can soar as soon
> To the corners of the moon. (Ll. 1013-17)

These regions are of course the same as those envisioned in the *Vacation Exercise*. No muses will return, nor does Blake want them to (easily overlooked is the fact that he does not plead for their revival). Instead "we on earth with undiscording voice" will "rightly answer" the "melodious noise" of Milton's *At a Solemn Music*, written just prior to *Comus*. That music sounds "everlastingly."

> O may we soon again renew that song,
> And keep in tune with heav'n, till God ere long
> To his celestial consort us unite,
> To live with him, and sing in endless morn of light. (Ll. 25-28)

"Mortals that would follow me," the Attendant Spirit concludes in *Comus*, "Love Virtue":

> She can teach ye how to climb
> Higher than the sphery chime. (Ll. 1018-21)

Although there is little doubt that the young Blake wished to follow, even an uncloistered Virtue would not be his guide. The muses dead or moribund, *his* attendant spirit will be Milton, who will, if he has not visibly done so already in *To the Muses*, "teach [him] how to climb"—or, in the words of *Paradise Lost*, teach him how

> to wander where the Muses haunt
> Clear spring, or shady grove, or sunny hill,
> Smit with the love of sacred song. (III,27-29)

In any case, imitation now is becoming (if it has not become) criticism.[41]

ANTITHETICAL
STRUCTURE

SOME TIME AGO Harold Bloom
identified the structure of *The Marriage of Heaven and Hell* as dialectical
and, before him, Frye confirmed the value of regarding *The Songs of Innocence and of Experience* as dialectically ordered.[1] Similarly the symbolic
mental warfare in Blake's prophecies is often externalized in at least the
semblance of dialectical debate, albeit sometimes obscured by the elaborateness and complexity of other aspects of his prophetic construct.[2] More
recently the splendid work being done on Blake's "composite art" has shown
conclusively that, in W.J.T. Mitchell's words, there is "an energetic rivalry,
a dialogue or dialectic between vigorously independent modes of expression"—that is, between verbal and graphic design; "the effect is a kind of
counterpoint in which each medium proceeds with its own independent
formal integrity, while interacting with the other to form a complex unified
whole."[3] Even without reference to the designs, however, we have not only
learned to perceive, say, the two sets of *Songs* as "arguing" with each other
(they are, after all, songs *of,* not songs *about*) but also individual songs as
embodying their own antitheses and dramatically enacting, singly as well as
cumulatively, a marriage or synthesis only in the total context of the combined work as coherent book. Anterior to such mature accomplishments,
not to mention the brilliantly conceived structural, verbal, and iconic rela-
tional complexities of *Jerusalem,* lie the simpler procedure of antithesis and
the more rudimentary notion of contrast.

Contrast is defined succinctly (and appropriately) by "the religious" in
Plate 3 of *The Marriage of Heaven and Hell:*

> Good is the passive that obeys Reason. Evil is the active springing from
> Energy.
> Good is Heaven. Evil is Hell. (E34)

And it is validated by the Devil in Plate 4 as the "Errors" promulgated by
"All Bibles or sacred codes":

> 1. That Man has two real existing principles Viz: a Body & a Soul.
> 2. That Energy. calld Evil. is alone from the Body. & that Reason. calld
> Good. is alone from the Soul. (E34)

Contrast, then, is essentially inert, a noninteractive (and, more crucially, abstract) relationship between "two real existing principles" or objects. Just as "Demonstration Similitude & Harmony are Objects of Reasoning" (Annotations to Reynolds, E648), so too are contrasts, which, as we say, "stand" in (nonenergetic) opposition to each other, or which engage in obvious conflict, each intent on effecting a "negation" of the other. For Blake this is corporeal war, the fallen world's version of mental war. As Milton says to his Spectre, Satan:

> I know my power thee to annihilate
> And be a greater in thy place, & be thy Tabernacle
> A covering for thee to do thy will, till one greater comes
> And smites me as I smote thee & becomes my covering.[4]

This cyclical smiting may be one of the reasons Blake abandoned his poem on *The French Revolution;* perhaps he saw (or even foresaw) that the glorious promise would inevitably, and inexorably, collapse into the world of time and therefore into self-renewing tyranny, the same round over again. In the later eponymous prophecy Milton goes on to remind us, as he eschews mortal combat with Satan:

> There is a Negation, & there is a Contrary
> The Negation must be destroyd to redeem the Contraries
> The Negation is the Spectre; the Reasoning Power in Man
> This is a false Body: an Incrustation over my Immortal
> Spirit; a Selfhood, which must be put off & annihilated alway.
>
> (40:32-36, E141)

The "positive" version of contrast is what Mitchell calls "complementarity":[5] in the composite of text and design the sort of "illustration" to the text that merely illustrates; in textual terms, a verbal equivalency or, to use Blake's word, similitude, a comparability of fragments relatable to a rationally conceivable whole. "I will not Reason & Compare," cries Los in *Jerusalem:* "my business is to Create" (10:21, E151), more specifically to create out of contrariety imaginative unity. In this light it is not without interest, then, that Blake never employs the word "contrast" as verb or noun in his poetry.

Somewhere between the reductiveness of this complementarity and the intellectual-imaginative vigor of dialectic there seems to me to be a middle ground, one that I should like to define in formal terms as antithetical structure—dialectic in its emergent form. Although all three structural modes will appear persistently throughout Blake's entire oeuvre (indeed the uses to which he puts each mode, and the interrelationships among them, may constitute a valuable, as yet largely unexplored, avenue into his purely verbal strategies from the *Songs* through *Jerusalem*), it is striking that even as early as the *Poetical Sketches* he began experimenting with them. If we cannot demonstrate with confidence the dialectical nature of the volume as a whole, it nevertheless rarely employs, and, as a volume, doesn't rest on, the poetic or structural or philosophical validity of mere contrast.

Some years ago I argued that *To Winter* not only contrasts sharply with the three preceding seasonal poems but perversely parodies their seemingly sequential development toward fulfillment and unity, while destroying any illusions readers might have about the validity, comfort, and consolations of seasonal cyclicity.[6] Somewhat similarly, *To the Evening Star* parodies *To Morning*, though with far less explicitly devastating consequences. I shall examine these two splendid poems more thoroughly in the next chapter, but it will be helpful here to notice certain aspects of their relationship to each other, as well as to the seasons poems. For example, as morning "issue[s] forth" to "awake the dawn that sleeps in heaven," lets "light / Rise from the chambers of the east," and brings "the honied dew that cometh on waking day," so evening comes forth lighting its "bright torch of love," and scatters its

> silver dew
> On every flower that shuts its sweet eyes
> In timely sleep.

As the "radiant morning" salutes the sun who is "Rouz'd like a huntsman to the chace" and appears "upon the hills," so evening puts on its "radiant crown" and speaks "silence" while the sun "rests on the mountains." Thus far but gentle parody if parody at all—the echoed phrasing only minimally insistent. But then as the Diana-like sun in *To Morning* quickly rushes off to the hunt, in *To the Evening Star* all too soon the Arcadian scene fades with the star's withdrawal, the

> wolf rages wide,
> And the lion glares thro' the dun forest.

Despite the familiarity of the lion-wolf-sheep trope in pastoral literature, Blake is at some pains here to absent the otherwise everpresent shepherd from the scene—indeed from the poem, which moves nonpastorally from lover to poet (perhaps) to an indistinct generalized "we." Thus although the flocks are "cover'd" with the evening star's "sacred dew," the poem concludes with only an earnest prayer that they will be protected "with thine influence." We are not told whether that influence works (or indeed how it *can* work once the evening star has withdrawn) or whether the sacred dew really does ward off raging wolves and glaring lions. Equally descendental, to use Hartman's apt term,[7] is the movement from the virgin world of morning to the human "loves" of "our evening bed" to the darkly ominous "dun forest" and its bestial rapaciousness. It takes little effort to see here, condensed and even truncated because of the nonconclusive fragmentariness of *To Morning*, at least something of the overall antithetical structure of the seasons poems; but if we are alert to Blake's shrewd use of Spenser's *Epithalamion* in both the evening and morning poems, we will have some better purchase on their striking unity in division.

It has often been pointed out that *To Morning* echoes Spenser's lines:

> Loe where she comes along with portly pace
> Lyke Phoebe from her chamber of the East,
> Arysing forth to run her mighty race,
> Clad all in white, that seemes a virgin best. (Ll. 148-51)

Seldom noted, however, is that Spenser's bride, like Blake's evening star (not his morning), is described as an "angell"—if not simply "fair-hair'd" as in Blake, still with "long loose yellow locks lyke golden wyre" (lines 153-54). Later in Spenser's poem "the bright euening star with golden creast" appears,

> Fayre childe of beauty, glorious lampe of loue
> That all the host of heauen in rankes doost lead,
> And guydest louers through the nightes dread. (Ll. 286-90)

Spenser's speaker then orders his bride's attendants away and like Blake's speaker in the *Evening Star* welcomes night:

> Spread thy broad wing ouer my loue and me,
> That no man may vs see,
> And in thy sable mantle vs enwrap,
> From feare of perill and foule horror free. (Ll. 319-22)

And, he continues, with Blake still listening intently,

> let stil Silence trew night watches keepe,
> That sacred peace may in assurance rayne,
> And tymely sleep, when it is tyme to sleepe,
> May poure his limbs forth on your pleasant playne,
> The whiles an hundred little winged loues,
> Like diuers fethered doues,
> Shall fly and flutter round about your bed. (Ll. 353-59)

But unlike Blake, who in *To Morning* transforms Diana into a sun goddess but absents her from his evening poem, Spenser has her appear as the moon, Cynthia, to bless the nuptial bed with fruitfulness; and the "powers which in the [stars] remayne" will

> Poure out your blessing on vs plentiously,
> And happy influence vpon vs raine. (Ll. 417-18)

As David Wagenknecht observes, what has happened to the epithalamic tradition in Blake's hands is that an urgent need for protection supplants the usual combination of watchfulness and beseeched fruitfulness; the positive saluting of life is negated by the fear of death and the assuredness of Spenser's "sacred peace" is diminished to only hopefully impervious "sacred dew." Wagenknecht goes on to demonstrate how *To the Evening Star* ramifies into the *Songs of Innocence* poem *Night* and thence into the well-known forests of the night where, if not wolves and lions, tigers rage and glare.[8] Even without such a forward glance, however, the diurnal patterning recalls that of Blake's four seasons. *To Spring* and *To Morning* are invocatory in precisely the same biblical terms, a parallelism accentuated by the overlapping of the two focal words: thus Spring initially appears looking "down / Thro' the clear windows of the morning." Both "issue forth," the "holy feet" of Spring to "come o'er the eastern hills," the "buskin'd feet" of morning appearing "upon our hills." Spring scatters its pearls of dew upon "our love-sick land" while Morning brings "the honied dew that cometh on waking day." Yet the patent eroticism of *To Spring* finds no counterpart in the virginal *To Morning,* any more than the *Epithalamion*'s Cynthia with her fructifying power is identifiable with the chaste Diana of Blake's morning poem. On the other hand, in *To the Evening Star* the "golden crown" that Spring (in *To Spring*) will bestow on the love-sick land becomes the star's "radiant crown" under whose aegis she will "smile upon our evening bed" and "on our loves."

What is missing from the diurnal poems is, of course, noon and afternoon: Blake's Summer in which noon rides "his fervid car" and his Autumn "laden with fruit." The latter's song in *To Autumn,* however, substantially does complete the diurnal analogy by summing up the erotic season sequence of courtship to consummation:

> love runs in her thrilling veins;
> Blossoms hang round the brows of morning, and
> Flourish down the bright cheek of modest eve.[9]

That leaves winter. When Autumn flees "from our sight," it is "o'er the bleak / Hills" that he goes, the same hills on which Morning appeared and on which the sun rests in *To the Evening Star*—and the same hills that are skeletalized into the "groaning rocks" and "cliffs" of *To Winter.* This studied parallelism invites us to associate that direful monster's rape of the land and the tyranny of his iron car, unchained storms, and scepter with the roving and unrestrained ravening of wolf and lion in *To the Evening Star,* an association that underlies Blake's later fusion of the metallic horror of the one and the bestiality of the other in *The Tyger:*

> What the hammer? what the chain,
> In what furnace was thy brain?

> What the anvil? what dread grasp,
> Dare its deadly terrors clasp? (E25)

While the context and full implications of *The Tyger* passage are obviously inapplicable, with respect to these early poems it seems to me not untoward to see the forests of the night prevailing over the effete pastoralism of sacred dews, stars' influence, and the joys of innocent love, Blake's antithetical structures here laying the groundwork for the parodic-dialectic of *Songs of Innocence and of Experience.*

Antithetical structuring in Blake, then, while falling short of parodic interanimation, is still an infusing of vitality and energy into the relative inertness and obviousness of contrast. It is "active," to use his own apt terminology in *The Marriage of Heaven and Hell,* as opposed to the "passive that obeys Reason," that sort of passiveness which produces the opposite of contrast as well, "similitude."[10] Contrast is the stuff of "Fable or Allegory . . . a totally distinct & inferior kind of Poetry";[11] antithetical structure is a mode of criticism, a verbal and figural intra- and inter-patterning that serves as a prelude to imaginative synthesis, the ultimate Blakean dramatic articulation of which is a marriage. Given the impressiveness of Blake's achievement in the seasonal and diurnal poems it can be, and has been, argued that those poems are almost surely the most mature of Blake's *Poetical Sketches,* and that therefore claiming them as anticipatory of later poetic developments is critically defensible, not to say comfortable. Perhaps; but what of the other poems in the *Sketches?* Despite unpromising titles and seemingly even less auspicious infrastructures, evidence of the persistence of pastoral (that is, seasonal and diurnal) oppositions is discernible in all of them. *Fair Elenor,* as we have seen, is a night poem, filled with death and horror: her lord, erstwhile "like a flower upon the brows / Of lusty May," "a star, in highest heav'n," and "the opening eyes of day," is "darken'd; like the summer's noon, / Clouded. . . ." *The Prologue to King John,* after its "patriotic" blood-bath and "the work of death," concludes with Albion's sons joying "as in the morning! Her daughters sing as to the rising year"; and *King Edward the Third* parodically celebrates the darkness of war, soldiers as "ravening wolves" and "lions rouz'd by light'ning from their dens," and bloody death as the pursuit of life and night, sunshine and morning, play and sport and dance, and the rebirth of spring (I cite here but a few of the relevant passages): Edward's troops "beam forth lustre on a darkling world" (note the echo of the opening of the Spenser imitation); the Prince "has danc'd in the field / of battle, like the youth at morrice play"; "Death doth sport / In the bright sunshine of this fatal day"; Dagworth's "heart dances" in anticipation of the battle, and he feels himself "as light / As the young bridegroom going to be married"; "Morning / Shall be prevented by their swords gleaming / And Evening hear their song of victory"; and, most extraordinary of all,

>   the bright morn
> Smiles on our army, and the gallant sun
> Springs from the hills like a young hero
> Into the battle, shaking his golden locks
> Exultingly. . . .[12]

The other major war poem, *Gwin, King of Norway,* is unrelievedly and un-parodically a night and winter poem: Gordred's "sons of blood" are "like lions' whelps . . . / Seeking their nightly food" and even their wives and children howl "furious as wolves / In the bleak wintry day"; his "nations" are "black," o'erclouding the day, and Gwin's host is "black as night, / When pestilence does fly," "scattering death / Thro' the red fev'rous night"; the stars "drop like fruit unto the earth, / Thro' the fierce burning night."

Although not a "war poem" proper, *Samson* too is a night piece: "Night, noon-tide of damned spirits, over the silent earth spreads her pavilion" and the land "groans . . . and seeks to hide her bruised head under the mists of night." Against this darkness Blake juxtaposes his invocation to truth, reminiscent, as we have seen, of that in the Spenser imitation: "O Truth, that shinest with propitious beams, turning our earthly night to heavenly day . . . thou visitest our darkling world with blessed feet" (cf. stanza 2 of *To Spring,* the "buskin'd feet" of *To Morning,* and the penultimate stanza of *Fresh from the Dewy Hill*—not to mention, of course, the later *And Did Those Feet in Ancient Time* prefatory to *Milton*). The *Imitation of Spencer* invokes "Golden Apollo," the sun, and his beams of truth to deck the poet's "darkling verses" and "enlight" his "sleeping brain." More nearly a morning-spring poem, though obviously clouded by the fact of absence, is *To the Muses* with its invocatory "chambers of the East" and "of the sun." The contrary of this may be found in the twin prose poems, *The Couch of Death* and *Contemplation.* The former invokes "veiled Evening" who, in good pastoral fashion, "walked solitary down the western hills . . . till the curtains of darkness were drawn." At the same time, we learn later in the poem that the seasonal setting is summer, with stars faintly glimmering in the sky; and the "consolation" for the youth's death is cast in the familiar imagery of Blake's seasons poems: "the sun shine[s], and the drops of rain glisten, the yellow harvest breathes" and the "breath" of the transformed "night slept among the leaves of the forest: the bosom of the lofty hill drank in the silent dew, while on his majestic brow the voice of Angels is heard" (cf. *Fresh from the Dewy Hill* as well). Finally, even the least likely of the *Sketches, Blind-Man's Buff,* participates in this overall motif-fabric as we have seen, for it is a winter night-piece whose Thomsonian social fireside is curiously turned by Blake to the muted violence of "the game."

My perhaps tedious spinning out of these citations is to suggest that the seasonal and diurnal paradigms so sophisticatedly exploited in the six poems that stand at the beginning of *Poetical Sketches* evolved gradually in at least a number of the volume's other poems rather than being superimposed *ab extra*. In these other poems the paradigm is rarely insisted upon, nor does it determine their structures. Rather, the structures as they aspire to antithetical inter- and intra-animation through other poetic strategies invite, as it were, the applicability and pertinence of the paradigm in a supporting role. That group of poems in *Poetical Sketches* simply entitled *Song* is a case in point. To accept for the moment without cavil Malkin's very early date for *How Sweet I Roam'd*, let me extrapolate from that "fact" a relatively early date for all the "songs" as the locus of Blake's discovery not so much of the paradigm itself (in its obviousness it needed no "discovery") as of the imaginative power inherent in the very obviousness of its constituent contrasts or antitheses.

In his excellent essay on "Blake's Songs of Spring" Michael Tolley has suggested that *When Early Morn Walks Forth in Sober Grey* dramatizes "the voice of experience expressing the pangs of jealousy" and is thus a contrary song to the preceding *Fresh from the Dewy Hill*, with its paradisal "times of innocence, and holy joy." "In retrospect, then," he goes on, "the first song betrays infatuation rather than ideal love: each field and village only *seemed* Edenic."[13] But while Tolley's perception of this internal relationship between the two songs is astute, his interpretation of the relationship is open to question—or at least to modification. That *Fresh from the Dewy Hill* is a song of spring goes without saying. More properly it is a song of spring and morning "married" in "times of innocence, and holy joy," of "heav'nly light" and angelic music. But the last stanza invokes not the sublimed pastoralism of "the morn" and "merry year" in which even the villages seem "the haunt of holy feet" but rather the physical realities of the mistress's village, of sleep, of night's shade, whose "innocence" is qualified by the experiential "more than mortal fire" that "burns in [the] soul" of the speaker. If that fire inspires his song, it also calls into question the reality or substantiality, the physical durability and final validity, of the song's fiction. For sleep and night's shade, no matter how sweet, are "timely," as Blake reminds us in *To the Evening Star*—that is, invocatory of the world of time as distinct from the angelic purity and timelessness of the Edenic first four stanzas where the maiden, "risen like the morn," beams "with heav'nly light" eternally "glitt'ring in the sky." She is at once the sunrise, noon's brilliance, the evening star, and the moon. Yet the antithetical perspective of the fifth stanza, which Blake signals by its initial "But," insists upon her humanity and thus her mortality: she does, every night, close "her eyes in sleep beneath night's shade" and the village where she lives is, though "sweet" to the speaker, nevertheless not "the haunt of holy feet" at all.

There is nothing necessarily ominous about this: the song does not go so far as *To the Evening Star* in its descendentalism, to use again Hartman's idea in a way he didn't quite intend. Yet the times of innocence and joy, the terrestrial paradise of Beulah in Blake's later mythology, are sustainable only by imaginative effort, song. In real villages real feet press real earth. In one sense, then, Tolley is right about *When Early Morn*, the immediately succeeding song, for the jealousy of the speaker there is bred of the realities of night and time and the ineluctable modalities of experience. Instead of the maiden arising like the morn, beaming with heavenly light, morn "walks forth in sober grey" clouded by the speaker's apprehension even before he sees the youth walking by his maiden's side "in stolen joy and pride." To put it somewhat too baldly, morning appears as if she were Milton's twilight or evening:

> Now came still ev'ning on, and twilight gray
> Had in her sober livery all things clad.[14]

Here in the coldness of psychological, if not physical, realities there is no innocence and holy joy but rather the external projections of the same non-innocent mind Blake drew so tellingly and frighteningly later in *Infant Sorrow* — a world perennially darkened by a perversely cherished pensiveness and "pleasing woe." The familiar literary love-sickness formula so rampant in the love lyrics of the Renaissance through the eighteenth century should not divert us from what Blake is about here — for he disrupts such an association by the virulence of

> O should she e'er prove false, his limbs I'd tear,
> And throw all pity on the burning air —

the last phrase a revealing echo (or anticipation) of the "burning air, / Where thousand deaths are posting up and down," into which the Prince "breathes" his hopes of avoiding war in *King Edward the Third*.[15] No "more than mortal fire" inspires his song here or reinvokes Edenic innocence; only the vague and weak surrender to cursing Fortune for his lot, dying in peace, and being forgot — that old hackneyed business which may be Blake's way of underlining the equally hackneyed unreality of pastoral Edens and delicious melancholy. The transformation of the latter in *Mad Song* gives it the final lie.

Although all this is quite neatly done, it is worth noting that it's done largely without what I have called significant allusion. In fact, *When Early Morn* is one of the least allusive poems in all of the *Sketches*. Instead Blake relies rather daringly upon the limp formulae themselves to establish the foolish fictions that are to be demolished by the experiential violence of real jealousy.[16] On the other hand, the fiction created by the lover's song in *Fresh from the Dewy Hill* owes at least something, rather startlingly, to Milton's *Nativity Ode*. In the latter's vision of the return of "the age of gold" the angels "are seen in glittering ranks"

> Harping in loud and solemn quire
> With unexpressive notes to Heaven's new-born heir.

"The shepherds on the lawn," chatting perhaps of their loves, are silenced by "such music sweet" and "holy song" sung by the "Divinely warbled voice." "Each field seems Eden," Blake summarizes; but for Milton, each village *is* the haunt of holy feet. The allusion intensifies the fiction of the first four stanzas virtually to absurdity, making it all the more vulnerable to the unallusive reality activated by the only negatively charged word in the poem, the "But" of stanza 5. Of course, we can now see, no "rising glories beam around [the lover's] head" at all, his feet only seem "wing'd," and hers are as far from "holy . . . angels' feet" as her tongue is from that of angels.[17] The world may seem Eden, the age of gold, just as "each village seems the haunt of holy feet," but, as *When Early Morn* makes clear, the "merry year" of love songs not infrequently appears as it does in *Paradise Regained* after a night of tempests and storm, "in amice grey" (IV,427). And black-eyed maids all too often "*prove* false" (my italics), Blake's verb a potent harbinger of demythification. Is this the reason he borrowed a single phrase from the Malbecco-Hellenore story in *The Faerie Queene?* The deceiving Hellenore we recall, after her affair with Paridell, deserts him for the satyrs

> Whom their May-lady they had newly made:
> She proud of that new honour, which they red,
> And of their louely fellowship full glade,
> Daunst liuely, and her face did with a Lawrell shade.   (III,x,44)

In *Fresh from the Dewy Hill* the speaker says that "Round [his] young brows the laurel wreathes a shade"—as if he were the king of the May—only to have *When Early Morn* reveal him to be a Malbecco after all: trying to die in peace and be forgot Malbecco in his abortive suicide leap, cursing what Blake calls with studied irony his "bright fortune for [his] mixed lot,"

> can . . . neuer dye, but dying liues,
> And doth himselfe with sorrow new sustaine,
> That death and life attonce vnto him giues.
> And painefull pleasure turnes to pleasing paine.
> There dwels he euer [in his cave/grave], miserable swaine,
> Hatefull both to him selfe, and euery wight;
> Where he through priuy griefe, and horrour vaine,
> Is woxen so deform'd, that he has quight
> Forgot he was a man, and *Gealosie* is hight.   (III,x,60)

If indeed the Malbecco-Hellenore story is embedded in Blake's imaginative construct here, the triggering phrase is a woefully insufficient prod to the memories of all but the most devoted and retentive Spenser reader. Although the allusion is marvelously apt (and I am inclined to believe it is there), it is certainly possible that Blake simply drew the laurel-shade locution from his ample store of other stock phrases, the more insistent Miltonic imagery and language indicating in themselves the direction of his thinking here. But let us move on to the other songs. In contrast to the fairly clear antithetical structures of the two poems just dealt with are such songs as *Love and Harmony Combine* and the deliberately *L'Allegro*-like *I Love the Jocund Dance*.[18] As I believe Blake, at least at first, perceived Milton's twin poems as not really interacting with each other even protodialectically,[19] so these two poems of his own do not "need" an *Il Penseroso* for their "completion." This is not to say that there are no penseroso poems among the songs of *Poetical Sketches: My Silks and Fine Array* and *When Early Morn* are surely two—though the latter, as I have shown, is a more "necessary" poem with respect to *Fresh from the Dewy Hill* than *My Silks* is to any other poem in the *Sketches*. What is interesting about *I Love the Jocund Dance*, though, is what Blake makes of it in *The Ecchoing Green* and more especially in the *Laughing Song* plate of *Songs of Innocence*, whose illustration stands in strikingly sober and static contrast to the exuberance and vitality of the text. But this is not the place for my view of that amazingly deceptive and allusively complex plate.[20]

Love and Harmony does have some interest beyond its insouciant idyllicism, however, by way of its Spenser allusions—indeed a kind of troublesome interest in the indiscriminate mixture the allusions create of proper and profane love. Blake's fourth stanza, for example, evokes the *Epithalamion* and its marriage of "innocence and virtue," "love and harmony," and song:

> Hark how the cheerefull birds do chaunt theyr laies
> And carroll of loues praise.
> . . . .
> So goodly all agree with sweet consent,
> To this dayes merriment.
> Ah my deere loue why doe ye sleepe thus long,
> When meeter were that ye should now awake,
> T'awayt the comming of your ioyous make,
> And hearken to the birds louelearned song,
> The deawy leaues among.   (*Epithalamion*, ll. 78-89)

In Phaedria's bower, however,

> Trees, braunches, birds, and songs were framed fit,
> For to allure fraile mind to carelesse ease.   (*FQ* II,vi,13)

And it is in the Temple of Venus that "litle loues, and sports, and ioyes" flock round (IV,x,42) and "the merry birds," "pricked" with Venus's "lustfull powres," "Chirpe loud to thee out of their leauy cages" (IV,x,45). Similarly, it is in the Garden of Proserpine that the tree bearing the "goodly golden fruit" grows (II,vii,53-55)—though it is quite possible, of course, that

Blake had in mind the more readily available golden apples of Hesperides. Despite the ominousness of these contexts, however, there is obviously no trace of Ate or Acrasia or Proserpina in Blake's poem. The *Epithalamion* allusion, on the other hand, is as apt[21] as the others are irrelevant—thus illustrating the distinction I drew earlier between imitation and allusion, or between "ornament" and a structurally and thematically enriching contextualized borrowing. The one is a bow to what oft was thought and ne'er so well expressed, the other an imaginative re-creation.[22] Of the latter Blake's most mature antithetical structures will be conceived, of the former *I Love the Jocund Dance.*

Some better sense of the distinction I have been drawing between poems that contrast with each other and those that interact antithetically with each other, or within themselves, may be derived from the poems orbiting in one way or another around *Mad Song.* Its obvious oppositeness, however deepened beyond mere penserosoism, to *I Love the Jocund Dance* is not interesting, much less illuminating. The contrast is passive. The same relationship subsists between *Mad Song* and *Love and Harmony Combine,*[23] whose allusiveness to Spenser is decorative, if generally supportive imagistically, as *L'Allegro* is to *I Love the Jocund Dance.* But if we juxtapose *Mad Song* to *My Silks and Fine Array,* for example, a revealing interanimation is triggered, one that amounts to a kind of bold self-satire as well as a typical Blakean attack on empty—or at least flaccid—literary convention (similar in kind to the undermining of cyclicity in the seasons and diurnal poems).

It is well known that *My Silks and Fine Array* participates in a poetic tradition that had become commonplace well before Blake's day, that of the sighing Strephon who will die of love (all too often, alas, without the invigorating pun on "die")—though, as W. H. Stevenson reminds us, it is rare in that tradition to find a woman as the speaker, the man disdainful and cold.[24] As interesting as that inversion may be, the total impact of the poem relies on the hyperbolic convention. As a result the contrasts within the poem are relatively inert: silks and fine array versus a winding sheet, smiles versus "mournful lean Despair," her lover's fair face so like morning and spring (cf. *Fresh from the Dewy Hill*) versus his heart "wintry cold" like the tomb, the mildness of spring versus the "winds and tempests" beating on her grave. Even the momentary and rudimentary transformation of these romantic fictions into the flower-May-star-morning/cloud-cold-tomb-real-corpse contrast in *Fair Elenor* is recognizably more alive. If some life is breathed into the formulae by Blake's technical achievement in the rhymes and verse form of *My Silks,* there is little or nothing in the poem to engage us in its feigning. In *Mad Song,* on the other hand, the wished-for "winds and tempests" and the lover's wintry heart are transformed into the torturing "wild winds," "tempests," and cold of a real storm and real grief, the dead convention startlingly reincarnated in the nameless and causeless state of the speaker's mind. Here is no self-deception as Bloom suggests:[25] that is precisely what the poem inveighs against in such self-indulgent fictions as the "languish'd air" of *My Silks* and the "pleasing woe" of *When Early Morn.* To look ahead, even circumspectly, for a moment, Blake's state of experience will have no room for fanciful conceits born of sentimental self-dramatization (except of course where the conceit itself is satirized as an unselfconscious fiction) nor will his innocence be "purely" pastoral.

Such relief from the wrenchings of grief as is available to the speaker of *Mad Song* is patently ambiguous, as well as diametrically opposed to the consolatory rest (or at least the psychological equilibrium) of a poetic death and self-elegizing. We know, for example, that the fourth line of *Mad Song* was printed as "And my griefs unfold," and that Blake hand-corrected the verb to "infold" in six of the extant copies of the volume.[26] Given his early acquaintance with Spenser's poetry it is at least possible that a passage from the first canto of Book II of *The Faerie Queene* surfaced in his mind during the composition of *Mad Song.* Guyon and the Palmer "by a forest side" suddenly hear the air rent "With percing shriekes, and many a dolefull lay," the cries of Amavia dying beside the slain Sir Mordant and holding tightly to her bleeding breast her child. She curses the "carelesse heauens" for their injustice and seeming "delight / To see sad pageants of mens miseries," and calls upon "sweetest death" to "take away this long lent loathed light" to free her captive soul "from wearie thraldome" (II,i,35-36). Rushing to her side, Guyon stanches her wound, lifts her up in his arms, and urges her to speak:

> Yet if the stony cold
> Haue not all seized on your frozen hart,
> Let one word fall that may your griefe vnfold,
> And tell the secret of your mortall smart;
> He oft finds present helpe, who does his griefe impart   (II,i,46)

It is a marvelous allusion if indeed it is creditable. But whether we catch it or not, we can still acknowledge what was perhaps Blake's original idea that sleep is a condition of the mind (and body) in which griefs could be unfolded and hence disburdened. In the poem no such unfolding takes place, for all too soon "morning peeps," precluding sleep and the solace of silent unburdening. In contrast, wrackingly awake the speaker finds no comfort or solace at all in the actual "imparting" of his grief, for there is no Guyon there to provide "present helpe."

On the other hand, Blake's inked changes of "unfold" to "infold" (even though they appear in only some of the extant emended copies of the *Sketches*) suggest either a recognition of the obscurity of the allusion or a simple correction of a printer's error (but why not then correct *all* copies?). In either case the effect is that instead of possibly finding "present helpe," the speaker of *Mad Song* hopes that sleep will quietly absorb all his grief and give him rest. The important thing is that the shallow fiction of *My Silks and Fine Array* is thrown into bold relief. Similarly the self-resignation to the mythical grave at the end of *My Silks* Blake warps into the insane insistence on maintaining a consistent world of darkness, cold, and storm, on even transforming the universe (heaven, earth, night, day) into a kind of satisfying reflection of the speaker's own psyche. Cold comfort to be sure, but somehow in the phantasmagoria of madness more comfortable than the conventional, yet in the world of the speaker's mind now perverse, restoratives of the sun's warmth and light.

One does not need to find in *Mad Song* the origins of Blake's Spectre to appreciate the expert demolition of poetic consolation, easy escape, and the inadequacies of literariness as an expression of human experience. Real madness lies in such fictions, for the grave is no escape, as Thel finds out all too rudely in Blake's later poem. Experience is neither to be surrendered to meekly nor avoided.[27] Even as *My Silks and Fine Array* is finally trivialized by Blake in *Mad Song,* the "error" of the latter is in man's foolish and ultimately tragic will to forcibly make his world fit his mind. The gravity of this error is underscored by Blake's angry retort near the end of his life to Wordsworth's notion in *The Excursion,* not that man willfully aligns his mind to the external world, but rather that such fittingness is both a fact and a desideratum. "You shall not bring me down to believe such fitting & fitted I know better," Blake writes (E656) alongside his transcription of lines 63-68 of "the conclusion of the first book of 'The Recluse'" (included in Wordsworth's Preface to *The Excursion*). His objection was at least threefold: (1) the premise inherent in Wordsworth's "fitting" of a viable reality "out there," distinguished from that of the mind; hence (2) the sanctification of what Abrams calls the "artifacts of reason," a Lockean contrast/comparison "incapable of reunion into a higher organization";[28] and (3) the validation of objects of sense as the equivalent of imaginative perception. No wonder, as Crabb Robinson reported of Blake, the passage "caused him a bowel complaint which nearly killed him."[29] If one must allow that Blake's point in these annotations is not precisely the burden of *Mad Song,* and even that the implications of inner-outer complementarity in the poem are sufficiently damning in themselves, Blake's attack on Wordsworth is still of interest in the total context of the poem. The next passage Blake copied (not quite accurately) out of this section of *The Excursion* on the fittingness of man to his world (which he translates as "to the vile Body") includes "madding passions mutually inflamd" and "Humanity in fields & groves" piping "solitary anguish" (E656). Did *Mad Song* cling to his memory so long (the Wordsworth annotations were made in 1826)?[30]

Two more points about that fascinating poem. Phillips observes that it is cyclical in structure, from night to day and back to night,[31] the self-entrapment of a forcibly consistent metaphysics doomed to repeat the same (though here hardly dull) round over again. Whereas the narrative of *My Silks and Fine Array* "proceeds" from beginning to end and thus surrenders, even panders, to time, *Mad Song* describes the cyclicity of a perverted eternity, a forced timelessness that merely exacerbates the trials of time. Phillips, then, may be correct in identifying the "light" as "that of visionary illumination," the tragedy of the poem lying in the speaker's refusal to embrace it despite the "frantic pain" with which it seizes his "brain."[32] In any case, if *Mad Song* is tragic at all — and it may, of course, look forward to the higher tragedy inherent in Los's prolonged inability (overcome finally) to assume his prophetic calling — *My Silks and Fine Array* is mock-tragedy, the death as well as the love in it experientially inconsequential.

This latter is almost certainly the reason that, all commentators on the poem notwithstanding, Blake did not model his *Mad Song* on those of Percy's *Reliques* — in which death and love (even madness itself) *are* equally inconsequential.[33] Blake's is no hyperbolic lament at the lover's cruelty, disdain, or unfaithfulness; indeed it doesn't deal with love at all but with a mythology of night, corroboration for, perhaps even the seeds of which, he found in Milton. If Phillips is correct about the light imagery, we should be reminded of Milton's own invocation of darkness as inspiration:

> Befriend me, Night, best patroness of grief,
> Over the pole thy thickest mantle throw,
> And work my flattered fancy to belief
> That heav'n and earth are colored with my woe;
> My sorrows are too dark for day to know. (*The Passion*, ll. 29-33)

While Blake's poem hardly evokes the specific context of *The Passion*, this allusion elevates his conception of night-woe-madness to a level of significance far beyond that of the trivialized and even humorous "lunacy" of Percy's examples. Other Miltonic echoes conspire to the same sort of elevation. It is the fallen Adam and Eve whose now corrupted fancy breeds in their minds "wings / Wherewith to scorn the earth" (*PL* IX,1010-11); and it is Satan and his fallen hosts who hurl defiance "toward the vault of ["star-paved"] heav'n."[34] The voices and "stunning sounds . . . all confused" that assault Satan's ear emerge from the realm of chaos and old Night (*PL* II,952ff.), and the thunder, clouds, winds, and "grisly specters, which the Fiend had raised / To tempt the Son of God with terrors dire" in *Paradise Regained* are stilled there by "Morning Fair" (IV,429-31, 426), leaving Christ as unscathed as Blake's speaker is forever scarred because of his perverse insistence on turning his back, as in Adam and Eve's exodus from the garden, on the comforts of the East.[35] And, finally, it is dark-veiled Cotytto who with Hecate rides her ebon car through the Stygian darkness in *Comus*, ruling the perverse and corruption-filled universe of night till

> The nice Morn on th' Indian steep,
> From her cabined loop-hole peep.   (Ll. 139-40)

Only the poet, like the Attendant Spirit of *Comus* sent from heaven "with his soft pipe and smooth-dittied song," can "still the wild winds when they roar" (lines 86-87), for unlike Blake's self-tortured speaker he does not suffer the light seizing his brain with frantic pain.

Far less dramatic than the antithetical structures I have been discussing, but no less important, are those of two other songs, one already mentioned, the other not. The latter is *Memory, Hither Come*. By itself it commands little attention with its all too familiar contrast between the sighing lover beguiled by pleasant memories, fancies, and dreams by day and enveloped in the shades of melancholy by night.[36] Yet in the context of *Mad Song*, the seeking of "fit" places for the indulgence of one's moods takes on some special interest. For *Memory, Hither Come* is, finally, a song of waste, of life avoided, not totally unlike Thel's though she is of concern to us because of her earnest attempts, however misguided or inappropriately managed, to understand what she regards as her "plight." Similarly we care for the speaker of *Mad Song*, however benighted he is, because his madness is movingly, frighteningly human. We should also appreciate, then, that *Mad Song* is a devastating parody of the triviality of precisely the same effort the speaker in *Memory, Hither Come* makes to confirm his whims in the landscape. Like *Mad Song*, it too is a cyclical poem, only here the cycle describes the emptiness and silliness of a consistent and enduring "innocence":

> And there I'll lie and dream
> The day along:
> And, when night comes, I'll go
> To places fit for woe;
> Walking along the darken'd valley,
> With silent Melancholy.

And when day comes he'll lie and dream, and so on: the same dull round, now very dull indeed.[37] The fatuousness of such a "life" is underscored by the intransitiveness of Blake's language. The speaker will "pore," "hear," "lie," and "dream." Fancies "pass" by in the steam, and though he fishes for them, the pleasure is clearly in the fishing and their passing rather than in his catching (which we are not told ever happens). Similarly memory simply "comes" just as night comes, the speaker's response to both equally languorous. Even the verbs of action pale, as well as pall: "go," "walking." The stagnancy of it all as well as its vacant and patent foolishness emerge only by way of the poem's proximity to *Mad Song*, the latter's Miltonic ambience clashing sharply with the only specific allusion in *Memory, Hither Come*, to Gray's elegy:

> There at the foot of yonder nodding beech
> That wreathes its old fantastic roots so high,
> His listless length at noontide would he stretch,
> And pore upon the brook that babbles by.
>
> Hard by yon wood, now smiling as in scorn,
> Muttering his wayward fancies he would rove,
> Now drooping, woeful wan, like one forlorn,
> Or crazed with care, or crossed in hopeless love.　　　　(Ll. 101-8)

This shrewd choice of the most languid passage of Gray's epitome of contemplation and "silent Melancholy" bespeaks eloquently Blake's sureness of touch here, transforming the poem's apparent insouciance into the deadened, and deadening, antithesis of the vigorous assertive joy, ebullience, laughter, and sport of *I Love the Jocund Dance*. It is no accident that no song of innocence or of experience develops out of *Memory, Hither Come* while the complex imaginative infrastructures of *Laughing Song* and *The Ecchoing Green* are born in the breathing innocence of *I Love the Jocund Dance*.

　　When Early Morn Walks Forth in Sober Grey in some ways constitutes a midway house between the flimsiness of *Memory, Hither Come* and the ferocious substantiality of *Mad Song*. I have already commented on the startling turn of the last stanza, but we should also note that here a landscape consistent with the speaker's mental state is not sought, but rather "becomes." Reversing Milton's "still ev'ning" whose "twilight gray / Had in her sober livery all things clad" (*PL* IV,598-99), Blake's speaker affirms the "early morn" as "sober grey," having taken on the coloring of evening's "dusky bow'r"; and the "vale darkens" of itself at the speaker's "pensive woe." This is more nearly Wordsworth's "natural" fitting and fitted than anything else in the *Poetical Sketches*. And it is that fittingness which is abruptly shattered by the sudden violence of the last stanza, where the speaker will "throw all pity on the burning air" in precisely the same way that the words of the speaker of *Mad Song*

> 　　　　strike the ear of night,
> 　　Make weep the eyes of day;
> They make mad the roaring winds,
> 　　And with tempests play.

If *When Early Morn* lapses weakly into the hackneyed cursing of fortune, the rage of the preceding lines is a sufficient experiential leaven to redeem (almost) the final surrender to conventional consolations. *A Poison Tree* of *Songs of Experience* is not far away.

　　I have reserved *How Sweet I Roam'd from Field to Field* till last since in some ways it is the most problematical of the songs of *Poetical Sketches*. Its problematic nature stems only partly from its intrinsic properties and rather in large part from the unlikely imaginative sophistication accorded it by some respectable critics. To be sure, it is hardly a "laughing song" or "idyl of the untroubled life," as Erdman once described most of the songs except *Mad Song*.[38] Bloom, relying largely on Frye, says it's "partly . . . an esoteric parable of the fall of nature, which Blake will expand on many years later. More simply, it is a first account of the movement from Innocence into Experience, with the deceptions of nature as the responsible agent of transition."[39] Damon early on saw it as an attack on marriage, aligning it with Quid's song on "Matrimony's Golden cage" in the later *An Island in the Moon*.[40] My own inclination is to regard it, as Frye himself does despite his forward leap to *The Four Zoas* to help explain it, as "a conventional Petrarchan love-story [which] has the ambiguous tone of one."[41] As such it stands in contrast to the "harmony" of *Love and Harmony Combine*, which emblemizes a conventional pastoral marriage in two intertwined trees, one "clad in flowers fair" (the "prince of love" in *How Sweet I Roam'd*, we recall, provides the speaker "lilies" for his/her hair), the other bearing "golden fruit" (surely the same as "the summer's pride" of *How Sweet I Roam'd*) which the speaker tastes. Love, figured as a turtle-dove, sleeps, sports, and plays among the branches in the sort of indissoluble unity that informs many of the *Songs of Innocence*.

But if the last two stanzas of *How Sweet I Roam'd* are a rudimentary image of experience (or of the fall from innocence into experience), that fall is initiated curiously and uncharacteristically by love itself, with an assist from "sweet May dews" (presumably Bloom's "deceptions of nature"). It seems to me, then, that any idea of the Fall here must be imposed on the poem from Blake's later work. It simply isn't there of itself. What "happens" in the poem is essentially a Spenserian (or Petrarchan) account of how the "prince of love" leads the speaker to and "through" the

> Gardins of Adonis fraught
> With pleasures manifold

of *The Faerie Queene*, the same garden, surely, in which "Love and harmony combine":

> There is continuall spring, and haruest there
> Continuall, both meeting at one time:
> For both the boughes doe laughing blossomes beare,
> And with fresh colours decke the wanton Prime,
> And eke attonce the heauy trees they clime,
> Which seeme to labour vnder their fruits lode:
> The whiles the ioyous birdes make their pastime
> Emongst the shadie leaues, their sweet abode,
> And their true loues without suspition tell abrode.[42]

But weighed down by the very sweetness of the dew that nourishes the produce of the gardens, the speaker, now unable to roam any longer "from field to field" and fired to angry complaint by Phoebus (who somehow is unable to dry the wings), is caught by the prince of love (not, given the syntactical patterning of the poem, Phoebus, as some readers have assumed) and shut in a golden cage. To assume that is "marriage" seems to me absurd—though the weight of evidence in Blake's later usage of the figure and in the literary tradition as cited by Lowery and others seems solidly to confirm such an identification. If it is marriage, one might ask the obvious "to whom?" Mona Wilson amusingly overstates the case by saying that an answer to this question "would mean the superfluous insertion of a second little bird sulking in the corner of the cage or trilling unheeded songs from an importunate throat."[43] But she is nonetheless absolutely correct, for the assumed "marriage" is, simply, the conventional Petrarchan idea of being imprisoned by love itself:

> In nets of golden wires,
> In pearl and ruby spangled,
> My heart entangled
> Cries and help requires.
> Sweet love, from out these briars
> But thou vouchsafe to free me,
> Ere long, alive, alas, thou shalt not see me.[44]

This is precisely the predicament of the speaker of *My Silks and Fine Array*, which, perhaps not so haphazardly, is the next poem in the volume's arrangement. Such a proximity conveniently argues for the speaker of *How Sweet I Roam'd* as also, unusually so given the ancestry of this poetic mode, feminine. Irene Chayes identifies her, persuasively, as Psyche; and thus, though the prince of love's (Cupid's) oppressive action "has a quality which might be recognized as already typically Blakean . . . it is also perfectly in accord with the [Cupid-Psyche] tradition represented by the illustrations to Montfaucon and Spence."[45] The *Antiquité expliquée* and *Polymetis* Blake probably knew, but the ubiquity of the story in text and design, from Apuleius to Blake's own day, hardly necessitates singling out a particular source. Partly as a result of this traditionalism, the contrasts within *How Sweet I Roam'd* (liberty and imprisonment) and between *How Sweet I Roam'd* and *Love and Harmony Combine* on the one hand and *My Silks and Fine Array* on the other are just that: contrasts. Underscoring this fact, aside from the passive acquiescence in cliché, is Blake's reliance on a kind of abstraction—love, liberty, despair, harmony, joy—that he will later associate with negations rather than contraries.

As a lyric, then, *How Sweet I Roam'd* may be indeed, as Frye says (and others seem to agree), "one of the finest" in *Poetical Sketches*,[46] but its demonstrably simple derivativeness and passive relationship to other songs serve more persuasively to validate Malkin's statement about its adolescent inception. Can we imagine Blake characterizing *Mad Song* as "vocal rage"?

As I noted earlier, there is no way of knowing how it was decided which of Blake's poems should be included in *Poetical Sketches* (or of knowing whether these poems are all that he had written—which is hardly likely) or, more to the point, what arrangement the poems should be accorded and on whose authority. Nevertheless Blake seems to direct us, if only by the titles, to consider the "Songs" together in some fashion. To be sure, they are not yet "Songs of . . . ," but they are nevertheless suggestively interrelated thematically as well as structurally. And *pace* Ehrstine and others who badly want to see in the *Sketches* a rudimentary Blakean mythology or "system," recognition of the antithetical interplay within individual poems and between or among poems seems to me a more valuable introduction to the poetic strategies and achievements of the Blake we all know. Beyond structure, the songs also show Blake's allusionary technique in emergent, if often in but elementary, form. For the most part the allusions, if not merely gratuitous, hover somewhere on the scale between solid imitation in the neoclassical critical sense and convenient ornamentation, what Jonson called lending "a kind of Majesty to style" and "a kind of grace like newnesse."[47] The specifics of the allusive contexts are generally ignored in favor of phrasal or imagistic felicitousness and/or the prevailing ambience of Spenser's and Milton's acknowledged sweetness and sublimity. Only *Mad Song*, it seems to me, significantly engages our minds, thanks to the Milton allusions (and the contexts of those allusions), beyond the obviousness of Percy's mad songs—though even here the mixture of *Comus*, Adam and Eve, Satan's fallen angels, *The Passion*, *Il Penseroso*, and *Paradise Regained*, stunningly ambitious as it is, seems finally odd or ill-assimilated. Blake will do much better.

CYCLE
AND ANTICYCLE

WHEN Northrop Frye pointed out that Blake's personifications in *To Summer* and *To Winter* evolve into the figures of Orc and Urizen; and when Hazard Adams perceived a relationship between the several seasonal poems and Blake's idea of the fallen world and apocalypse; and when Bernard Blackstone observed in the four seasonal poems "the broad outlines" of the four Zoas,[1] they were providing invaluable critical entrées into the world of Blake's later poetry. But by focusing attention upon these harbingers of Blake's later vision we have often misread, or inadequately understood, his general relationship to *his* past. As uneasy as we might well be about Frye's categorical assertion that "Blake's masters in poetry were Gray, Collins, Chatterton, and Ossian," we ought to be more uneasy about saying that the *Poetical Sketches* "shows Blake's symbolic language in an emergent and transitional form."[2] More accurately, although "Blake is organically part of his literary age," in the *Sketches,* as Frye notes, he "shows a receptivity to a poetic environment which only a young poet of confident and assured originality would dare to assume."[3]

That Blake was receptive to the seasonal-landscape poem of his own artistic environment is an unassailable fact; but how receptive he was to the older traditions of seasonal poetry (individual and cyclical), landscape poetry, and the pastoral is almost impossible to determine. What we know of his reading is largely a product of our extrapolation from his allusions— clear, near, or (all too often) conjectural; and our knowledge about his personal library is pitifully minimal.[4] Moreover, as Rosemond Tuve properly has warned us, "The commonplaces of seasons poetry are . . . not traceable to any 'influence' except life under the same stars. . . ."[5] In this dilemma critics have turned inevitably to the most obvious "source" for Blake's season poems, Thomson—and, in so doing, have made a signal mistake in "placing" those poems. Very simply, Blake's *To Spring, To Summer, To Autumn,* and *To Winter* are like Thomson's *Seasons* only if one glances casually at their surfaces. In total conception and plan, diction, imagery, handling of personification, and other aspects of technique and content, Blake's poems represent a mature transfiguration of his poetic inheritance for purposes fundamentally different from Thomson's—as well as from those of other seasons poets. It would have been virtually impossible for Blake to be unaware of *The Seasons,* but his own "versions" are a remarkable testament to his ability to subsume and to triumph over rather than merely to assimilate his material—as well as dramatic evidence of that "assured and confident originality" Frye spoke of.

The reasons for this critical error are important not only for the study of Blake's seasons but also for the literary history of the eighteenth century. Although it is quite clear, and readily demonstrable, that Thomson's poem (as well as William Kent's famous illustrations) exerted a considerable influence on the blank verse and on the landscape poem of the next hundred years, imitations of the complete cyclical-seasonal poem are remarkably few in the eighteenth century. And of these few, William Mills, Jr.'s translation of the *Georgics* in 1780 is symptomatic of the closed nature of Thomson's influence. For Mills acknowledges having taken Thomson and John Philips (whose *Cyder,* published in 1706, was a Miltonic imitation of Virgil's pastorals) as his models.[6] Although he does not develop the point, Ralph Cohen in *The Art of Discrimination* is the first critic to suggest this discrepancy in the pattern of critical assumptions made about Thomson's poem.[7] Thomson's sources in the *Georgics,* John Armstrong's *Winter* (which he had seen in manuscript), William Hinchcliffe's *The Seasons,* and perhaps Ambrose Philips's *To the Earl of Dorset,* all employ and exploit conventions found in seasons poetry from Virgil and Ovid through the Middle Ages to Spenser, Milton, and Pope—few of which survive in Blake's poems untouched by his iconoclasm. These conventions, which largely constitute what Tuve calls the "commonplaces" of seasons poetry, also form the substance and fabric of most seasons poems, and passages on the seasons, after Thomson.

> Now cheerful Spring the circle leads
> And strows with flowers the smiling meads;
> Gay Summer next, whom russet robes adorn,
> And waving fields of yellow corn;
> Then Autumn, who with lavish stores the lap of Nature spreads,
> Decrepit Winter, laggard in the dance,
> (Like feeble age oppres'd with pain)
> A heavy season does maintain,
> With driving snows, and winds and rain;
> Till Spring, recruited to advance,
> The various year rolls round again.

This passage, from Johns Hughes's *An Ode to the Creator of the World* (published in 1713), a précis not of Thomson of course, who had not as yet written, but of Spenser or Virgil, illustrates the kind of conventional structure and imagery that are used for a variety of purposes on a variety of occasions in virtually all the seasons poetry immediately preceding and following Thomson.[8]

This situation—the great influence of Thomson's Miltonic blank verse and the language of his description, the fact that his *Seasons* spawned almost no direct (if many bastard) progeny, and the prominent inclusion of Virgilian and Spenserian elements in his major poem—has led critics and literary historians into a peculiar contradiction, one that may be regarded as defining the poetical milieu out of which Blake's seasonal poems emerged. For example, Patricia Meyer Spacks writes baldly that Thomson had "many imitators," yet names none; nor does she demonstrate or clarify in any way the nature of these "imitations."[9] Douglas Grant writes in a similar vein and with an equally sweeping vagueness: "A glance through any book of poetry written after its publication will show that every considerable poet thereafter was affected either directly or indirectly by this extraordinary work."[10] And Margaret Lowery assures us that "the periodicals and miscellanies were filled with poems imitative of one or all of Thomson's seasons"—though she gives but three examples.[11] On the other hand Calvin D. Yost in his survey of the poetry of the *Gentleman's Magazine* demonstrates persuasively that "there was little real nature poetry after Thomson";[12] while R. F. Jones, in addressing the complex problem of the relationship between the pastoral and the descriptive nature poem, generally subscribes to a line of influence defined by the poet Collins's admission that Pope's *Pastorals*, not Thomson, were responsible for his seasonal descriptions and, by implication, for much of the descriptive verse, and particularly the use of the temporal cycle, in the eighteenth century.[13] That *The Seasons* is not a conventional pastoral poem is generally agreed, but there is far less agreement on what seems to me equally clear, that much of the nature poetry of the eighteenth century is based on, or imitative of, a tradition well established before Thomson wrote. As Jean Hagstrum observes with respect to Thomson's "pictorialized natural personification," his technique has predecessors in *Windsor Forest*, more rudimentary in *Annus Mirabilis*, and back of these Milton, the Jonsonian masque, Ovid, and "the whole tradition of classical pictorialism."[14] While one must agree, then, that the immense popularity of *The Seasons* ensured the continuity of a combined use of an already commonplace poetic diction and of personification, as well as the familiar reduction of "Virgil's didactic fourfold" into "varied if still cultic celebrations of the English countryside,"[15] to assume that Blake's (or for that matter any other poet's) use of such a form and manner was stimulated only by Thomson is absurd. John Aiken's complaint in 1777 was not unique: "Descriptive poetry has degenerated into a kind of phraseology, consisting of combinations of words which have been so long coupled together, that like the hero and his epithet in Homer, they are become unseparable companions. . . . An ordinary versifier seems no more able to conceive of the Morn without rosy fingers and dewy locks, or Spring without flowers and showers, loves and groves, than any of the heathen deities without their useful attributes."[16] And before 1777, or indeed before Thomson, there is Pope, Dryden, Milton, Spenser, Virgil, and so on.

In view of this extraordinary complex of possible "sources," most of which may be (and often are) mere analogues, and the resultant confusion inherent in advancing easy and sweeping claims for Thomson's influence on the later century, it is manifestly inaccurate to say that Blake's seasons "are clearly indebted to Thomson's blank verse descriptive poem, *The Seasons*."[17] And to pronounce, as Lowery does, that "the first twenty lines of Thomson's *A Hymn to the Seasons* outline Blake's four seasons"[18] is to misconstrue completely Blake's poems and to force upon them an eighteenth-century idea of order and a "varied God" that Blake was not only suspicious of but was already attacking. On the other hand, one must allow the possibility that the titles of Blake's poems owe something to Thomson, and that the diction and imagery of the poems owe something to the poetical milieu Aiken bewailed; but the overriding conception of Blake's seasons owes almost nothing to the eighteenth century.

More recently than the criticism with which I have been dealing thus far, Blake's seasons "suite" (as Irene Chayes aptly calls the four poems)[19] has suffered a totally different, but I think equally misleading, critical formulation—that derived from the paradigm of the "progress poem." Capitalizing on a hint by Hagstrum, Geoffrey Hartman has developed an intricate theory, most fully worked out in his analysis of Blake's diurnal poems (to which I shall turn in the next chapter), of the traditional "westering" of the poetic spirit (as in Collins, for example) from the orientalism of the Bible to England—adumbrated in *To Spring* and culminating in *To Summer* and *To Autumn*. In *To Winter*, however, "by shifting from one historical scheme to another," that is, from an east-west to a north-south axis, Blake "puts in doubt the historicity of either Progress, and so reinforces his thought that poetry is coterminous with man and not with a region."[20] This insistence on the immediacy or directness of the source, the eternal presentness of the language of the true myth as Hazard Adams defines that,[21] constitutes then an antiprogress, an occlusion of historicity and linear time. Chayes modulates this conception into a progress-of-the-poet pattern, confining the progress of poetry to *Spring* ("the Oriental spirit of Hebrew sacred poetry") and *To Summer* ("the Graeco-Roman tradition"), and asserting that it is the latter which Blake's speaker, as "product of [his] time, a complacent Neoclassical poet," accepts (*To Summer*'s last stanza constituting Blake's "ironic" indictment of such complacency). *To Autumn* to Chayes represents Blake's turning back to Milton and (somehow) Marvell to "establish that it is from the tradition of English poetry as it already exists that the speaker will learn his art in his new phase"—Autumn's "golden load" being "that tradition as a whole." *To Winter*, according to this formulation, must then be prophecy proper, not merely of the return of spring but of "the emergence of a new and higher order of life for man and nature alike—a revival and re-creation, which will require a still newer kind of poetry as its expression, beyond both lyricism and prophecy." To confirm this radical reshaping of Blake's intent in the poems Chayes concludes by literally reshaping the "suite" herself: "Blake's Seasons suite as a history of the growth of the poet properly begins with 'To Summer' and moves through successive inner and outer 'states' to what is now the first poem; when 'To Spring' is read *after* 'To Winter,' it acquires a meaning that makes it the climax of the whole sequence."[22]

I dwell on these interpretations, despite my disagreements with them, to welcome them as the fullest recognitions we have of the remarkable maturity of Blake's seasons poems—and, by extension, of much of the *Poetical Sketches* volume as a whole. Yet their error seems to me closely akin to that inherent in superimposing Thomson's order on Blake's—though, as Hartman suggests, his own perception of the nonsequential nature of the "suite" and the satiric or parodic aspects of *To Winter* share the views I expressed over fifteen years ago of Blake's overall *structural* intent here. For not only is Winter antithetical, in the sense of my earlier use of that term, to Spring-Summer-Autumn; it is their contrary in Blake's maturest dialectical sense. Or, alternatively, not only does the winter poem serve, in Chayes's words, as "an infernal contrary . . . of each [of the other poems] in turn,"[23] but the apparent sequence defined by the others is repeatedly frustrated by the linguistic and imagistic denials of temporality or sequentiality within each of them. Their constituting an antiprogress in Hartman's sense should thus be escalated into their being a nonhistory of any kind, least of all a fundamentally autobiographical, hence linear account of "the growth of the poet" as that requires us to see *To Spring* "the second time around."

Although he limits himself to commentary on *To Spring*, Michael Tolley's view, it seems to me, is sounder. If I may extrapolate on his point about the one poem for a moment, Blake "tries to induce his readers to see a present eternity in and through the mortal" seasons.[24] In the first three poems it is the "time" that returns again—as in Milton's *Nativity Ode,* and in precisely the same sense that Blake later on describes the "Eternal Image" of any thing being renewed "by its seed": "the Imaginative Image returns by the seed of Contemplative Thought" (*Vision of the Last Judgment*, E545). The verb *renew* is crucial, Blake's marvelously apt "translation" of *return:* it evokes a repetition in the infinite (not Coleridge's "finite") mind of the eternally new, the Eternal Now. Hence it is a repetition that does not repeat, a renewed and renewing vision of eternal images and "individualities" as distinct from "the things of Vegetative & Generative Nature," which, like the oak, die "as well as the Lettuce" (*Last Judgment*, E545). Only "prophets illustrate these conceptions of the Visionary Fancy by their various sublime & Divine Images as seen in the Worlds of Vision" (ibid.). Herein lies the most fundamental and radical difference between Blake and Thomson, for the latter's "worlds" are Pope's "worlds on world" that "compose one universe" in which "system into system runs"—but which " 'Tis ours to trace . . . only in our own" (*Essay on Man* I,21-25).

Even while subscribing to Tuve's observation that the paradigm of the seasons and months, of vegetative and generative Nature, is as old as art and literature themselves, I believe that the particular formulation of it that Blake employs is Spenser's, in Book VII of *The Faerie Queene*—from which Pope also borrowed, and thence Thomson and Collins (though it must be acknowledged that Collins's untraditional Winter, who "yelling through the troublous air" "rudely rends [the] robes" of Evening, is the winter Blake chose for his purposes). Conflating aspects of Spenser's seasons and months in their triumphal procession at the behest of Order to prove Mutabilitie's case for sovereignty over all, Blake also was intensely aware of the debate constituting the context for the procession—that between Nature and Mutabilitie herself. The opening of the canto presents Nature, "great goddesse," issuing forth as Blake's Spring does, and being throned in the bright "pauilion" (*FQ* VII,vii,5, 8). Spenser's Spring, "all dight in leaues of flowres" (Blake's "perfumed garments"), "forth issew'd" as Love, accompanied by "thousand birds . . . / That sweetly sung, to call forth Paramours" (VII,vii,28). His Summer, "iolly" and clad "in a thin silken cassock," after his labors "now would bathe his limbes, with labor heated sore" (VII,vii,29). Autumn is "laden with fruits that made him laugh, full glad," but Winter, unlike Collins's, is "feeble," "faint," and "weak with eld," consonant with his more usual personification (VII,vii,30-31). Paralleling their seasonal equivalents the months follow. April comes "for his loues delight" and "*Cupid* selfe about [May] fluttred all in greene" (VII,vii,33-34). Like Summer, June is "iolly," July so "hot . . . boyling like to fire / That all his garments he had cast away" (VII,vii,35-36). September is "heauy laden with the spoyle / Of haruests riches," October "full of merry glee," his head dizzy from his treading the winepress whose "ioyous oyle [and] gentle gust / Made him so frollick and so full of lust" (VII,vii,38-39). Again Winter, in the person of February, is too old and feeble to walk in the train and must ride "in an old wagon" (VII,vii,43). With them also come day and night and the "*Howres, faire daughters of high Ioue*" (Blake's "daughters of the year") all "fit to kindle loue" (VII,vii,44-45). Despite this display of her overwhelming power, Mutabilitie is defeated by Nature, who finally "the silence brake" with her case:

> I well consider all that ye haue sayd,
> And find that all things stedfastnes doe hate

And changed be: yet being rightly wayd
They are not changed from their first estate;
But by their change their being doe dilate:
And turning to themselues at length againe,
Doe worke their owne perfection so by fate:
Then ouer them Change doth not rule and raigne;
But they raigne ouer change, and doe their states maintaine.

Even so, this idea of "eterne in Mutabilitie" (III,vi,47) would clearly appeal to Blake less than Nature's idea of the "time" that "shall come" when "none no more change shall see"

But stedfast rest of all things firmely stayd
Vpon the pillours of Eternity.

Such a vision, Spenser recognized (as well as Blake), is achievable only through "that Sabaoths sight," the divinely imaginative perception (and eternal creation, "re-newal") of "that great Sabbaoth God."[25] In such a vision Winter no longer exists "Really" much less "Unchangeably":[26] in natural terms, like Blake's Winter as well as the wild boar that slew Adonis, he is

firmely . . . emprisoned for ay,
That [Venus's] sweet loue his malice mote auoyd.
In a strong rocky Caue, which is they say,
Hewen vnderneath that Mount, that none him losen may.

(III,vi,48)

Blake's distinct echo of these lines at the close of *To Winter* corroborates the connection, the power of the Spenser passage (especially "imprisoned for ay" and "none him losen may") confounding the efforts of the unimaginative to establish Winter's return to his caves as but a "proper" temporary respite. For Blake, then, it might fairly be said that at least here, in the Garden of Adonis and the Mutabilitie Cantos, Spenser's allegory is "Vision or Imagination . . . a Representation of what Eternally Exists. Really & Unchangeably" (*Vision of the Last Judgment*, E544). And his Mutabilitie is Blake's Vala, "the shadow of Jerusalem."[27]

That later mythological naming, however, is not necessary to Blake's conception in his seasons poems, which depend upon structure, as a kind of antimyth, to furnish elements of the linguistic "rough basement" undergirding those later prophecies. Basically that structure is antithetical, though its fruition blooms in the dialectic between temporal cycle and the atemporality of imaginative vision;[28] for the poems at once describe a cycle and deny the viability of that cycle. The cycle is of course that of the seasons, but Blake flattens it into a sequence describing the coming of Love (and Imagination) to the earth and the destruction of Love, a theme clearly anticipative of Blake's states of Innocence and Experience, his unfallen and fallen worlds, his garden of love that becomes in the winter of holiness the *Garden of Love* of *Songs of Experience*. In addition, of course, it anticipates Los the creator and Urizen, the destructive, tyrannical "god of this world." Even more fundamentally the apparent temporality of the sequence becomes but a symbolic surrogate for an atemporal state of eternal becoming—that is, a vision of the eternal Now. The sequence itself looks back to the Lucretian Venus, Nature or Spring, who "is the creatrix, the personification of the life-giving principle in the universe. At her coming all creatures rejoice . . . bulls and bleating flocks obey her behests, birds sing and flowers bloom. Concord reigns; the power of love is universal, the very burgeoning of the trees figure forth marriage."[29] This notion, so common in classical literature, most notably in Virgil, emanates from the theoretical union of Aether and Earth which informs so many of the literary treatments of the seasons through the Middle Ages on into the Renaissance. Blake, however, does not employ the medieval and Renaissance commonplace parallel of the four seasons, the four humors, and the four elements, though there is an analogy between his conception and that suggested by the *Secreta Secretorum,* in which in Spring "þe earthe holy takys his worshippe and fairhede, and bycomes as a fair damoysele, a spouse semly dighte of ryche ornementes and dyuers colours, to be shewyd to were yn þe feste of weddynge."[30] Although it is unlikely that Blake had any knowledge of this tradition of the seasons except insofar as he found it in Spenser and in the general association of pastoral poetry and love, such an analogy as I suggest indicates how remote Blake's conception is from the conventional pastoralism of the eighteenth century and the morally colored landscape of Thomson and others. Instead, as Tolley has shown, his conception in *To Spring,* at least, originates in the Bible. "The Song of Solomon," Tolley correctly observes, "is for Blake the classic account of a *true* vision of spring" (my italics): an overwhelming number of the substantive words in Blake's poem are biblical, and of those all but a few are found in the Canticles. Tolley also suggests that the "strategy" of those sources is "fully and almost exclusively Miltonic," by which he means the Englishing of the orientalism of their origins.[31] The mediator of this Englishing for Blake is, as I have suggested, Spenser, the familiar Blakean prophetic "line of vision," from the Bible to England's two great prophets to himself, thus being not merely in its formative stages but already established.

The erotic note of the Canticles is immediately obvious in *To Spring,* as the season is implored first to look down on the longing earth, then to visit and impregnate the land "whose modest tresses were bound up for thee" in the traditional gesture of chastity and continence that Blake probably found, appropriately, in Spenser's *Epithalamion* (line 62). The land is "love-sick," "languish'd,"[32] mourning for the death of her lover (an echo of the Venus-Adonis myth), longing to kiss Spring's "perfumed garments," to taste his breath, to be decked forth with his "fair fingers," to be kissed upon her bosom, and to be crowned with Solomon's crown: "behold king Solomon with the crown wherewith his mother crowned him in the day of his espousals, and in the day of the gladness of his heart."[33] Spring, then, is Love (precisely as that identification is found in *Amoretti* IV), a fructifying male spirit, the sun turning its eyes after the blackness of winter "upon our western isle," Christ who is besought to "let thy holy feet visit our clime" and whose garments are kissed by the winds. The coming is the apocalyptic coming of Christ the Bridegroom, Love, and Imagination, the eternal morning of Christ's nativity and its "courts of everlasting day." As in Milton's *Nativity Ode* it is the advent of the Christ whose eternal dayspring triumphs over "the winter wild" of his birth, whose "holy feet" (Milton's adjective is "blessèd") shall "visit our clime," and whom our western isle's "full choir hails" (Milton's "angel quire"). Blake's "verse" and "hymn" and "solemn strain" is thus Milton's, "to welcome him to this his new abode."

Yet, at the same time that Blake makes use of Spenser, invokes Christ's coming, aligns his poem with Milton's ode, reverses the roles of The Song of Solomon while retaining its basic analogies, and refers to Thomson almost as a challenge to the reader to see that he will not emulate Thomson in any way—at the same time we have the familiar Renaissance and neoclassical poetic diction of "dewy locks," "pearls" of dew, "fair fingers," "modest tresses," and so on. Indeed, we should hear Collins's music:

> When Spring, with dewy fingers cold,
> Returns to deck their hallowed mould—

his "decking" of the dead totally subsumed in Blake's epithalamic ritual.[34] Or, hearing another tune entirely, we may see a flash of Thomson's sun mounting

> his throne; but kind before him sends,
> Issuing from out the portals of the morn,
> The general breeze to mitigate his fire. . . .   (*Summer*, ll. 639-41)

Or, again Thomson:

> . . . through the lucid chambers of the south
> Looked out the joyous Spring—looked out and smiled.
>
> (*Winter*, ll. 15-16)

But it is again Spenser whose words and melody linger, his "beames of the morning Sun, / Forth looking through the windowes of the East" (*Colin Clout*, lines 604-5).

To Summer, the details of which Lowery regards as taken from Thomson's *Spring* and *Summer*, which Pierre Berger identifies as having no sex, and which Bloom interprets as the coming not of a season but of "a youthful Apollo" into "a poet's paradise," Wimsatt sees more accurately as an example "of the Biblical, classical, and Renaissance tradition of allegory as it approaches the romantic condition of landscape naturalism." The season descends into the landscape and is fused with it, a "blurring of literal and figurative," a "fusion of ideas with material"[35] that is a remarkably mature adaptation by Blake of technique to subject. The bridegroom or Love has now arrived in all of his heated passion and virility ("strength"), and having come to court the earth and to be courted, he is properly the subject of Love. As will be the case with Blake's later tyrants, he is both enslaver and enslaved; or more properly, given this innocent Edenic context, he is, like all men, in the language of *The Marriage of Heaven and Hell*, at once prolific and devourer. Were he merely to oppress the "vallies" with his "fierce steeds" and the "heat / That flames from their large nostrils,"[36] he would be but another form of Winter's tyranny. But, as Psalm 84 tell us, "Blessed is the man whose strength is in thee; in whose heart are the ways of them. Who passing through the valley of Baca make it well."[37] Thus Summer gives heat, life, light, and love (imagination), while the earth, as devourer, absorbs them all; at the same time the earth, as prolific, provides him shade (the same pattern Blake puts to good use in *The Little Black Boy* of *Songs of Innocence*),[38] a clear stream, song, dance, and love—for "Our vallies love the Summer in his pride."

The eroticism of *To Spring* is thus maintained throughout the poem—in Summer's "ruddy limbs" and "flourishing hair" (an echo of the Song of Solomon 5:10-11 that counterpoints the female land's bound tresses of *To Spring*), the nakedness and rushing into the stream of stanza 2, and the simple last line of the same stanza. Specific eighteenth-century analogies are even fewer here than in *To Spring*, though the music and diction of the last stanza and a few of the details—the too-oft repeated "ofts," for example—have that familiarity born of ubiquitous use from the Renaissance to Blake's day. If this is what Eliot meant by assimilation, he was right. As in *To Spring*, however, in and through such assimilation Spenser and Milton assert themselves distinctly and vigorously—and are transformed. I noted earlier that Blake recalls Spenser's July "boyling like fire" and casting away all his garments, as well as his Summer's bathing "his limbes, with labor heated sore." But elsewhere in *The Faerie Queene* "firie-mouthed steeds" draw "the Sunnes bright wayne" (V,viii,40), and Summer's pride is a commonplace in both Spenser and Milton. To ameliorate his Summer's apparent tyranny, Blake divests Spenser's figure of his scythe and sickle (and hence, by implication, the Greco-Roman origins of the sun-chariot figure) and thoroughly Miltonizes his into Christ and Creation by equipping him with a "fervid car" and having him ride "o'er the deep of heaven":

"Silence, ye troubled waves, and thou deep, peace,"
Said then th' omnific Word, "your discord end."
   Nor stayed, but on the wings of Cherubim
Uplifted, in paternal glory rode
Far into Chaos and the world unborn;
For Chaos heard his voice. Him all his train
Followed in bright procession to behold
Creation, and the wonders of his might.
Then stayed the fervid wheels, and in his hand
He took the golden compasses. . . .[39]

Of *To Autumn* Bloom writes: it "is a dialogue between this poetic land and a mature harvest bard who sings a song of fruition. . . . The assimilation of sexual joy to natural flowering here is so frequent in mythic thought as to be a commonplace. What is more characteristic of Blake is the dual advent of song and achieved sexuality in the . . . final lines" of stanza 2.[40] Apparently convinced by Lowery that the last two lines of the poem are an echo of the conclusion of *Lycidas,* Bloom interprets them as a reminder of the poet's mortality analogous to that of the season. Except for the *Lycidas* allusion, which seems to me neither verbally nor ideologically close to Blake's lines,[41] Bloom's emphasis on the erotic nature of the poem and the relationship of sexuality (Blake would prefer "sensual enjoyment") to artistic creation is clearly correct. But I do not see the "dialogue" quite as he does. Love now is united with the land: earth and season are one. Blake accents this union by assigning to Autumn himself (not a "harvest bard") the song of praise for what the land does under Autumn's auspices—just as the "western isle . . . in full choir" hailed the approach of Spring, just as the land lacked "not songs, nor instruments of joy" to offer to Summer.[42] No longer, in *To Autumn,* does the earth or land regard the season as a lover to be invited, besought, offered to, but one to ripen in the presence of Autumn; the song of the season and the songs of the land are the same songs. Autumn indeed is definable now only in terms of its union with the earth: it is "laden with fruit"; it is "clust'ring Summer"; it is, in succession, poetry, dance, fruits and flowers, buds and beauties, the sun, love and the blood pulsing through human veins, blossoms, morning and eve (thus linking it nonlinearly with the "morn and evening" of *To Spring*), song, spirits of the air, joy, gardens, trees. The dissociation of Autumn from his "golden load" marks the end, not of a cycle or sequence, but of the vision. Autumn may be "fled from our sight," but his "golden load" is clearly the wholeness of the seasons as Blake's vision has just revealed that to us.

   The first-person singular, to which Blake changes in this poem (not in *To Winter* as Bloom says), is clearly *the* Poet's, both the voice that has made articulate the longings of the lovesick land and that of the poet-prophet whose very being is a product of the union of earth and season, sense and imagination, female and male, love and joy. Summer's "golden tent," in which he rested and slept half apart from, half of, the land, has now become Autumn's "golden load." Concomitantly in this time of oneness, fruition, and creation, it is no accident that Blake has "*all* the daughters of the year" dancing—all seasons and months and days and hours.[43] Sequence or cycle proceeds only in the eyes of the nonpoet, the prisoner of the senses, Spenser's Mutabilitie, Thomson's "varied god," and the pastoral poet who sees in the four seasons merely the progression from birth to youth to maturity to old age and death.[44]

To accommodate her thesis, Chayes elaborates on the significance of what she finds to be "the relatively few literary associations of both [Autumn's] song and the framing poem."[45] Nothing could be further from the fact—though the error is pardonable once we recognize that Blake now alludes less to Spenser, Milton, and the Bible directly than to his own *To Spring* and *To Summer* and their incorporated allusions. If his *To Autumn* seems to invoke Spenser's, which is, as we have seen, "laden with fruits that made him laugh," Blake makes him no Spenserian reaper holding "in his hand a sickle."[46] Instead he *is* his fruits—just as he is all the following: Spring with his "narrow bud," sun and blossom; "clust'ring Summer" with his flowers, fruit, and song (hence Blake's transformation of Spenser's "iolly Summer" into a "jolly Autumn" and his ignoring of Spenser's yellow-clad Autumn); the beauty of morning and the "bright cheek of modest eve"; all the "Howres," which are the "faire daughters" of Blake's apocalyptic "year"; perhaps even the winepress of the biblical apocalypse itself.[47] Autumn flees, but only from corporeal vision, over the same hills, now bleak to sight, that Spring comes o'er in *To Spring*. Coming and going are thus united—in a vision of what eternally exists really and unchangeably.

The sureness of Blake's technique here, even amid the remnants of conventional, even hackneyed, phraseology and diction, strongly suggests the seasons poems as among his most mature in the *Poetical Sketches*. Emerging through his fusion of cause and effect, tenor and vehicle, literal and figurative, and multiple disparate allusions is a poetical structure that does not, as in Thomson or Pope or Collins, depend for its unity so much upon the presence of a personified season "iconically invested with appropriate signa" as upon a symbolic antinarrative, the main characters of which, while retaining iconicity (what Wimsatt calls "solidity of symbol and the sensory verbal qualities"),[48] are ideas, concepts, not percepts. Or, to put it another way: Blake's poems originate not so much in his response to natural objects or events as in a conception that demands a heightened perception of reality to give formal dimensions to it. For his conventional poetic contemporaries such a "vision" is naturally iconicized in personification; for Blake it iconicizes itself, as it were, in mythological characters whose being is not merely describable and thus presentable in sensory terms, but rather is knowable only by an act of imaginative perception akin to the creative act itself.

I have said that Blake's vision is complete with the end of *To Autumn,* in its totality inherent in and symbolized by Autumn's "golden load" as well as ontologically verified by his disappearance from sight. "Complete" is not entirely accurate, of course, for Winter *does* come, "really," as the final poem of the "sequence" reminds us all too trenchantly. The imaginative achievement of oneness, fullness, and joy is ever threatened with destruction.[49] The "bleak hills" on the periphery of Autumn remind us of this, as do the mourning in *To Spring* and the fierceness of Summer's steeds, as does the full seasonal cycle of mutability's reign that continually presses its claim upon our senses. Blake's *To Winter,* then, is both a terminus of that sensual cycle and a "vision" parallel to that defined by the first three poems, horribly parodying their imaginative fusion of all into one. It is, to use Hazard Adams's apt term, an "anti-myth."[50]

Little need be said, I think, about the poem's function as the end of the cycle. All its imagery is destructive of or antithetical to life, redolent with death; Winter advances on the world uninvited and conquers it. The hope for relief that Blake expresses in the last stanza is deliberately conventional, cast in what Hartman felicitously calls "an inspired period cliché":[51]

> . . . till heaven smiles, and the monster
> Is driv'n yelling to his caves beneath mount Hecla.

The suggestion that "heaven" inevitably smiles is canceled effectively by the temporary flight, not death, of the "monster." Such an interpretation is lent strength by Blake's allusion to the "yelling monsters" who are the progeny of Sin and Death in *Paradise Lost:*

> when they list, into the womb
> That bred them they return, and howl and gnaw
> My [Sin's] bowels, their repast; then bursting forth
> Afresh, with conscious terrors vex me round,
> That rest or intermission none I find.   (II,795, 798-802)

Indeed for Milton, Death himself is "the monster" who moves "with horrid strides; hell trembled as he strode" (II,675-76). In *Paradise Lost* Sin and Death are conquered, as we know, by Christ's sacrifice; for Blake in the seasons poems they (or Winter) are conquered by his eternal coming and being—which is to say, in Blake's later formulation, Error, created by fallen vision, "will be Burned Up & then & not till then Truth or Eternity will appear It is Burnt up the Moment Men cease to behold it" (*Vision of the Last Judgment,* E555).

The seasonal cycle for Blake *is* that error, epitomized in its paradoxical "completion" in Winter's destructiveness. If Winter comes, can Spring be far behind is a nonquestion; for the cycle is not victory but repeated defeat, not an occasion for enduring joy but the certainty of terror and the bondage of time—that is, death. Thus Blake's *To Winter* is best seen as a spectrous parody, in proper sequence, of Spring-Summer-Autumn.[52] In its first stanza, after the invocatory "O" that heretofore signaled an eager invitation, instead of prayerfully beseeching Spring to "issue forth" and "Come o'er the eastern hills," Blake's speaker vigorously orders Winter to "bar" his "adamantine doors," to stay in his "dark / Deep-founded habitation" in "the north." Summer's "fervid car" and "fierce steeds" riding "o'er the deep of heaven" become Winter's "iron car" thundering heavily "o'er the yawning deep"; "our longing eyes" being "turned / Up" to the "bright pavillions" of the sun and Spring, in *To Winter* are downturned and the speaker dares "not lift" them; the "golden crown" bestowed by Spring on the earth's "languish'd head" is transformed into Winter's "sceptre" which he rears "o'er the world"; and displacing Summer's throwing his "Silk draperies off" to "rush into the stream" and Autumn's clothing the earth with buds and blossoms, fruits and flowers ("Till clust'ring Summer breaks forth into singing"), Winter

> withers all in silence, and his hand
> Unclothes the earth, and freezes up frail life.

Seated upon the cliffs, which are perhaps an extension of the "bleak / Hills" of *To Autumn*, Winter leaves his iron load in direct contrast to Autumn's "golden Load."

To underscore the significance of this parodic antimyth, Blake radically alters the image pattern of his first three poems and their eighteenth-century flavored language of natural description to that of artificial, man-made, "unnatural" elements: "adamantine," "doors," "Deep-founded habitation," "roofs," "pillars," "iron car," chains, sheaths, "ribbed steel," "sceptre." Not only is Winter a monster, not a person; a hater, not a lover; a rapist, not a bridegroom; a lustful animal, not a poet—he is also, in a sense, a *thing*. Properly, then, Blake makes of him a simple, unmergeable personification, an abstraction given sensory form. With a searing irony he is the human form of unhumanity, an all-consuming devourer innately undifferentiable as well as separate in all respects from the other seasons, his home a "cave," cold and dark, not the heavens.[53]

Yet conscious of the mythic power of the prevailing seasonal paradigm, and sensitive to its undergirding of conventional belief, Blake alludes to the received wisdom of Warton, Collins, and Thomson on such matters. Warton, for example, in his *Ode XI: On the Approach of Summer* mentions "iron-scepter'd Winter," and Thomson's *Winter*, when it is not an occasion for social converse and cozy firesides, "On every nerve"

> . . . deadly . . . seizes, shuts up sense,

> And, o'er [man's] inmost vitals creeping cold,
> Lays him along the snows a stiffened corse.　　　(*Winter*, ll. 317-20)

In addition to Blake's clear allusion (cited earlier) to the Winter figure at the end of the *Ode to Evening*, Collins adds another important dimension to Blake's use of the paradigm, on the authority of Thomson as well as Dryden, in his *Ode to Peace*. There it is War who in his "iron car" drawn by vultures "bade his storms arise" in Britain.[54] Thomson's own vision, however, dominates the conclusion of Blake's poem, illuminating the otherwise curious exclamation of pity for the wretched mariner.[55] In his impressive *Winter* storm scene, where the "sullen seas / . . . will rest no more / Beneath the shackles of the mighty north" (lines 997-99), he adds rather tamely, "Ill fares the bark, with trembling wretches charged" (line 1004); and, more fiercely again, in the gloom "is heard the hungry howl / Of famished monsters, there awaiting wrecks":

> Yet Providence, that ever-waking Eye,
> Looks down with pity on the feeble toil
> Of mortals lost to hope, and lights them safe
> Through all this dreary labyrinth of fate.　　　(Ll. 1018-23)

Blake's transformation of this passage is shrewdly managed. Not only has he severely condensed Thomson's sublime effusiveness, but *his* wretch "cries in vain." No clear "Providence" responds to "light him safe" out of the "labyrinth of fate"; and such pity as there is emanates not from Thomson's Miltonic "ever-waking Eye" (cf. *PL* V,711-17), but from the speaker of the poem in his oddly sentimental exclamation. Heaven may smile and the monster be driven back home, but the clichéd salvation has already been effectively sabotaged. Similarly, perhaps to confute his predecessor's wisdom further, Blake seems to adopt some of the imagery of *To Winter* from Thomson's *Summer:*

> . . . the rage intense
> Of brazen-vaulted skies, of iron fields,
> Where drought and famine starve the blasted year;
> Fired by the torch of noon to tenfold rage,
> The infuriate hill that shoots the pillared flame;
> And, roused within the subterranean world,
> The expanding earthquake, that resistless shakes
> Aspiring cities from their solid base.　　　(Ll. 1092-99)

The cumulative intensifications these apparent allusions effect are of the conventional framework of the cycle, the death, destruction, and even the warfare all geared to support the efficacy, perhaps even the miracle, of

Spring's (and Peace's) ultimate victory over the temporary status of tyranny. The suffusion of *To Winter* with Miltonic allusions tells another story entirely, almost as if to put right Warton, Collins, and Thomson in their borrowings from the same source. If Christ comes in *To Spring,* rides his "fervid car" in creation in *To Summer,* and unites with the land in *To Autumn,* the obvious parody of this coming and consummate union is the coming of the Antichrist and his progeny, Sin and Death and their "yelling monsters."[56] Winter's doors are thus the "gates of burning adamant / Barred over" to "prohibit all egress" for Satan and his fallen crew (*PL* II,436-37); yet they are also the "adamantine gates" of death, chaos, and old Night that, once unbolted and unbarred by Sin, are unclosable (II,853-97). Blake also echoes Satan's arrogant charge to Gabriel in Book IV: "Let him [God] surer bar / His iron gates, if he intends our stay / In that dark durance" (lines 897-99). Following Isaiah (14:13) both Milton and Blake assign Satan to "the quarters of the north" (V,689) and Blake's "dark / Deep-founded habitation" is a truncated quotation of Michael's description of hell:

> strict fate had cast too deep
> Her dark foundations, and too fast had bound.
> . . . .
>   Hell at last
> Yawning received them whole, and on them closed,
> Hell, their fit habitation . . .   (VI,869-70, 874-76),

in itself an echo, Blake surely recognized, of the Creator in the *Nativity Ode* casting "the dark foundations deep" of the universe. Beelzebub's speech in Book II (lines 310 ff.) adds to Blake's clustering images the "iron sceptre" (thus firmly contextualizing Warton's simpler Miltonic borrowing noted earlier), and, with an eye to his own Summer poem, Blake would also have remembered Satan

>   overcome with rage;
> But like a proud steed reined, went haughty on,
> Champing his iron curb.   (IV,857-59)

Blake's odd locution, "Nor bend thy pillars with thine iron car," refers not to the destruction of some pillared edifice but rather to Satan's artillery in Book VI, lines 572-73:

> A triple-mounted row of pillars laid
> On wheels . . . —

some of brass, some of iron, some of stone, levied against (that is, bent against) the armies of heaven. Although Milton does not use the word "car" in this description, Blake boldly appropriates it (as Collins, Dryden, and Thomson may have as well) from "the gilded car of day" of *Comus* (line 95)

and, of course, his own Miltonic usage, noon's "fervid car" of *To Summer.*
Blake's phrase "rides heavy" recalls Satan's troops who, prior to "bending"
their pillars, "with heavy pace" approach "gross and huge" (*PL* VI,551-52);
and his "storms . . . unchain'd" are the disgorged ammunition of the iron
pillars: "Their devilish glut, chained thunderbolts and hail" (VI,589).

Blake's choice of Hecla, then, as the mountain beneath which Winter is
driven Typhon-like is a shrewd one: not only is it in the frigid zones of
Iceland, but it was widely believed to be one of the gates of Purgatory.[57]
Finally, Satan himself, as he metamorphoses into serpent form, suggests
Blake's "monster, whose skin clings / To his strong bones":

> His visage drawn he felt to sharp and spare,
> His arms clung to his ribs. . . .   (X,511-12)

In all, then, the Miltonic-Satanic character of *To Winter* is as astonishingly
complete as its structure is built on studied inversions of the verbs, nouns,
and adjectives of Spring-Summer-Autumn. To say, though, that Winter is
thus "destructive energy bursting out of repression" and that the mariner
passage signals somehow the giving to the poet of a "kind of control over the
desolate scene that eluded him at the beginning" is completely to misconstrue the poem as well as the sequence—as is Hartman's view of Winter as
"the Genius of the North" (Ossian, et al.) who confounds the normal
westering of the poetic spirit with a North-South movement.[58] The poet's
"control" (whatever that may mean) and the progress (or nonprogress) of
poetry are not the issue. Our perception is. If we lean on the comforts of a
conventional rebirth of Spring to console our sense of loss in Winter, we
have capitulated to the very mythological construct and tradition Blake is at
some pains to subvert. Time is not *the* Time. Even the prophetic Los in
Blake's later myth forgot for a time that his is the "vigorous voice [of]
prophecy" (*Four Zoas,* E301) and, succumbing to his fallen wars of love and
hate with Enitharmon, satisfies himself with controlling "the times & seasons,
& the days & years"[59]—that is, with emulating Spenser's Mutabilitie.

Citing Spenser in connection with this most un-Spenserian poem, I'm
aware, must seem perverse; but as I indicated briefly, earlier in this chapter,
the Garden of Adonis section of *The Faerie Queene* has not only an indirect
pertinence, by way of the Mutabilitie Cantos, to the seasons suite as a
whole, but a direct relationship to the "conclusion" of the cycle (*To Winter*)—
and, most especially, to the concluding lines of that conclusion. Adonis, we
recall, is he "that liuing giues to all" (III,vi,47) and hence, in the garden, "he
liueth in eternall blis" (stanza 48).

> Ne feareth he henceforth that foe of his,
> Which with his cruell tuske him deadly cloyd:
> For that wilde Bore, the which him once annoyd,

She [Venus] firmely hath emprisoned for ay,
That her sweet loue his malice mote auoyde,
In a strong rocky Caue, which is they say,
Hewen vnderneath that Mount, that none him losen may.

(Stanza 48)

The parallels to Blake's conception in *To Winter* are obvious: Venus-Adonis as Blake's Spring-Summer-Autumn, suffused with love; the boar as Blake's Winter; the mount as Blake's "mount Hecla." But just as obviously something is awry: Spenser's mount and Blake's Hecla are hardly like in the same way that the other two pairs are; indeed Blake seems to have perverted Venus's mount to the boar's (to Winter's), thus suggesting, in the context of the cyclical paradigm, that the boar-winter is not indeed "emprisoned for ay" but will rise again with each new year, only to be chased to his cave so that he may rise yet once more. For however much Adonis "is eterne," his eternity subsists only "in mutabilitie"—as all things do in the Mutabilitie Cantos. No "Sabaoths sight" obtains in Spenser's vision here, or there—or in *The Shepheardes Calender*—and hence no "real" (that is, Blakean) eternity is perceived. This "state of life" is "tickle," Spenser laments (*FQ* VII,viii,1), and it is precisely that tickle state that the cycle of the seasons and the Garden of Adonis celebrate. If "by succession" Adonis is "made perpetuall" (III,vi,47), the perpetuity of succession in Blake's seasons is but a rehearsal of dyings. The boar, not Adonis, is the victor; and Spenser's grand conception is but "mere" allegory after all. Blake's imaginative vision (and, he earnestly hopes, ours) sees through such allegory, which is addressed to the corporeal powers alone, in his seeing unveiling the true lineaments of that sublimer allegory addressed to the intellectual powers. And it is the latter that, paradoxically, is energized by the contrarious antimyth of *To Winter*.

In his *A Vision of the Last Judgment* among its host of imaginative-allegorical figures is Seth, higher in Blake's painting than Noah, beneath whose feet the four seasons are represented as "the Changed State" of things "made by the flood." Seth "is a higher state of Happiness & wisdom than Noah being nearer the State of Innocence"; and beneath his feet are only two seasons, "Spring & Autumn," the inception and the "autumn ripeness" of "The Divine Vision." By Seth's side is Elijah who "comprehends all the Prophetic Characters," in his "fiery Chariot bowing before the throne of the Saviour" (E550). I cite Blake's grand apocalypse here not to impose it upon his seasons suite, but rather to demonstrate the continuity of conception he inaugurated in those early poems, especially as that continuity sustains the Spring-Autumn axis of Blake's overall structure. If we, like the speaker of *To Winter,* are intimidated—not merely by the season's power and rule, but by his self-constructed and self-dramatized vision of the way things are—to turn our eyes downward, if we do not dare lift up our eyes, we shall, of course, not see; and we shall be thankful only for the momentary respite from our pain that heaven's smiling affords us in the eternal round of seasons, years, and months and days.

MORNINGS
AND EVENINGS

BLAKE'S *To the Evening Star* and *To Morning* have been justly praised over the years. In addition to *Mad Song* and *To the Muses* (and more recently the four seasonal poems), they have been regarded as the most accomplished and mature of his early poems. I have no quarrel with that judgment, so often voiced that references here to its occurrences would be superfluous. As we have seen in previous chapters, there is clear evidence of literary indebtedness in the other poems just listed, but *To the Evening Star* and *To Morning* have been cited regularly as among the most imitative of the *Poetical Sketches*, virtual pastiches, however splendidly individualized, of Spenser's *Epithalamion*. For example, except for her somewhat labored analysis of what Blake does *to* Spenser in his *Imitation of Spencer*, Margaret Lowery's entire case for Spenser's influence throughout *Poetical Sketches* would be largely vitiated were it not for the *Epithalamion* parallels she cites.[1] It seems, then, that what elicits the steady praise for these poems is the expertness of Blake's poetic quilting or, more generously (and accurately), his ability somehow to rise above his source and create something that approaches, at least, what H. D. Traill claims for the poems ("perfection . . . not to be matched by any poet of the eighteenth century") or Swinburne's judgment that they are "at once more noble and more sweet in style [than anything] ever written."[2] Swinburne's inappropriate terminology aside, I share such sentiments—for reasons not only quite distinct from Traill's and Swinburne's but also largely unconsidered by Blake's critics.

Let me begin by acknowledging (as well as escalating and qualifying) the obvious: there is no doubt that Blake read the *Epithalamion*, the *Prothalamion*, and the *Amoretti* as "something of a revelation," that "he read them again and again until . . . [they] were a part of the texture of his mind,"[3] and that there is abundant evidence in *To the Evening Star* and *To Morning* of such absorption. It has gone completely unnoticed, however, that in *To Morning*, at least, Blake omits any reference to the first 147 lines of the *Epithalamion*, instead choosing to begin his poem with Spenser's lines 148-51:

> Loe where she comes along with portly pace
> Lyke Phoebe from her chamber of the East,
> Arysing forth to run her mighty race,
> Clad all in white, that seemes a virgin best.

Spenser immediately follows this passage in Song of Solomon fashion with a description of his bride, something that Blake also omits together with, even more significantly, Spenser's subsequent attribution of moral perfection to the bride:

> There dwels sweet loue and constant chastity,
> Vnspotted fayth and comely womanhood,
> Regard of honour and mild modesty,
> There vertue raynes as Queene in royal throne,
> And giueth lawes alone.
> The which the base affections doe obay,
> And yeeld theyr seruices vnto her will.   (Ll. 191-97)

Moreover, Blake makes no mention of the marriage or the marriage celebration (lines 204-77), concluding instead with images of the sun "Rouz'd like a huntsman to the chace" and of Morning herself appearing "upon our hills" with her "buskin'd feet." *Amoretti* LXVII ("Lyke as a huntsman") has been suggested as a possible source for Blake's "comparison of the groom with a huntsman,"[4] but this seems to me wrong on two counts: (1) Spenser's sonnet as a whole has little bearing on Blake's hymn, and (2) there is no "groom" in Blake's poem at all. Michael Tolley is more nearly correct in identifying the poem as a song of spring-morning "fused together into a single 'time'" symbolic of "a present eternity in and through the mortal spring."[5] As in Blake's *To Spring* there are three characters, the speaker, the sun, and Morning (in *To Spring* the speaker, Spring, and the earth, or "this love-sick land"), so that the poem immediately veers sharply from Spenser's intensely personal first-person dramatic narrative-song. Yet whereas *To Spring*, capitalizing on the Canticles, annunciates a fructifying "marriage" between the season and the land, there is no comparable union in *To Morning*, despite the telling repetition of the epithalamic phrase "issue forth" and the repeated attribution of the source for both Spring and Morning to the chambers of the east.

Blake, then, has in some sense reversed Spenser, his "bride" not being compared to the sun or morning but rather the morning to a forthcoming bride.[6] Morning is called upon to "salute the sun," light rises to accompany the issuing forth of Morning, and the sun seems roused like a huntsman at the same time that Morning appears "upon our hills" in her own buskins. While one needs to proceed gingerly in such matters, it is worth noting that this last phrase, in precisely the same context (spring-morning, Tolley's "apocalyptic . . . time when the holy feet again visit our clime"), recurs in *Jerusalem*'s resounding conclusion:

> Awake! Awake Jerusalem! O lovely Emanation of Albion
> Awake and overspread all Nations as in Ancient Time
> For lo! the Night of Death is past and the Eternal Day
> Appears upon our Hills. . . .[7]

This passage too is squarely in the epithalamic tradition rather than that of merely hymning the dawn of a new day and the sweetness, light, and joy it brings round again.

Blake's intention to "reverse" Spenser is confirmed by his speaker's importuning of Morning to "Unlock heav'n's golden gates" and "issue forth," in contrast to Spenser's bride entering the gates of the church:

> Open the temple gates vnto my loue,
> Open them wide that she may enter in,
>
> . . . .
>
> That commeth in to you.   (Ll. 204-5, 209)

Instead of Spenser, Blake at this point may have recalled Milton's frequent use of heaven's gate—as, for example, in the opening lines of Book VI of *Paradise Lost:* "Morn, / Waked by the circling Hours, with rosy hand / Unbarred the gates of light."[8] And a few lines later in Milton (9) it is "Light" that "issues forth," a phrasing that Blake conflates in his Morning's issuing forth and the "light" rising "from the chambers of the east." While the "issue forth" formula is a commonplace, especially ubiquitous in Spenser, there is no context I have found in any poet other than Milton that incorporates it with morning, awakening, unbarring or unlocking, gates, and light. And there is no comparable "unlocking" in Spenser anywhere. On the other hand, in Blake's *The Four Zoas* Urizen asks, "What Chain encompasses in what Lock is the river of light confind / That issues forth in the morning by measure & the evening by carefulness" (IX, E376-77). This ominous context, deriving clearly from *To Morning,* should make us somewhat less startled to find in Milton that Sin, forbidden by God "to unlock / These adamantine gates," nevertheless does so with her "fatal key" (*PL* II,852-53, 871), loosing upon the new-created world not only her own power but that of Death and, of course, Satan himself. This self-parody by Milton of his various openings of heaven's gate would not have been lost on Blake, whose hymn to light in *To Morning* consequently aligns itself with the elder poet's poignant opening to Book III ("Hail, holy Light"), his "saluting" not only of the sun, as in Blake, but of the "Bright effluence of bright essence increate" in God (III,1-6). Milton's antithetical language and verbal patterning thus effectively contravene any emphasis we might place on *To Morning* as a conventional epithalamion, at the same time confirming Blake's inversion of the basic Spenserian metaphor.

What is not "explained" by the Milton references or the *Epithalamion* is Blake's climactic hunting metaphor for both sun and morning. The most obvious analogy, as Lowery tentatively suggests, is to "chaste Diana" and she cites a quite persuasive passage from Drayton's *Endimion and Phoebe.*[9] One might add Jonson's "Queene and huntress, chaste and faire." Without denying the likelihood of these allusions, the firm Spenserian and Miltonic context of Blake's poem should urge us to look to those two poets first for some precedent for Blake's radical shift from standard epithalamic patterns to a hunting image. Belphoebe in Book II of *The Faerie Queene* seems the obvious Spenserian candidate since she is buskined and associated with both Diana and chastity. But the whole passage in Canto iii (stanzas 27-29) that presents her in this fashion is not even vaguely related to Blake's poem. In any case, as Roger Lonsdale observes, "passages . . . describing healthy maidens usually based on Diana with buskins and bow, are relatively common," especially in the eighteenth century.[10] A more pointedly moralistic "source," in Milton, is the Elder Brother's citing "the old schools of Greece" to convince his younger brother of the invulnerability of their sister despite her entanglement in Comus's woods. Antiquity, he says, testifies to

> the arms of chastity [.]
> Hence had the huntress Dian her dread bow,
> Fair silver-shafted queen for ever chaste,
>
> . . . .
>
> . . .[to] set at naught
> The frivolous bolt of Cupid; gods and men
> Feared her stern frown, and she was queen o' th' woods.
>
> (*Comus,* ll. 439-46)

But despite the first line of *To Morning,* chastity and its power are essentially as irrelevant to Blake's poem as the absence of conventional epithalamic patterns are relevant; and there is nothing in the *Comus* passage to explain Blake's curious metamorphosis of the sun and Morning into hunters. Long ago H. G. Hewlett suggested Collins's *The Passions: An Ode for Music* as Blake's source. There "Cheerfulness" appears clad in "buskins gemmed with morning dew," and though Damon roundly pooh-poohs Hewlett's "usual" pedantry, he is no further off the mark than others have been since the 1870s.[11] Despite the fact that the language, and indeed the total conception, seem to be most unlike, lines 122-24 from *Il Penseroso* more probably contain the hint of Blake's point. Morning there appears "civil-suited" as appropriate to the penseroso mood, "not tricked and frounced as she was wont / With the Attic boy to hunt." If Blake knew that the "Attic boy" was Cephalus, the great hunter beloved of Aurora, the apparent epithalamic theme would metamorphose into the dalliance of goddesses with mortals— the content of that dalliance the ebullient joy of *L'Allegro* as well as of

Blake's own *Poetical Sketches* prose poem *Contemplation:* "the youthful sun joys like a hunter rouzed to the chace: he rushes up the sky, and lays hold on the immortal coursers of day; the sky glitters with the jingling trappings."[12]

If all of these possibilities conspire to undercut severely epithalamic intent, the apparent allusion to Psalm 19 that everyone cites (verse 5) seems to restore such a consideration. But even there God is described as having "set a tabernacle for the sun, / Which is as a bridegroom coming out of his chamber," precisely Blake's inversion of Spenser's trope in the marriage hymn. And David's hymn continues with what may be yet another of the origins of Blake's huntsman reference: "the sun rejoiceth as a strong man to run a race." To return to Milton, then, we find in *L'Allegro* that "the hounds and horn" of the early morning hunters "cheerly rouse the slumb'ring morn" and appear "on hillocks green, / Right against the eastern gate, / Where the great sun begins his state" (lines 53-60). This version of the "tricked and frounced" morning who is "wont / With the Attic boy to hunt," so inveighed against in *Il Penseroso,* is joined by Blake, interestingly, with the *Penseroso* passage on the bee. Employing the word *honied* for the only time in his career, Blake transforms Milton's bee, hidden "from Day's garish eye" and "with honied thigh" singing "at her flow'ry work," into "the honied dew that cometh on waking day"—that is, in the full blaze of "Day's garish eye" (lines 141-43).

Although the precise phrase, "honied dew," Blake may have recalled from Drayton's *Endimion and Phoebe*[13] (or, indeed, elsewhere in his Renaissance reading, for it is a commonplace), his own mixture of allegro-penseroso mirth-melancholy (underscored by Drayton's association of the dew with evening—as in Blake's companion poem, *To the Evening Star*), his studied manipulation of the simpler and more obvious contrasts of Milton's companion poems, and his use of the curious verb *unlock*—all this leads us, more unerringly than my earlier passing citation of it suggests, to the opening of Book VI of *Paradise Lost* as the locus classicus of Blake's total conception in *To Morning*. Milton's language and the passage's hymnic structure and tone corroborate the connection: his morning, "Waked, . . . with rosy hand / Unbarred the gates of light"; Blake's dawn "sleeps in heaven" as night (or darkness) holds sway, while in Milton "light and darkness in perpetual round / Lodge and dislodge by turns" within "the mount of God," light "issu[ing] forth" after "obsequious darkness" (perhaps an echo of *Il Penseroso*'s melancholy shades) reenters the mount "at the other door" (lines 2-9). Although there is obviously no huntsman in the passage, the day-night pageantry leads directly to the pageantry of the heavenly armies standing in readiness (lines 15-21), and Blake's appropriation of it to swell and enrich his allegro-penseroso borrowings—thus modulating the more obvious Spenserian-epithalamic "narrative"-allegoric structure of the poems—is in many ways a remarkable achievement.

Additional Miltonic allusions complete the metamorphic amalgamation of the epithalamic tradition and provide a solid ground for Blake's conception of morning as both male *and* female—more precisely, morning as the latter, the sun as the former. Through line 5 of the poem, however densely textured with the allusions I have cited and however marvelously Blake has harmonized those allusions, there is little beyond the joyousness occasioned by a natural phenomenon, as glorious as that may be. With line 6, though, the poem takes a crucial turn, precipitated largely by the commonplace adjective *radiant* and the almost uniquely un-Blakean word *salute*. The former occurs so frequently in eighteenth-century poetry as to preclude identifiable allusions—it is a favorite, for example, of Thomson, Akenside, and Thomas Warton, all of whom may well have derived it from Spenser and/or Milton; but Collins, who is not only a "discriminating . . . Miltonian"[14] but a poet to whom for various reasons (as we have seen) Blake was attracted, in his first Persian *Eclogue* employs the line, "The radiant morn resumed her orient pride" (the *only* use in his poetry of *radiant*), in the inverted epithalamic configuration noted earlier (that is, Collins's "morn" is an "eastern bride").[15] As so often in Collins, such a unique word-usage derives from *Paradise Lost*, here the epic's usual morning of "Orient beams" and "radiant sun," the latter a naturalized or secularized version of "the radiant image" of God's glory (that is, "His only Son") as well as of Uriel, "regent of the sun."[16] Thus, even if "radiant morning" is borrowed from Collins (it does not appear in Milton) Blake's maintenance of the associative ganglion obtaining in Milton's use of the two words is a measure of his triumph over simpler Miltonic imitations or borrowings.[17] Just so in Blake's use of the verb *salute:* aside from two (solidly conventional) occurrences in *An Island in the Moon* this is the only appearance of the word in his work (it is absent entirely from Collins's poetry). Although the verb is unusual in Milton as well (and does not appear at all in the Bible), its two appearances there conform to the natural-secular-religious amalgam inherent in his *radiant*.[18] In *Song: On a May Morning*, for example (a spring-morning song in Tolley's sense), May is "hailed," in Douglas Bush's words, with "restrained and elegant simplicity and urbanity":[19]

> Thus we salute thee with our early song,
> And welcome thee, and wish thee long.

But that simple urbanity, parallel to Blake's in his opening five lines, Milton elevates in *Paradise Lost* and *Paradise Regained* into the joyous solemnity of the angel's address to Mary in Luke 1:28:

> And the angel came in unto her, and said, Hail, thou that art highly favored, the Lord is with thee: blessed art thou among women.

In *Paradise Regained* Mary, troubled at her Son's nonreturn home,

[81]

> and oft to mind
> Recalling what remarkably had passed
> Since first her salutation heard,   (II,105-7)

ponders her situation in Luke's terms:

> "O what avails me now that honor high
> To have conceived of God, or that salute,
> 'Hail, highly favored, among women blest!'
> While I to sorrows am no less advanced,
> And fears as eminent, above the lot
> Of other women, by the birth I bore [?]   (II,66-71)

This "holy salutation" (V,386) seems to me precisely Blake's, as it was Gray's in *The Bard* (the "Swarm" that hovers round Edward III's court is described as "Gone to salute the rising Morn"—lines 69-70)—though the latter's severely ironic usage, of course, is not Blake's.

As is perhaps all too obvious, however, the "holy salutation" in Blake's poem is delivered, or will be delivered, by the morning (female) to the sun (male), both about to set out on a chase over the hills. Luke's annunciation scene (as well as Milton's references to it) is thus severely wrenched, virgin-morning-Angel-radiant-Christ-Diana merged somehow as irretrievably as light-sun-Christ-Phoebus-Mary. In this extraordinary (even startling) confusion, one can see better, perhaps, what Blake has "done" both to the Spenserian-epithalamic tradition (which resurfaces in muted, even transmuted, form in *To Morning*'s last lines) and to Milton's naturalistic-religious imagery—not to mention to the fading residuum of classical mythology so baldly and awkwardly exploited in *An Imitation of Spencer*. The final success of the resultant melange, it seems to me, however delicately lovely the poem as a whole, must be called into question. If the virginal morning and Diana seem somehow to "belong" together, the concluding huntress-huntsman image even more strongly pulls the poem in a direction for which its first six lines leave us totally unprepared. Similarly, if Blake's morning, like Spenser's bride,

> comes along with portly pace
> Lyke Phoebe from her chamber of the East,
> Arysing forth to run her mighty race,
> Clad all in white, that seemes a virgin best,

Spenser's bride-morning dons no buskins but, with "modest eyes abashed," affixes them upon "the lowly ground" (lines 158, 161). Moreover the *Epithalamion* speaker-bridegroom makes no reference whatsoever to hunting; and Blake's last lines emerge in no way out of his Miltonic borrowings or the Luke annunciation.

It has been suggested, with reason, that *To Morning* is at the very least a "sketch" for Blake's *To Spring*, even a parallel poem. Certainly the diurnal-seasonal analogy is predictable, especially given Blake's reference to morning and evening in both *To Spring* and *To Autumn*. But if such a relationship is examined carefully, the hunting trope in *To Morning* all the more stubbornly thwarts our expectations—expectations engendered by precisely those allusions (to Spenser and Milton) to which he seems to have led us so purposively. While Blake's reasons for this thwarting may not be entirely clear in the poem as it stands, there are some clues in the entirety of the seasonal suite and in *To Morning*'s companion poem, *To the Evening Star*. As we have already seen in the seasons, Blake elaborately fashions out of poetic tradition a set of structural expectations that derive from his correct assumption of our assent to the conceptual validity of that tradition—the cycle of the seasons. Once trapped in this "round," we find it difficult (some have found it impossible) to straighten the cycle into a sequence (or, more accurately, to fuse it into a moment) that imaginatively describes an eternal truth comparable to the rational simplicity of "perfection" inherent in the circle-cycle metaphor. *To Morning* performs something of the same prestidigitation upon us, leading us to expectations of a marriage celebration, the birth of Christ, and perhaps even the truth newborn of Milton's *Nativity Ode,* only to detour us—somehow delicately without the trauma of wrenched expectations—into a *Windsor Forest* hunting scene that has no relation at all to what *seems* to spawn it. That the tone of the last line (as distinct from its allusive implications) does not echo (or anticipate) the concluding ominousness of *To the Evening Star* should not blind us to Blake's rejection of conventional conclusions. Indeed, it might well be said that *To Morning* doesn't conclude at all: the sun and morning merely "appear upon our hills."[20] Still, "appear" is a powerfully charged word in Blake, embodying the idea of eternal reality made, or becoming, visible to the sensory eye—an "incarnation" as it were.[21] Here it signifies light humanized, not "a round Disk of fire somewhat like a Guinea" but *like* a virgin huntsman: male and female, sun and morning fused into at least a kind of "giant form."[22] Appear to do what, however? Hardly to love, to celebrate Hymen, to honor the newborn God, to defend chastity, or even to hymn, like Milton's Adam and Eve, the glories of God's creation. Indeed, we are not "told" what sun-morning will do, just as we are not told what "happens" at the end of *To the Evening Star*. To be sure, in that poem the wolf rages, the lion glares, the evening star disappears; and, rather deflatingly as well as illogically, the vanished star is called upon to protect the sheep with its "influence." What "happens," then, is unacted, is merely inherent in the prayer to "protect." From one point of view Blake seems to say that doing is not the point; being is, epiphanically appearing. Even so, there is a kind of muted, suppressed violence inherent in "Rouz'd," "huntsman," and "chace" that bursts into the open in the Minstrel's song of *King Edward the Third*. The seeming quiet of the "concluding" clause, "appear upon our hills," thus assumes a function precisely parallel to the specious quiet of the *Evening Star*'s "protect them with thine influence," the former noncommittal yet anticipative, the latter a conventional wishful thinking hardly commensurate with the "dun" reality of the forests of the night (even if the fulness of Blake's later symbolic enrichment of that phrase remains here unevocable).

To press this point beyond suggestion seems untoward, if not unwarranted, given Blake's generally positive stance in *To Morning* and the richly powerful affirmation of "appear." Nevertheless the negative force of "unlock" (why should "heav'n's golden gates" *ever* be locked?[23]), the prevailing tone of beseechment for what clearly is not occurring, and the curious earthly guise of both morning and the sun must give one serious pause. In any case, our total "experience" of the poem depends in large measure on its being but part of the total context of dawn-morning *and* evening-night, just as our imaginative sense of the "truth" of the seasons depends upon our perception of Winter's role in the suite. It is well, then, that we turn now to the "penseroso" half of Blake's diurnal paradigm.

Although we know nothing of their compositional history, it would be absurd to assume that the seasons poems do not "belong together" or that they "originally" might have been in some other sequence. A similar situation seems to exist with Blake's mini-sequence of *To the Evening Star* and *To Morning,* functioning as they do parallel to the seasons. Hartman and Chayes have made much of the sequential nature of the seasons poems, as we have seen, both stumbling (I think) in distinctly different though related ways because of their very adherence to the *idea* of sequence—that is, of fulfilled expectations. As Chayes herself points out, Hartman's narrative patterning of the migration or "progress" of the poetical spirit to England forces upon Blake's four poems a structure applicable to only two of them; but after establishing her own patterning, she repositions *To Spring* as the final poem, *To Summer* as introduction, and *To Winter* the prophecy of the return of Spring. "Whether it was Blake or someone else—the bookseller, the author of the patronizing preface, the printer—who determined the quaternary arrangement we now have," she concludes, her arrangement is best, or at least what Blake wanted.[24]

As I suggested in the previous chapter, if there is sequence in the seasons poems, it derives from a tradition that raises expectations Blake is at some pains to demonstrate as false—or at least based on false premises. The "logic" of cycles, "progress," and sequence is shown to be imaginatively suspect by Blake's frustrating of expectation, his refusal to supply a neat closure, and his superimposition of an antisequence on top of that seemingly formed by the first three poems. In this light, it really doesn't matter who determined the arrangement of the poems, for however grouped or sequenced they militate insistently against "arrangement." That *To the Evening Star* precedes *To Morning* in *Poetical Sketches* as printed may seem on the surface to reinforce Chayes's point about the seasons, and about *To Winter* especially; but if we apply her argument to the diurnal poems we end not in Blakean prophecy of "both the return of spring [or morning] and the emergence of a new and higher order of life" that "will require a . . . newer kind of poetry as its expression,"[25] but rather in a return to classical mythology, Diana, buskins, and an outmoded pastoral chase. In fact, as in the antipattern within the morning poem, the "sequence" of the two poems is neither from evening to morning nor morning to evening—though once again Blake tempts us into that kind of thinking.

To the Evening Star is an intricate and richly textured poem, only its most obvious conformations (as those in *To Morning*) deriving from Spenser's *Epithalamion.* Yet so powerful are the resonances from that poem that they have almost totally obscured Blake's daring originality in their use. As in his companion poem, Blake's borrowings from Spenser in the *Evening Star* are actually minimal, and what he omits from Spenser is as revealing as what he borrows, perhaps even more so. Despite its obviousness, and despite the problems of sequence discussed above, the fact that Blake's two poems as they stand in the volume reverse the "sequence" of Spenser's has received no attention. As is traditional, Spenser proceeds from morning to noon to evening to night, from the coming forth of the bride to the consummation of the marriage. *The Epithalamion,* whatever else it is—a numerological puzzle, a dazzling piece of artistry, or any number of other critical descriptions to which it has been subjected—is a "tymely" poem. It functions necessarily in time, it is in many ways about time, it is (more famously) "for short time an endlesse moniment," and it abounds in time-signals: "for it is time" (line 74); "first come ye fayre hours which were begot / In Ioues sweet paradice, of Day and Night, / Which doe the seasons of the yeare allot" (lines 98-100); the repetitive "now," "evermore" (as well as "ever" and "never"), "still," "endlesse," the longest day and shortest night; "tymely sleep, when it is tyme to sleepe," "timely seed," "timely fruit," and "tymely ioys"—the list goes on. The poet's achievement, of course, is to stop time, to effectuate the eternal Now that only art is capable of. The "dew time" necessary for the "many ornaments / With which my loue should duly haue bene dect" is cut off *by* time, but the eternal presentness of the poem itself constitutes "a goodly ornament" that both rolls all time into a ball (to adapt Marvell's famous image) and unrolls it into eternity. The woods, called upon finally to "no more vs answer," answer endlessly, the echo of "short time" ringing joyously in the timeless (as well as spaceless) poem. The powerful present and future constructions dovetail with the fourteen appearances of the word *now* and the twenty-one versions and synonyms of *forever* to encapsulate all time in the moment of the monument.

Once again, then, as in *To Morning,* it is worth noting at the outset what Blake omitted from Spenser in his "imitation" epithalamion. Simply stated, he left out everything before line 286, "And the bright euening star with golden creast." The verbal affinities in Blake's poem to the several lines after 286 are striking: Spenser's "Fayre childe of beauty," Blake's "fair-hair'd angel of the evening";[26] "glorious lampe of loue" and Blake's "bright torch of love" (conflated, of course with Spenser's earlier "bright Tead" of Hymen);[27] "How chearefully thou lookest from aboue, / And seemst to laugh atweene thy twinkling light" Blake condenses to "smile upon our evening bed! / Smile on our loves";[28] Spenser's "silken courteins" are transformed, with ample poetic precedent, into the "Blue curtains of the sky" that the evening star "drawest";[29] Spenser's call for silence (lines 313-14, 353-56), Blake's "speak silence with thy glimmering [Spenser's "twinkling"] eyes";[30] Spenser's "let the night be calm and quietsome, / Without tempestuous storms or sad afray" and "let stil Silence trew night watches keepe" are truncated and particularized into "let thy west wind sleep on / The lake; speak silence"; and, finally, Spenser's "tymely sleep" for his bride becomes, curiously, the "timely sleep" of Blake's flowers.[31]

But after inviting us into Spenser's "bridale bowre" and leading us to the brink of consummation, to the prayers for nonviolation by outside forces of this "paradise of ioyes" and for "timely fruit," and to the supplication of heaven's "thousand torches flaming bright" and "all ye powers which in the same remayne" to

> Poure out your blessing on vs plentiously,
> And happy influence vpon vs raine,

Blake swiftly detours us to the withdrawing of the evening star—not merely soon but all too soon: "Soon, full soon." That sudden withdrawal and the consequent onset of darkness are intensified by the absence of Spenser's moon peeping in the bedchamber windows and, even more startlingly, by a bold leap into the forest wilderness where wolves rage and lions glare—perhaps a daringly perverse throwback to Spenser's invitation to the "lightfoot mayds which keepe the deere" and who "With . . . steele darts doo chace" "the wylde wolues which seeke them to deuoure."[32] If in this distinctly ominous context "the fleeces of our flocks are cover'd with" the evening's "sacred dew"—as the "silver dew" earlier is scattered "on every flower that shuts its sweet eyes / In timely sleep"—it is impossible now to have confidence that the dew's "protection" is other than sleeping unawareness, a vulnerability not in the least qualified by Blake's closing Spenserian prayer: "protect them with thine influence."[33] The epithalamic conventionality of "sacred peace" reigning "in assurance" as "Silence trew night watches keepe" and the stars' "thousand torches" flame bright "in dreadful darknesse" to "lend desired light"—all of this is hollowed to the dreadful ineffectuality of supplicating a disappearing, even totally "withdrawn," protector. Although *To Morning* does come next in the volume as printed, auguries of its succession are as notably absent from *To the Evening Star* as Spring is from Blake's *To Winter.*

As in that latter poem, the powerful, even rude, frustration of our expectations in *To the Evening Star* turns us back upon what we, caught in Blake's allusive trap, had assumed to be a proper cycle—or at least a conclusion. If there is in the seasons poems a clear adumbration of Blake's later famous quaternaries, it must also be recalled that Blake's fours are eternally one. To add them up is to create the grounds of cyclicity or narrative sequence; to subtract one is to judge: "Bring out number weight & measure in a year of dearth" (*Marriage of Heaven and Hell*, E35). Thomson's *Seasons,* Blake knew, were initiated by his *Winter,* however they were finally arranged. *Verbum sat.* Blake's wisdom in *To the Evening Star,* iconicized in his language and energized by the perverse seductiveness of his *Epithalamion* allusions, is revealed in other borrowings as well—although some of them are so thoroughly absorbed into the epithalamic base that they are difficult to recognize. Nevertheless, with a firm grasp on what Blake, *pace* Kathleen Raine,[34] thought was *the* tradition—the Bible, Spenser, and Milton—we may venture to proceed. For Blake the Bible-Spenser-Milton line was not only that of prophecy (or, this early, perhaps simply "true" poetry), it was also a verbal line. By "verbal" I mean something other than "diction" in the sense that we describe that as being biblical, Spenserian, Miltonic, or merely "poetic." Diction in that sense is what makes imitators, who for the most part succumb to the power of their source—willingly or unwillingly.[35] Thomson is Miltonic, but Wordsworth is Wordsworthian despite, as it were, his Miltonic heritage. Keats triumphs over his early Spenserianism to become himself despite his persistent Spenser allusions, while Collins only rarely subdues his poetic ancestry and Gray only when he turns to "the grand Bardic manner" of Norse mythology. Macpherson's derivativeness is evidenced, finally, in his extraordinarily limited range, in the monotony of his cadences and languages, in what Mark Schorer acidly described as his "melodramatic inflations that fill the gap of content."[36] If Collins can be distinguished in obvious ways from the Wartons, and Smart from Gray, such distinctions are rarely verbal in my sense, but rather triumphs of spirit and imagination over a borrowed manner.[37]

By "verbal" I refer to something like what A. C. Hamilton claims for Spenser,[38] the exquisite and finely tuned sensitivity to the resonances and invested power of significant words, or to the contextual riches of a phrase. *To the Evening Star* has a number of these significant words and phrases, some of which I have commented upon already in my notes, and they are freighted with a transformational energy that informs the substratum of Blake's inversion of Spenser's *Epithalamion.* Before focusing on a few of these quite literally seminal words and phrases, however, it is important to notice that Blake has juxtaposed to the already short-circuited epithalamion pattern the even larger pattern of *Paradise Lost* IV,598-609, which begins with evening:

> Now came still ev'ning on, and twilight gray
> Had in her sober livery all things clad;
> Silence accompanied, for beast and bird,
> They to their grassy couch, these to their nests
> Were slunk, all but the wakeful nightingale;
> She all night long her amorous descant sung;
> Silence was pleased. Now glowed the firmament
> With living sapphires; Hesperus that led
> The starry host, rode brightest, till the moon
> Rising in clouded majesty, at length
> Apparent queen unveiled her peerless light,
> And o'er the dark her silver mantle threw.

It is after this prelude that Milton has Adam address Eve (in a passage I cited in an earlier note) on the appropriateness of retiring, "since God hath set / Labor and rest, as day and night to men / Successive"—the "timely dew of sleep" falling not as in Blake upon the flowers but "with soft slumbrous weight" upon their eyelids (lines 612-16). Nature wills such rest, Adam says, and Eve antiphonally invokes "All seasons and their change," all times of day, which please more sweetly and dissolve into the timelessness of Eden's eternal spring when shared with him (lines 635-58).

> Thus talking, hand in hand alone they passed
> On to their blissful bower   (ll. 689-90)

where Eve "decked first her nuptial bed, / And heav'nly quires the hymenean sung" (lines 710-11). Milton too then sings his own hymeneal celebrating "the rites / Mysterious of connubial love" (lines 742-43) in the justly famous "Hail, wedded Love" passage (lines 750-75).

The fulness of this bliss is anticipated in time by the structural recollection of Adam's crucial conversation with Raphael in Book VIII, a passage that validates Geoffrey Hartman's suggestion that *To the Evening Star* is "really" a morning poem.[39] Bringing his "story to the sum of earthly bliss" (line 522) Adam concludes:

> To the nuptial bow'r
> I led her blushing like the morn; all heav'n
> And happy constellations on that hour
> Shed their selectest influence; the earth
> Gave sign of gratulation, and each hill;
> Joyous the birds; fresh gales and gentle airs

Whispered it to the woods, and from their wings
Flung rose, flung odors from the spicy shrub,
Disporting, till the amorous bird of night
Sung spousal, and bid haste the ev'ning star
On his hill top, to light the bridal lamp.

(Ll. 510-20)

If the echoes of this passage in Blake's diurnal poems are obvious, the counter-echoes are not. These latter consist in the extraordinary silence of both of Blake's poems, most particularly *To the Evening Star,* a silence that slides menacingly from the welcome silence of Spenser's marriage bed to the ominousness of its being broken, not by Milton's natural choirs or the nightingale's amorous descant, but by the wolf's raging wide and the unarticulated but ineffectively suppressed growl of the lion. Similarly, while "happy constellations" firmly "shed their selectest influence" on Adam and Eve's nuptial couch and the firmament "glowed . . . / With living sapphires" coterminous with the moon's "peerless light" apparent (IV,604-8), Blake's star withdraws, no moon rises, the forest is "dun," and the total scene is "illuminated" only by the lion's "glare." To be sure, Blake's "dusk" is "washed" with silver just as "o'er the dark" Milton's moon "her silver mantle threw" (IV,609), but the uniqueness of Blake's diction here, within *Poetical Sketches* (and, retrospectively, even within his entire oeuvre), should alert us to his careful skewing of the apparent parallels.

The noun *dusk* appears in neither Spenser nor Milton, though the latter uses it adjectivally three times: "exhalation dusk and moist" which the hills supply to the heavens to help supply the deluge (*PL* XI,740ff.); the "pathless desert, dusk with horrid shades," that constitutes the wilderness into which Christ, as "our Morning Star," is led (*PR* I,291-96); and the "dusk faces" of empire with which Satan taunts Christ in Book IV of *Paradise Regained* (lines 76ff.). While such uses obviously convey ominous implications, and while Blake's verbal memory was unusually acute, I find it difficult, however tempting and attractive, to credit him with so ambitious a triune recall. There is no doubt, though, about his recall of *Comus:*

The star that bids the shepherd fold
Now the top of heav'n doth hold,
And the gilded car of day
His glowing axle doth allay
In the steep Atlantic stream;
And the slope sun his upward beam
Shoots against the dusky pole,
Pacing toward the other goal
Of his chamber in the east.

(Ll. 93-101)

With its pointed relationship to both *To Morning* and *To the Evening Star,* this passage also may have suggested to Blake his justly acclaimed line, "wash the dusk with silver"; for Milton's picture, as Blake's painterly eye would surely have seen, is of the sun dipped below the ocean's watery horizon, yet shining upward momently to silver the descending dusk.[40] Cowper no doubt took his "dusk of eve" from Milton's lines, as did Thomson in *Summer* and *Autumn,* but neither of these capitalizes on Milton's context: Comus's setting of the scene, amid (as the stage direction describes it) "a rout of monsters headed like sundry sorts of wild beasts" making "riotous and unruly noise," and with perverse hymeneal "torches in their hands" lighting this parody of Adam and Eve's (or, more properly, given the date of *Comus,* Spenser's) nuptial rites:

> What hath night to do with sleep?
> Night hath better sweets to prove,
> Venus now wakes, and wakens Love.
> Come, let us our rites begin;
> 'Tis only daylight that makes sin,
> Which these dun shades will ne'er report.   (Ll. 122-27)

Blake's strikingly sophisticated appropriation of this passage and its implications hinges on another word unique in *Poetical Sketches* (as well as, like *dusk,* in the whole of his work). Arthur Sherbo has claimed that *dun* is a Miltonic word,[41] despite its being used but twice by Milton in his poetry (aside from his reference in *Vacation Exercise* to the River Dun). Given its full context in *Comus* and the uniqueness of Blake's contrarious usage in an epithalamionlike structure, whether it is merely "Miltonic" or not in Sherbo's sense is beside the point. For *Blake* it was what I have called a "significant" word, an imaginative epiphanizing of a total context whose appropriateness to his perverse design must have appeared in his brain like a revelation. The "dun night" of Collins (his only use of the word), Thomson's "dun umbrage," "dun expanse," and "mantle dun," Shenstone's "the dun far distant grove," Thomas Warton's "dun void" and "dun clouds," and Beattie's "dun gloom" are of a piece: simplistically evocative of melancholy, part and parcel of the loco-descriptive tradition,[42] contextually irrelevant to Milton's complex montage of riot, lust, bestiality, Cotytto, Hecate, Stygian darkness and so on. The differences need not be pursued perhaps but the closest approach of all of these to Milton and Blake may be taken, generously, as typical. It is from Thomson's *Summer:*

> Evening yields
> The world to Night; not in her winter robe
> Of massy Stygian woof, but loose arrayed
> In mantle dun. . . .
> . . . .

> Sudden to heaven
> Thence weary vision turns; where, leading soft
> The silent hours of love, with purest ray
> Sweet Venus shines; and, from her genial rise,
> When daylight sickens, till it springs afresh,
> Unrivalled reigns, the fairest lamp of night.　　(Ll. 1684-87, 1693-98)

The passage prepares the way for neither epithalamion nor anti-epithalamion but for "serene Philosophy," with whom Thomson will "crown [his] song," predictably and characteristically, in a hymn to "Him, / The world-producing Essence, who alone / Possesses being" (lines 1730-31, 1746-48). The extremity of the contrast between Blake's and Thomson's borrowings from Milton, however, remains yet to be seen. It inheres in a radical reshaping of Milton heretofore unacknowledged in the early Blake. Again a word almost unique in Blake (*glares*) triggers the effect quite marvelously.

The verb occurs several times in Thomson, always evoking Milton, always de-Miltonizing its impact. For example, in the "first fresh dawn" of "the gladdened race / Of uncorrupted man"

> The herds and flocks commixing played secure.
> This when, emergent from the gloomy wood,
> The glaring lion saw, his horrid heart
> Was meekened, and he joined his sullen joy.
> For music held the whole in perfect peace.
>
> 　　　　　　　　　(*Spring*, ll. 242-43, 263-67)

In *Paradise Lost* Satan, having penetrated into Eden to spy on Adam and Eve's state,

> 　　　　Around them round
> A lion now he stalks with fiery glare.[43]

Blake's lion "glares through the dun forest" with Banquo-like ferocity[44]—just as, in a different but related context, the Minstrel of *King Edward the Third* stirs the King's troops to bloodthirst with:

> O sons of Trojan Brutus, cloath'd in war,
> Whose voices are the thunder of the field,
> Rolling dark clouds o'er France, muffling the sun
> In sickly darkness like a dim eclipse,
> Threatening as the red brows of storms, as fire
> Burning up nations in your wrath and fury!
>
> Your ancestors come from the fires of Troy,
> (Like lions rouz'd by light'ning from their dens,
> Whose eyes do glare against the stormy fires)
> Heated with war. . . .
>
> 　　　　　　　　　　　　　(E428)

The lion's glare in *To the Evening Star,* then, is no mere gesture, nor on Blake's part but a gestural invoking of primal fears:[45] it is Satanic and warlike, destructive of love and loving silence and timely sleep, and most of all of "our flocks" and the entire fond fiction of pastoralism, however seemingly "protected" by a covering of dew, however fervently prayed for.[46] Milton's Satanic wolf completes the destruction of pastoral innocence as well as of wedded love:

> As when a prowling wolf,
> Whom hunger drives to seek new haunt for prey,
> Watching where shepherds pen their flocks at eve
> In hurdled cotes amid the field secure,
> Leaps o'er the fence with ease into the fold;
> . . . .
> So clomb this first grand thief into God's fold.   (*PL* IV, 183-87, 192)

For all the "foulness" of the "descent" Satan must now "constrain" himself

> Into a beast, and mixed with bestial slime,
> This essence to incarnate and imbrute,

so "that destruction wide may range" (IX,164-66, 134). The echoes of *Comus* in this passage were not lost on Blake either.

Hartman has argued that *To the Evening Star* defines an "interlunar moment," a "power failure or dangerous interval, a moment when the light goes out. The evening star rises in that space, on that loss"; but, he adds, "however strongly it rises there is often the fear of new withdrawal . . . and the dangerous sense that 'sacred dew' or starry 'influence' no longer prevails."[47] While such an interpretation seems to me generally correct, Hartman's tentativeness in the latter part of this statement leads him to a final confusion: "Blake's evening star, therefore, rises upon the twilight of English and classicizing poetry with the energy of dawn: it is, already, the morning star."[48] One may accept the idea of the twilight of "classicizing poetry," but there is a significant error in the assumption of "progress" from evening to morning, one that rests all too comfortably on the epithalamic power of Blake's Spenserian allusions while ignoring the counterthrust of the significant words I have noted. But even without these latter, Blake's severe truncation of the diurnal cycle should alert us to something unusual, untoward. Morning yields to no noon. It merely "appears." And while that natural fact may be an occasion for joy and confidence, the subtle shift from the sun's "race" in Psalm 19 to a hunt lends the poem, as we have seen, something more than what Bloom calls "a faintly sinister quality."[49] Bloom's qualifier here blurs Blake's clear signs. The hortatory verbs of *To Morning* parallel those of *To Spring* but lead to no present-tense summer (noon); and even if the sun is already "rouz'd" and the morning "radiant" by the close of the poem—and there is some question in my mind as to whether that "really" happens, given the rhetorical structure—all the poem's "action" hinges on the disturbing verb "unlock." The unanswered questions that this word raises in *To Morning* are, for example, totally absent from Enion's great speech "from the Caverns of the Grave" in *The Four Zoas* VIII. For her

> the time of Love
> Appears upon the rocks & hills in silent shades but soon
> A voice came in the night a midnight cry upon the mountains
> Awake the bridegroom cometh I awoke to sleep no more.
>
> (E369-370)

No unlocking here, no need to unlock. The bridegroom cometh, I awoke, love appears, I sleep no more. This reworking of *To Morning* is perhaps illegitimately invoked here, but I cite it as an example of Blake's frequent "spelling out," later on, in *The Four Zoas* particularly, of the implications of his earlier perceptions.

As I have said, Spenser's *Epithalamion* proceeds in time even as it concenters all time in the moment. His speaker's exhortations emanate in action: "it *is* time." Noon, evening, and night succeed, and the diurnal round becomes the image of eternity in much the same way as Spenser manipulates the details of the Garden of Adonis. Neither occurs in *To Morning* and the hunter-huntress of the concluding lines will find mythological-classical-pastoral buskins ill-fitted for dealing with raging wolves and glaring lions. If indeed Blake's "unlock" evokes "that golden key / That opes the palace of Eternity" (*Comus*, lines 13-14), the rest of the poem inspires little confidence in St. Peter's iron key being alchemized to gold (see *Lycidas*, lines 110-11). In precisely the same fashion, but with deepened ominousness, *To the Evening Star* fails also to proceed or succeed. The star is invoked by the optimistic speaker, but what "happens" in the poem is an absenting, an assertion of pastness. The only effective present tenses are the wolf's raging and the lion's glaring; and although the flocks are covered with sacred dew, that seems as poor a protection against the power of night and its ravening denizens as the hunter-huntress of *To Morning* is an ineffectual finder of the keys to the gates.

I must confess that such a somber reading of these lovely lyrics is disturbing, especially in light of the triumphant eternal moment of Spring-Summer-Autumn in the seasonal poems—the anticycle or antisequence of *To Winter* notwithstanding. What makes the diurnal poems different from these is their focus on the marginal moments of dawn and evening. They must *become* day and night, and the force of the invocatory rhetoric tends to evoke the power of night before the dawn ("unlock") as well as of day before evening. The triumphs of time inhere in such emphases. While these marginal moments may not be, as Wagenknecht suggests in a slightly different context, "a failure of the imagination,"[50] to eternize their loveliness and paradisal peace and joy clearly requires more than sacred dew, starry influence, and queen and huntress chaste and fair. In *To Morning* and *To the Evening Star* the imaginative effort to transform cyclical time into illusory sequence and hence into eternal moment must be ours, not the poet's or the poems' as in the seasons suite.[51] Again Frye's observation comes to mind: there is in Blake "an inevitable affinity between the continuous and the unreflecting."[52] If by "unreflecting" he means unimaginative, the power of ominousness—indeed the presence of the *idea* of death (emblemized even in the exclusivity and self-enclosure of locked gates, heavenly or otherwise)—is its surrogate here, inhering as it does in the thrust of the two poems toward continuousness or sequentiality. Pastoralism, from shepherd's calendars to epithalamia, is an insufficient imagination, even if it is a more comfortable conceit.

The eternal moment is there, of course, as it is in the first three seasons poems, albeit more obscurely shining. Furthermore it is there in precisely the same position structurally, the first three-quarters of the cycle or sequence. The gates are opened, morning issues forth, the dawn awakes, light rises, the dew cometh, and day wakens at precisely the same moment as Spring-Summer-Autumn arrives. The "golden load" of Autumn is the radiance of the morning as well as the crown and smile of the evening star. There is no before or after. As Blake makes clear in *The Four Zoas*, "the impressions of Despair & Hope for ever vegetate" in "the shadows of Valas [Nature's] Garden," the "land of doubts & shadows sweet delusions unformd hopes" (IX, E380). The "ancient golden age" renews, Blake tells us in the resounding apocalypse of the same poem, when the sun, moon, and stars are consumed "like a lamp blown out," when time and sequence and cyclicity give way to the "Expanding Eyes of Man":

> One Earth one sea beneath nor Erring Globes wander but Stars
> Of fire rise up nightly from the Ocean & one Sun
> Each morning like a New born Man issues with songs & Joy
>
> (E380, 391)

Then (that is, now) the plowman's labor becomes the shepherd's rest and vice versa; and the new-born man

> ... walks upon the Eternal Mountains raising his heavenly voice
> Conversing with the Animal forms of wisdom night & day
> That risen from the Sea of fire renewd walk oer the Earth.
>
> (E391)

It is only the "*Spectre* of Prophecy" (E392; my italics) who says: If winter's here can spring be far behind; or if night is here the morning soon will break. The true prophet is he who sees eternity in the moment, in the ruins of time.[53] He is Blake—even the Blake of the seasons and days of *Poetical*

Sketches. His morning and spring *are,* not will be, "the Prince of Light" of Milton's *Nativity Ode,* whose reign as "greater Sun," we should recall, begins on a wintry night and is signalled as well as heralded by "Heaven's youngest-teemed star" (lines 62, 83, 240). Blake's seasonal and diurnal hymns, then, like Milton's, are calculated to "enwrap our fancy long" so that "Time will run back and fetch the age of gold,"

> And heav'n as at some festival
> Will open wide the gates of her high palace hall.

(Ll. 134-35, 147-48)

The sound notably absent in Blake's two poems, in Milton's rings out gloriously, eternally, so that he may allow his own to lapse into time ("Time is our tedious song should here have ending"—line 239). Blake's music is the music of the poems themselves. Arising out of, yet eternally in, "the chambers of the East, / The chambers of the sun," it shall not, in our imaginations, cease from "antient melody." The "antient love" abandoned by the modern bards in *To the Muses* is here enjoyed once more—and still to be enjoyed.

WORLDLY WARS
AND MENTAL FIGHT

THE FOCUS of virtually all criticism of *King Edward the Third* has been upon two main points: (1) its evident Shakespeareanism and its dramaturgical ineptness, the latter being the "cause" of the play's fragmentary state; (2) the question of whether it is Thomsonian jingoism, attributable to Blake's youth, or an ironic subversion of "patriotic" war-mongering. Of these, the first seems to me a nonquestion. Alicia Ostriker has claimed that "there is something ineffably Shakespearean about the texture of the versification," but the fact is, as she admits almost immediately, that Blake's blank-verse line is "absurdly" varied.[1] Similarly Frye notes that Blake has no sense of, or perhaps did not want to develop, a Shakespearean verse paragraph, and showed himself to be either incapable of handling a pentameter line or impatient "with the obtrusiveness of recurrent accents."[2] It is not surprising, then, that Lowery's painstaking search throughout Shakespeare's plays yields very little in the way of concrete, or even plausible, allusion in Blake's *King Edward*. With some perseverance we may discover a few general likenesses between *Henry V* and *Edward III*, but to say that Blake's drama "has *Henry V* for its spiritual father" seriously overstates the case.[3] Frye's demurrer seems to me apposite: the play is a less than successful "exercise in the idiom of Elizabethan drama" where, as Erdman sensibly remarks, Blake would have found (among other things of course) the idiom of "the blustering talk of warriors before battle"[4] that appeared to him appropriate for a war play.

Although it is not until after the turn of the century that Blake speaks directly about "history," there is no reason to suppose that it took him that long to make up his mind about its relative "truth." He himself suggests an early date for at least some of his convictions in an 1809 comment on his painting, *The Penance of Jane Shore in St. Paul's Church:* "This Drawing was done above Thirty Years ago [i.e., about the time of *Poetical Sketches*], and proves to the Author, and he thinks will prove to any discerning eye, that the productions of our youth and of our maturer age are equal in all essential points."[5] History, for him, consists in the acts of history: "Reasons and opinions concerning acts, are not history. Acts themselves alone are history." Historical art, however, whether verbal or graphic, deals with "spiritual agency," not probabilities or impossibilities; truth, not doubt; the imagination, not reason or nature. "If you have Nature before you at all you cannot Paint History."[6] For all his admiration of Shakespeare as an example of "the extent of the human mind" whose works "cannot be surpassed" since they are products of "the gift of God, the Holy Ghost," Blake was uneasy, I think, with the history plays, based as they were (and as he knew) on "self evident action and reality" (*Descriptive Catalogue*, E535, 534). Rarely, if ever, does he refer to them with approbation except as certain characters transcend their historical origins and confines, as Chaucer's do, to become "visions of . . . eternal principles or characters of human life" that "appear to poets, in all ages" (*Descriptive Catalogue*, E527). Thus the witches in *Macbeth* are "the Goddesses of Destiny" and Shakespeare's "Fairies . . . are the rulers of the vegetable world" (ibid., E526). Similarly in Blake's art the choice of Shakespearean character, incident, or scene reveals this same focus on visionary history, predicated firmly on his marvelous conception of the genius of Shakespeare as a "Fiery Pegasus."[7] *Brutus and Caesar's Ghost* (a confrontation not dramatized but only reported by Brutus), *Hamlet and the Ghost of His Father*, *Jaques and the Wounded Stag* (a "visionary" extrapolation of *As You Like It* IV,ii), *Lady Macbeth and Duncan* (a scene absent from the play), *Lear and Cordelia*, *Macbeth and the Ghost of Banquo*, *Oberon and Titania*, *Pity*, from *Macbeth*, and *Richard III Assailed by Ghosts*, for example, either "translate" the "facts" of Shakespeare into mythological (or at least thematic or symbolic) form or focus upon the realities of unreality, those forces that animate, control, and create true—that is, imaginative—history. Even the *Lear and Cordelia* watercolor, which seems a simple, human illustration, violates Shakespearean truth by locating their reconciliation in a prison from which, in Milton's *History of Britain* (Blake's source for much of his mythologized or poeticized history), Lear is released to regain his throne and to be succeeded by Cordelia. This latter is the "truth" of the matter, as David Bindman points out, since in the mythological history of Britain Lear appears as the last of the line descended from Brutus of Troy who brutalized the early "savage Britons" in his apocryphal invasion and settlement of the isles—an idea employed by the Minstrel in Blake's *King Edward the Third* as well.[8]

Let us return now to that play. What may have attracted Blake to Shakespeare was his sense that the idiom of visionary history was buried under the panoply and idiom of kings and war, in other words that the Poetic Genius was demonstrably alive, if struggling, under the yoke of historian. As he says in his *Descriptive Catalogue*, "historical fact" is only true when seen "in its poetical vigour"; and its poetical vigour inheres in "miracle or prodigy" operating in the lives of men and the march of events.[9] His own

Edward the Third accordingly may have been intended as a kind of re-
generated Shakespearean "history," a revelation that Shakespeare, like
Milton, was of the devil's party without knowing it, and that the powerful
Renaissance political forces had infected and channeled his genius in the
cause of British glory rather than inspiring "visions of . . . eternal principles"
that "appear to poets, in all ages" (*Descriptive Catalogue*, E527). The degree of
success such a regeneration of Shakespeare's historical truth could achieve
would depend perforce on Blake's expertness in subverting the Shakespearean historical idiom, a tactic that consists largely of planting revela-
tory ironies in the substratum of apparent imitation. Conversely, his ultimate abandonment of the project may have been due to a gradual recognition, something like Keats's growing awareness of the overinsistent Miltonism
of *Hyperion,* that it was his "imitations" which were triumphing—a "triumph"
amply testified to by modern critical judgments about the Shakespearean
derivativeness of the entire piece. Intimidated, perhaps even taken in, by
Blake's Elizabethanism, we have tended to focus almost exclusively on the
vehicle; and when the tenor has been addressed, it has been pronounced an
achievement of ineffable Shakespeareanism.

Erdman's extended analysis of *King Edward the Third* as an abortive "vast
moral pageant rather than a drama" or an historical poet's account of
historical verities is thus all the more impressive. Relying on Froissart, the
pseudo-Shakespearean *Raigne of King Edward the Third,* Rapin's *History of
England,* and Joshua Barnes's *History of Edward III* as Blake's likely "sources"
both for historical fact as well as historical ironies, Erdman nevertheless
fashions his interpretation in terms of the Great Plague of 1348 (not mentioned in Blake's play) that "lies in wait for the warriors of Edward's ill-
starred invasion of France": a prophetic vision of judgment to be visited
upon those whose minds are self-enslaved by visions of glory, conquest, and
gain—"invisible chains," as Blake says, "but heavy." The enabling means to
this end, Erdman says, is Blake's abandonment of "his characters as human
beings in order to plant ironies in their speeches," ironies that he admits are
all too frequently hidden beneath Shakespearean "expression." To expose
them Erdman concentrates on a number of key phrases and pieces of
dialogue within the play and, more heavily, on the facts of Edward's invasion
and its historical consequences as well as their employment in eighteenth-
century British jingoistic pamphleteering and poeticizing in the cause of
stamping out the American Revolution. "To grasp the full ironic contrast,
however," Erdman concludes, "we should have the unwritten sequel to
these opening scenes—first the furious war unchained at 'Cressy,' and then
the 'Fire, Pestilence and Famine following'—a sequel indicated not only in
America but in the narratives of Barnes and Rapin, in the titles of Blake's
war paintings, and in *The Couch of Death,*" the last of which Erdman reads,
erroneously I think, as a plague document.[10] It is always difficult to quarrel

with a persuasive analysis of what might have been, and I shall not attempt that here. Rather, I suggest that Erdman's conclusions about the prophetic nature of *Edward the Third* are inherent in the play as it stands, albeit so ineffectively (or at least incompletely) exploited as to lead Blake to abandon the effort—and to forsake Shakespeare as well. When, after many years, he took up his mythological-historical pen once again, he did so only after experimenting graphically in mythologized history as the ambitious list of historical subjects in his *Notebook* shows (E661). Bindman correctly interprets that list as "a view of Blake's interpretation of the whole panorama of English history from its mythological origins to the apocalyptic future."[11] The climactic subjects Blake proposes to himself are *A Prospect of Liberty* and *A Cloud*. Both of these figure prominently in *The French Revolution*, which, as William Halloran has shown with studied attention to its cloud imagery, is a "visual account of the death of an old order and the birth of a new," an "imaginative recasting of Revolution."[12] Like *King Edward the Third* this poem too is "unfinished," if we can credit Blake's title-page promise of an epic "in seven books." Bloom has argued, though, that with the "token of fulfillment" inherent in the revolutionaries' sitting "in peace . . . beneath morning's beam" at the end of the poem as we have it, "Blake had nothing to add, and the course of events had little to add to Blake's desired consummation." Halloran agrees: "Whatever Blake may have intended at first, the focus as we have it is essentially complete."[13]

While I should be loath to advance the same argument for the completeness of *King Edward the Third*, I am equally reluctant to rely on what might have been its full development and conclusion to explain its present "meaning" or intent. Patently more interesting is Blake's seeming abandonment not only of the play itself but of the *idea* of drama as a mode of prophecy. Although it is possible, even probable, that he was aware of the common critical judgment (in his own age and earlier) of the Book of Job and Revelation as both dramatic and prophetic, I believe that he tended to distinguish between dramatic values, even formal dramatic constituents, inherent in prophecy, and prophetic implications and power emanating out of dramaturgical structures. Attracted as he was, even as early as the *Poetical Sketches,* to Milton's *Samson Agonistes,* for example, his own version of Samson's "drama" (or, more accurately, his "response" to Milton's prophetic drama/dramatic prophecy) is cast deliberately in nondramatic form. But what of the later oft-quoted phrase, "Visionary forms dramatic" (*Jerusalem* 98:27, E255)—and, more pointedly perhaps, what about *The Ghost of Abel* which is not only among his last poetic works (the colophon date is 1822) but returns almost defiantly to the form of *King Edward the Third* and familiar dramatic paraphernalia (scene setting, stage directions, even a "Curtain" that "falls" at the work's end)?

The two "problems" are related, as we shall see, but the *Ghost of Abel* is the easier of the two to address, since its form is clearly a deliberate effort to mimic Byron's in *Cain.* Indeed, as Martin Bidney has shown, Blake's work is not merely a "reply" to Byron but rather "an alternative ending to it."[14] The particulars of Bidney's persuasive essay need not detain us here, but it is noteworthy that while Byron subtitles his play "A Mystery," prefatorially aligning it with "the ancient . . . dramas on similar subjects, which were styled 'Mysteries or Moralities,'" Blake subtitles his rewrite of the final fifth of Byron's third act as "A Revelation In the Visions of Jehovah, Seen by William Blake."[15] Rather than "Biblical drama," as George Steiner characterizes *Cain,*[16] Blake's "drama" is a revelation seen *in* a vision *by* vision. Its form, then, is Revelation's, not Byron's or Shakespeare's, and what I have called its dramatic paraphernalia are but ironic concessions to Byron's "imprisonment" by such formal imperatives, however much Blake may have been struck, even surprised, by Byron's "Blakean" location of his dramatic conflict in "Cain's own consciousness." (Perhaps he even recognized that *Cain* was "like" his own prophetic books in attaining its ends "as an interiorized exploration of mental conflict.")[17] Byron is thus "in the Wilderness" still, as Blake's dedication to him charges, irremediably bound to "Nature" despite his heroic efforts to be Elijah, his characters not yet "Visionary forms dramatic" but only dramatic forms with "some Vision."[18] Clumsy as it may seem, my phrasal shift of emphasis is an accurate reflection of Blake's fundamental difference from Byron. But, that aside, the difference most crucially lies in the nature of "conversation." The "Visionary forms dramatic" that "bright / Redounded" from the tongues of the Eternals in the apocalypse of *Jerusalem* are forms, not words: "every Word & Every Character / Was Human," and it is those breathing "exemplars of Memory and of Intellect" that "walked / To & fro in Eternity as One Man reflecting each in each & clearly seen / And seeing" (98:27-40, E255). Even "the Words of the Mutual Covenant Divine" ride majestically, but humanly, "on Chariots of gold & jewels" (41-42). Ten plates earlier we are given another version of this visionary conversation:

> When in Eternity Man converses with Man they enter
> Into each others Bosom (which are Universes of delight)
> In mutual interchange, and first their Emanations meet
> Surrounded by their Children. if they embrace & comingle
> The Human Four-fold Forms mingle also in thunders of Intellect
> (88:3-7, E244)

"Blake avoids the Shakespearean style," Damrosch has observed, "because he does not want it. Putting the matter baldly, it is too human," however much its "flexible movement and dramatic immediacy . . . transforms common speech into art."[19] Human drama may yield some vision, prophetic inklings as it were, but by virtue of its very mode it demands the narrative (and conversational) continuity, sequential event, statement and reply that Blake associated with nonimaginative (later, fallen) discourse as well as with history. Perhaps this is the reason for the circling inanities of that antidrama, *An Island in the Moon,* which Blake wrote two years (or less) after the printing of *Poetical Sketches;* and it is certainly the reason that, after *The French Revolution,* "conversation" in Blake's poetry more nearly approaches that in Shelley's *Prometheus Unbound* (or perhaps in grand opera) than in conventional "theater." In any case, to subvert history, or to transform it into mythology, "scenes," exits and entrances, and "realistic" dialogue quickly proved themselves imaginatively inadequate.[20] Inextricably tied to time and place, such action and dialogue required "visionary interludes" and a healthy admixture of the language of biblical prophecy even to approach the concentration of all time in the moment of history or the holding of infinity in the palm of one's hand. The bardic song that "concludes" *King Edward the Third* with a false or parodic apocalypse may be, in this light, a more appropriate closure or denouement than we have tended to allow. Gray was right in his historical "imaginations," Shakespeare wrong. Some years later when Blake tried a kind of "drama" once more in *The French Revolution,* dramaturgy is largely sacrificed to the long speechifying increasingly characteristic of Blake's prophecies, and to a "narrative" in which we are urged by the language and imagery to see all events taking place in the prophetic moment. If, in his earnest attempt to subdue the linear power of history, the myth-making machinery of that poem rather clankingly obtrudes (his almost immediate awareness of that driving him to the progressively greater subtleties of *America* and *Europe*), the imaginative transformation of history into at least a proto-vision in *The French Revolution* is nevertheless demonstrably on its way to the remarkably accomplished and subtly coherent mythography we all know.

What is most interesting in *King Edward the Third* are the tentative beginnings of that transformation, not via Shakespeare but, as we have come to expect in the *Poetical Sketches,* via Milton — as well as the egregious jingoism of Thomson's Miltonism.[21] Long ago Frye described much of the play as "simply 'Rule Britannia' in blank verse." Misled by the expertness of Blake's tonal borrowings from Thomson into believing that there is "no use looking for irony here," he blamed Blake's succumbing to the British party line upon "the sterility" of the environment out of which his "ideas developed logically." And although he regarded *Edward the Third* as "an early sketch of the parallel between English and Hebrew history which is the ground plan of *Jerusalem,*" he charged Blake with casting that sketch "in terms of a symbolism he later repudiated."[22] If Frye is wrong here, as I think he is, the fault is less his than Blake's, for there is more than an ineffable Thomsonianism about the play, exacerbated by an inadequacy of countering allusion. But "inadequacy" is not quite correct: the allusions are there, but often frustratingly impacted. Extracting them will afford us a firmer purchase on what Blake at least thought he could accomplish in this early effort at revelational prophecy.

The play opens propitiously with the King's invoking of God's aid in his enterprise against the French. Blake underscores the outrageousness of this common presumption of God's sanction and guidance before battle by casting the invocation in the language of Isaiah's prophecy of Armageddon:

> Come near, ye nations, to hear; and hearken, ye people; let the earth hear, and all that is therein; the world, and all things that come forth of it.
> For the indignation of the LORD is upon all nations, and his fury upon all their armies: he hath utterly destroyed them, he hath delivered them to the slaughter. (34:1-2)

The full implications of Isaiah's vision, which for Blake implicitly characterizes Edward's army as already "delivered . . . to the slaughter," already "utterly destroyed," are immediately aligned with Gray's bardic prophecy:

> "Ruin seize thee, ruthless king!
> Confusion on thy banners wait,
> Though fanned by Conquest's crimson wing
> They mock the air with idle state.
> Helm nor hauberk's twisted mail,
> Nor even thy virtues, tyrant, shall avail
> To save thy secret soul from nightly fears."[23]

This passage (and *The Bard* in general) is a pervasive force in Blake's total conception in *King Edward*. Erdman has noted the pertinence of the Bard's prophecy of "the doom of Edward [I] and his entire line,"[24] a prophecy that actually, not merely prospectively, weaves "the warp and . . . woof, / The winding-sheet of Edward's race." Poetic prophecy thus has not merely the proleptic power of Isaiah but the effectuating power of God's fulfillment of it. Despite Edward's prayer, "Confusion" will rage and on his banners wait, Gray's whirlwind "hushed in grim repose" (as Edward says it is in Brittany) will sweep "its desolating army" to sow the land with destruction. Edward's doom (in Gray's words) is thus ratified. Further, Blake's Black Prince sees himself as a successful warrior cutting a track "into the heaven of glory, / Leaving a track of light for men to wonder at" (3:247-75, E424), whereas in Gray it is the murdered Bards, still prophetically puissant, who soar "in yon bright track, that fires the western skies" (line 103). Such triumph as is alluded to in *Edward the Third*, then, becomes for Blake the ignominious defeat of Kings and Princes, the apotheosis of the prophet, and the actualization of Isaiah's apocalyptic vision of paradise regained (a vision, incidentally, that is grossly parodied in Dagworth's speeches in 5:27-38 and 49-61, and in Brutus's speech in the concluding Minstrel's song, 6:39-60).

Having established the efficacy of prophecy, both biblical and bardic,

Blake then moves with remarkable sureness to his ideal modern prophet, Milton, his robe instinct as always with biblical power. To address the latter first, perhaps the most striking expression of such power in the remainder of the King's opening speech is his address to his son:

> . . . be strong; thou fightest for a crown
> That death can never ravish from thy brow,
> A crown of glory.   (Ll. 21-23)

Peter's first epistle (5:3) cautions the faithful to be not "lords over God's heritage" but rather "ensamples to the flock." Thus abjuring the very strength Edward urges on his son, Peter prophesies that "when the chief Shepherd shall appear, ye shall receive a crown of glory that fadeth not away" (5:4). Isaiah employs the same image twice (28:5, 62:3). Intensifying these allusions is another (in lines 25-28) to Revelation 3: "He that overcometh, the same shall be clothed in white raiment; and I will not blot out his name out of the book of life"; instead "Him that overcometh . . . I will write upon him the name of my God, and the name of the city of my God, which is new Jerusalem, which cometh down out of heaven from my God: and I will write upon him my new name" (verses 5, 12). It has been suggested that the King's address to his son is Blake's parody of God's words to his Son in *Paradise Lost* (III,311ff.), but the connection between the two passages seems to me tenuous at best, however much one may wish otherwise. Edward sues for aid in the cause of liberty, but rather than a mental liberty (the very loss of which he attributes to his enemy) his is the "freedom" to exact a "just revenge" (line 43). The misguidedness of this allegiance is defined succinctly in *Paradise Regained:*

> What wise and valiant man would seek to free
> These thus degenerate, by themselves enslaved,
> Or could of inward slaves make outward free?   (IV,143-45)

These chastising words are delivered by Christ to Satan whom, we should recall, Gabriel accuses of passing himself off as a "Patron of liberty" (*PL* IV, 958). Christ then goes on to turn against itself Satan's tempting of him with the glorious crushing of worldly emperors:

> Know therefore when my season comes to sit
> On David's throne, it shall be like a tree
> Spreading and overshadowing all the earth,
> Or as a stone that shall to pieces dash
> All monarchies besides throughout the world.   (Ll. 146-50)

Edward's ambitions seem hardly so grand (though it is possible that Blake intended deliberately to escalate them), but the Isaiah-like prophecy of Milton's final two lines sets Edward's cause (and, we should add, that of the

French whom Blake clearly considered no better) directly in the middle of that apocalyptic "season."

Although the *Paradise Regained* passage is marvelously apt for Blake's purposes, one must acknowledge its obscurity, isolated as it seems to be. But it is not nearly so isolated as it appears. One way to read *Paradise Regained*, of course, is as a sustained debate about the nature of glory. Lowery has suggested that the theme upon which Blake constructed his characterizations and "which seems to be the purported theme" of the whole of *Edward the Third* is fear.[25] While discussions of fear abound, particularly by Dagworth, glory seems to me much more central, for it is in the thematic context of glory-mongering that the allusions to *Paradise Regained* function. For example, in his initial speech King Edward calls upon "Liberty" to "blaze in each countenance, and fire the battle," but it is the "crown of glory" he really seeks, the gaining of that "brightest fame" he himself images as a star out-blazing all others and upon whose "splendor" "the astonish'd world, with up-turn'd eyes" will "stand only for to gaze." In Book III of *Paradise Regained* Satan tempts Christ with precisely such glory:

> wherefore deprive
> All earth her wonder at thy acts, thyself
> The fame and glory, glory the reward
> That sole excites to high attempts the flame
> Of most erected spirits. (Ll. 23-27)

Christ's response is clearly that of the silent prophetic Blake hovering like Gray's Bard behind his lines: "What is glory but the blaze of fame" (line 47); Edward's "astonish'd world" is but a "miscellaneous rabble, who extol / Things vulgar" (lines 50-51);

> They err who count it glorious to subdue
> By conquest far and wide, to overrun
> Large countries, and in field great battles win,
> Great cities by assault. What do these worthies
> But rob and spoil, burn, slaughter, and enslave
> Peaceable nations, neighboring or remote,
> Made captive, yet deserving freedom more
> Than those their conquerors, who leave behind
> Nothing but ruin wheresoe'er they rove,
> And all the flourishing works of peace destroy. (Ll. 71-80)

Edward's self-righteous (one might say Satanic) view of the worthiness of his enterprise may allude as well, at least indirectly, to these final lines of Christ's speech: "we, that wander from our native seats, / . . . beam forth lustre on a darkling world" (lines 35-36). In Scene 3, Edward pronounces "each man . . . worthy / Of a triumph" (lines 74-75), just as Satan in Book VI of *Paradise Lost* finds all his

> companions dear,
> . . . worthy not of liberty alone,
> Too mean pretense, but what we more affect,
> Honor, dominion, glory, and renown.   (Ll. 419-22)

Edward's son too is worthy of his high command; indeed, the King pontificates, "the man / Were base who were not fir'd to deeds / Above heroic" in having such men under his command (3:79-80) — an extraordinary echo of Milton's characterization of Christ's actions in *Paradise Regained* as "deeds / Above heroic."[26]

This evolving pattern of allusion is fostered by a comparable pattern drawn from *Paradise Lost*, again concentrated in Edward's opening speech. "Like the mounting flame," he exhorts,

> We spring to battle o'er the floods of death [.]
> And these fair youths, the flow'r of England,
> Vent'ring their lives in my most righteous cause,
> O sheathe their hearts with triple steel, that they
> May emulate their fathers' virtues.

The penultimate line activates the richness of the allusion by summoning up Milton's description of the fallen angels in debate, whose "vain wisdom" and "false philosophy" excite "fallacious hope" and arm "th' obdurèd breast / With stubborn patience as with triple steel." So contextualized, Edward's claim that his triple-steel-sheathed warriors "may emulate their fathers' virtues" takes on added perversity, for the particular fallen angels Milton is speaking of are the "others more mild" who counsel submission to *their* "father" (or at least acceptance of their lot) and arm themselves not with sword and shield but with patience.[27] Earlier Satan had berated his entire army for such submission: as the "flow'r of heav'n" (Edward's "flow'r of England") his cohorts must, he says, "Awake, arise, or be for ever fall'n" (*PL* I,316, 330). Their "cause," to Satan, is of course as "righteous" as Edward's, and both fore-defeated kings thus lexically mock Christ's congratulations to his angelic Host:

> "Stand still in bright array, ye saints, here stand,
> Ye angels armed, this day from battle rest;
> Faithful hath been your warfare, and of God
> Accepted, fearless in his righteous cause."[28]

Both Edward and Satan marshal their forces to the combats of glory so that their names, already "written equal / In fame's wide trophied hall," will be gilded "to make them shine with gold / That never tarnishes" (*Edward the Third* 1:25-28). But their "sons" (who "shall rise from thrones in joy, / Each one buckling on his armour"), those "powers that erst in heaven sat on thrones," will not only not effectuate Edward's promised "victory" but will, as Satan's crew, earn "no memorial" in "heav'nly records," their names "blotted out and razed" from "the Books of Life."[29] Christ appears "with radiance crowned" and "all his Father in him" shining, but Blake makes it abundantly clear in the King's speech that, win or lose, Edward's soldiers' emulation of "their fathers' virtues" shall not "beam a radiance, to fire the breasts / Of youth unborn."[30] Or, if it does, that radiance will be but the tarnished glitter of bloody fame and the wages of Sin and Death. The latter, we recall, is Satan's son (begot of his copulation with Sin) whom he urges, as Edward does his son, to "be strong" in the combined assault with Sin on man; and Death's rape of Sin produces the "yelling monsters" Blake alludes to earlier in Edward's vision of "yelling death" running "up and down the ranks."[31]

Finally, Edward's extended analogical contrast between warriors who are ordinary stars and those that blaze the brightest is also taken directly from *Paradise Lost.* To the King "the world of men are like the num'rous stars" (Satan's "host / Innumerable as the stars of night"), each "clad in glory according to his sphere" just as Milton's heaven is populated with the "ethereal quintessence of heav'n / [Fled] upward" and "turned to stars": Each had his place appointed, each his course."[32] Satan's fall and that of his legions, then, are also the shattering of the starry heavens, a conception Blake will use richly and consistently later in his works. In *Edward the Third* is the seed of that use. The King envisions himself (the "we" he employs clearly the royal plural) as wandering from his appointed place and course, like Lucifer "brighter" than "that star the stars among" (*PL* VII,132-33). Lucifer's fall "into his place" of darkness and diminished lustre (VII,135) Blake subtly reverses in Edward's fancy of himself rising (and growing larger) till he shines so brightly that an astonished world must look up to gaze upon his splendor and that of his troops beaming "forth lustre on a darkling world" (1:35-42). Opulently, even dazzlingly allusive, Blake's cosmic picture in the opening 42 lines of the play is thus complete except for a final reference to Satan. Cast entirely in night imagery and now linked firmly with the idea of glory explored in the rest of the play, Edward's speech soars at its close to Satan's vast "Plutonian hall" where

> his high throne, which under state
> Of richest texture spread, at th' upper end
> Was placed in regal luster. . . .
> . . . .
> At last as from a cloud his fulgent head
> And shape star-bright appeared, or brighter, clad
> With what permissive glory since his fall
> Was left him, or false glitter.   *(PL* X,444-47, 449-52)

And like Edward's "astonish'd world," Satan's host look up "all amazed / At that so sudden blaze."[33] This stunning analogy cannot but remind us of

Satan's later shrinking to "monstrous serpent on his belly prone," his host in "horrid sympathy" changing also to hissing serpentry:

> down their arms,
> Down fell both spear and shield, down they as fast,
> And the dire hiss renewed, and the dire form
> Catched by contagion, like in punishment
> As in their crime. (X,514, 540-45)

No such apocalyptic transformation occurs in *Edward the Third*, of course, but this powerful evocation may suggest something of how the play might have developed had Blake decided to pursue what he had begun so eloquently.

What does develop in the play as it stands, as I have suggested, orbits around the triune deity Ambition-Glory-War, the ardent pursuit of which warps the constant clarion call of Liberty into a hollow breast-beating. As the ubiquity of the idea of glory in Milton's works surely inspired Blake to his task, Shakespeare's heroic warriors just as surely served him as historical exemplifications of Satan's vainglory. To examine in detail all of Milton's discussions beyond those I've already cited, however, is beyond our present need. But there are a few others that are particularly germane to Blake's play. In Scene 3, Chandos, who is described by Peter Blunt later in the play as "the wise man" (a judgment shared by Dagworth and others), counsels the bloodthirsty Black Prince, who loves "the noise of war," in the ways of more sober contemplation to curb the "heat" of his youth (lines 232-61). Blake subverts that seemingly good advice by having Chandos later pronounce "the armed field and noisy war" as "a thing of course" that will "pass over as a summer cloud, unregarded," to him who gets used to it (lines 247-49). The Prince accepts this wisdom eagerly, acknowledging that "youth has need of age to point fit prey" (line 269). Mentally so armed he will not "fear to beat round Nature's wilds, / And rouze the strongest prey; then if we fall, / We fall with glory" (lines 263-65). Similarly in *Paradise Lost* Sin counsels death to "devour unspared" whatever "Time mows down,"

> Till I in man residing through the race,
> His thoughts, his looks, words, actions all infect,
> And season him thy last and sweetest prey. (X,606-9)

And Satan himself resolves (if, as he says, he "must contend") to take on "best with the best, the sender not the sent; / Or all at once; more glory will be won, / Or less be lost" (IV,851-54). Now abjuring Chandos's urging of mature contemplation as quickly as he accepted it as wise, the Black Prince openly subscribes to Satan's conviction that

> years, and to ripe years judgment mature,
> Quench not the thirst of glory, but augment.

The more one grows in years, "the more inflamed / With glory" (*PR* III, 37-38, 40-41).

Finally, in *Paradise Lost* Michael's vision of the postlapsarian world includes prominently, for Adam's edification,

> Cities of men with lofty gates and tow'rs,
> Concourse in arms, fierce faces threat'ning war. (XI,640-41)

So violence

> Proceeded, and oppression, and sword-law
> Through all the plain, and refuge none was found. (Ll. 671-73)

To Adam's question about who these men are that thus deal death

> Inhumanly to men, and multiply
> Ten-thousandfold the sin of him who slew
> His brother, (ll. 676-79)

and that "massacre / Make . . . but of their brethren, men of men" (lines 679-80), Michael answers:

> in those days might only shall be admired,
> And valor and heroic virtue called;
> To overcome in battle, and subdue
> Nations, and bring home spoils with infinite
> Manslaughter, shall be held the highest pitch
> Of human glory, and for glory done
> Of triumph, to be styled great conquerors,
> Patrons of mankind, gods, and sons of gods. (Ll. 689-96)

"Rightlier called," Michael concludes, they are

> Destroyers . . . and plagues of men.
> Thus fame shall be achieved, renown on earth,
> And what most merits fame in silence hid. (Ll. 697-99)

Into this framework Blake fits the various other pieces of his play, including those that are most often discussed and that form the staple of Erdman's fine interpretation: the Thomsonian jingoism and celebration of commerce sanctioned by religion in Scene 2 (compare, for example, *Liberty* V,569-73); the startling profanation and perversion of Psalm 19.5 and the Song of Solomon 2.8 (the sun as bridegroom) in the opening lines of Scene 3 and in Dagworth's rededication of himself to the King's cause later in the same scene (lines 144-50); Dagworth's parable about fear in Scene 3, as well as the immediately ensuing harvest, sport, and sunshine imagery in the King's speech (lines 133-43); Chandos's muted references to Satan as a "self-dependent . . . free agent" who rejects servitude (Scene 3, lines 194-203), and the King's antiphonal hymn to Liberty immediately following that; the discussion of ambition, sin, and guilt in Scene 4, where Dagworth's man William seems to present himself as a sort of self-portrait of Blake—especially in his frustrated desire to tell a parabolic "story" presumably illustrating the history of ambition, sin, and guilt (is his "story," to us, *King Edward the Third?*); the "love" of war-songs at the end of Scene 4; and finally the exaltation of death in battle in Scene 5 where fallen thousands will rise "in victory" to the "heavenly fields" as "the flowers of immortality . . . blown" (lines 28-36).

In this fifth and concluding scene to the play proper Blake continues to sprinkle his language tellingly, if sparingly, with Milton's, most pointedly the description of Death snuffing with delight the "scent of living carcasses designed / For death, the following day, in bloody fight" (*PL* X,272, 277-78). Blake's lines, spoken by Sir Walter Manny, are "I seem to be in one great charnel-house, / And seem to scent the rotten carcases" and hear "the dismal yells of death."[34] Since Blake was already an accomplished biblical student Milton's probable source in Isaiah was surely not lost on him either:

> Come near, ye nations, to hear; and hearken, ye people: let the earth hear, and all that is therein; the world, and all things that come forth of it.
>
> For the indignation of the LORD is upon all nations, and his fury upon all their armies: he hath utterly destroyed them, he hath delivered them to the slaughter.
>
> Their slain also shall be cast out, and their stink shall come up out of their carcases, and the mountains shall be melted with their blood. (34:1-3)

This prophetic voice, conjoined with Milton's, Blake clearly intends to appropriate as his own in *Edward the Third.* If its proleptic power, as Erdman observes, remains distressingly obscured by the rhetoric of empire and glory[35] (though Blake's persistent use of the "significant" allusive word or phrase makes it less obscure than Erdman allows), such opaqueness as does obtain may be attributable as often to the inadequacy of our command of Milton as to the excessive subtlety of Blake's technique or the inadequacy of his pen to the grandeur of his conceptions. Perhaps indeed he thought his "play" complete after all, its antithetical structure and "inconclusiveness" matching those of his evening and morning poems, apocalypse sounding loudly in and through his Minstrel's false prophecy and antiphonally played out in Milton. In *The French Revolution* no battle ensues either. Apocalypse, Blake may have believed even this early, exists within those very moments of time the ruins of which build mansions in eternity. "The flowing waves / Of time" may roll over Brutus's breast in the Minstrel's song, but those waves guarantee only the false apocalypse of time as the song's concluding words make clear, the same vainglorious vision accorded England's golden cities and shining spires in the opening lines of Scene 2 (perhaps the shining cities whereby Satan tempts Christ in *Paradise Regained*). Nevertheless Blake recognized, I think, that the structural formulae, conventions, and other requisites of drama constituted but a poor vehicle for prophecy; even his character William (if it is *his* William) in *Edward the Third* comes off as a pallid imposture. However insistently the notes of Gray's Bard are echoed by Edward's Minstrel and the authorial "voice" behind Blake's dialogue, the prophetic genius demanded the lyre in *propria voce.* The ringing sounds of its strings and the accents of the voice it accompanies we hear only once in sustained fashion in *Poetical Sketches,* in *Samson.* There, as we shall see in the next chapter, Blake proves to himself that he can, indeed must, be his own hero in all the wars of the mind.

The remaining three "political" poems in *Poetical Sketches* are at once ancillary to, and thematically descendant from, *King Edward the Third.* Erdman has argued persuasively that Blake intended *A War Song to English-men* to be included in the "finished" version of *Edward the Third.*[36] Part of his "evidence" is Peter Blunt's mention in Scene 4 of a "war-song" that "a musician" or "minstrel" will write; it will be, Blunt says, "about all us that are to die, that we may be remembered in Old England, for all our blood and bones are in France" (lines 44-51). Essentially a parody of any number of the biblical prophets' calling upon the nations to prepare for Armageddon, the *War Song* thus incorporates, perhaps more clearly than anywhere else in *Edward the Third,* the voice of true prophecy echoing through a call to carnal war. This antithetical pattern is established in the first stanza, where for king and nobles the "Angel of Fate" is said to scatter the lots of death "out upon the darken'd earth." (In Revelation it is an angel of God who "having a golden censer . . . took the censer, and filled it with fire of the altar, and cast *it* into the earth"—8:3, 5.) In the second and third stanzas the prophesied "glorious victory" of knightly armies in their "cause" (never identified by the singer-minstrel) on the "well-fought field" is a redaction of the last-judgment prophecy of Revelation 20: 11-15:

> And I saw a great white throne, and him that sat on it, from whose face the earth and the heaven fled away . . .
> And I saw the dead, small and great, stand before God; and the books were opened: and another book was opened, which is the book of life: and the dead were judged out of those things which were written in the books, according to their works. . . .
> And whosoever was not found written in the book of life was cast into the lake of fire.

This book may be the "fatal scroll" of Blake's Minstrel, the "lot" cast by the Angel of Fate; but the "cause" here is obviously God's, not the unnamed cause of earthly battle. The fourth stanza of the *War Song* concludes with a vision of the "realms of light" to which the slaughtered soldiers aspire—an allusion, rather brilliantly reversed, to the realms from which Satan fell in *Paradise Lost:* now

> how changed
> From him, who in the happy realms of light
> Clothed with transcendent brightness didst outshine
> Myriads though bright. . . .   (I,84-87)

These are also the realms described in Revelation: with the "holy Jerusalem, descending out of heaven from God, Having the glory of God" (21:10-11)

> the city had no need of the sun, neither of the moon, to shine in it: for the glory of God did lighten it, and the Lamb is the light thereof.
> And the nations of them which are saved shall walk in the light of it: and the kings of the earth do bring their glory and honour into it. (21:23-24)

The entire *War Song,* moreover, is cast with even greater parodic energy in the form of Satan's exhortations to his fallen troops, an additional subverting (if we miss the biblical-prophetic notes) of the "prophecy" of the Minstrel: "Arm, warriors, for fight," Satan cries;

> "Let each
> His adamantine coat gird well, and each
> Fit well his helm, gripe fast his orbèd shield,
> Borne ev'n or high; for this day will pour down,
> If I conjecture aught, no drizzling shower,
> But rattling storm of arrows barbed with fire."   (VI,537, 541-46)

In the subsequent battle those arrows rain down from the "chariot of Paternal Deity" (VI,750); "in celestial panoply all armed," Christ ascends, "at his right hand Victory" sitting "eagle-winged," beside him "his bow / And quiver" (VI,760-64). On the other hand, "All resistance lost, / All courage," Satan's legions

> down their idle weapons dropped;
> O'er shields and helms and helmèd heads he rode
> Of Thrones and mighty Seraphim prostrate.   (VI,838-41)

Christ pressing his advantage, "On either side tempestuous fell / His arrows" to drive the Satanic rebels "into the wasteful deep."[37] In earthly conflict there will be no rising "to meet our fathers in the sky," only an endless fall "headlong . . . / Down from the verge of heav'n" (VI,864-65).

Neither of the two "prologues" is related so directly to *King Edward the Third* as the *War Song,* but the one *Intended for a Dramatic Piece of King Edward the Fourth* may be regarded usefully as a kind of self-proclaimed counterpoint to the *War Song.* Whatever "dramatic piece" Blake contemplated, the *Prologue* as it stands has nothing whatever to do with Edward IV except insofar as he was a noble, a king, and a most successful military leader.[38] Its links to the *War Song* are most clearly visible in the relationship between the two speakers. Whereas Edward the Third's minstrel conducts a kind of pep rally for the troops in France, assuring them not only of their cause's worthiness but, in effect, of their salvation—the true voice of prophecy only insinuating itself into the rhythms and language of glory-mongering—the Edward IV *Prologue* gives that true prophetic voice full vent. The biblical tonalities are largely (though not entirely) derived from Revelation but, perhaps predictably, Milton plays a role as well.[39] Milton's God is a sometime thunderer, of course, but it is rare to find him speaking, as the prophet of the *Prologue* wishes *he* could, with "a *voice* like thunder."[40] His are more usually the thunders of warfare, clearly not what Blake wanted to evoke here, divinely righteous and heavenly or not. On the other hand, the biblical prophets commonly refer to the thunder of God's voice in his wrath at his people, the locus classicus behind Blake's usage being probably Revelation 14:2—which also rather surprisingly provides an additional link between the Edward IV *Prologue* and the *War Song* on the one hand, and *King Edward the Third* on the other:

> And I heard a voice from heaven, as the voice of many waters, and as the voice of a great thunder: and I heard the voice of harpers harping with their harps:
> And they sung as it were a new song before the throne. . . .

Here, as well as in the Psalms (33:3, 96:1, 98:1), is Peter Blunt's "new song" that he says the musician-minstrel is "going to play before the King" (the Minstrel's song in Scene 6 as well as the *War Song*); and here also is the "voice from heaven" with which Blake's prophet in the *Prologue* endows himself. In Revelation, furthermore, the only ones who "could learn that song" were those "which were redeemed from the earth" (14:3). They "are without fault before the throne of God" (14:5), the same throne from which the equally biblical "whirlwind of fury" descends in Blake's *Prologue*. Blake's speaker prophesies the nations being driven together as Isaiah, Ezekiel, Zephaniah, and other biblical prophets do, the gathering of the tribes for God's final destruction of the unredeemed: "And he gathered them together into a place called in the Hebrew tongue Armageddon" (Revelation 16:16). More extensively, here is Zephaniah: ". . . for my determination is to gather the nations, that I may assemble the kingdoms, to pour upon them mine indignation, even all my fierce anger: for all the earth shall be devoured with the fire of my jealousy" (3:8). Against such a divinely ordered gathering the prophets regularly set the phrase "who can stand" or some variation thereof. For example, "Who can stand before his indignation?" cries Nahum (1:6); "who may abide the day of his coming? and who shall stand when he appeareth?" asks Malachi (3:2); and in Revelation "the great day of his wrath is come; and who shall be able to stand?" (6:17)

But there are at least two other kinds of gathering-together in the Bible. One is God's calling of witnesses "that ye may know and believe me, and understand that I am he: before me there was no God formed, neither shall there be after me. I, even I, am the LORD; and beside me there is no saviour."[41] The other is epitomized in the speech of the "angel standing in the sun" in Revelation:

> Come and gather yourselves together unto the supper of the great God;
> That ye may eat the flesh of kings, and the flesh of captains, and the flesh of mighty men, and the flesh of horses, and of them that sit on them, and the flesh of all men, both free and bond, both small and great.
> And I saw the beast, and the kings of the earth, and their armies, gathered together to make war against him that sat on the [white] horse [that was "called Faithful and True, and in righteousness . . . doth judge and make war" (19:11)] and against his army.
> And the beast was taken, and with him the false prophet. . . . (19:17-20)

From Milton's point of view the gathering for Armageddon includes prominently Satan and his hellish crew, on whom falls Isaiah's "Lord . . . with fire, and with his chariots like a whirlwind, to render his anger with fury, and his rebuke with flames of fire" (66:15). But it is also, at least implicitly, the gathering of the purveyors of violence, oppression, and sword-law in *Paradise Lost's* vision of futurity accorded Adam by Michael. They are, says Adam in language Blake may well have recalled for his *Prologue*, "Death's ministers, not men" (XI,676); their hectorings Milton describes, in a line Blake did remember, as the roarings of "the brazen throat of war" (XI,713).

In the same part of Michael's speech Enoch is advanced as the prophet who, amid the steady carnage, "spake much of right and wrong, / Of justice, of religion, truth and peace, / And judgment from above" (XI,666-68). As the Epistle of Jude puts it:

> Enoch . . . prophesied of these, saying, Behold, the Lord cometh with ten thousands of his saints,
> To execute judgment upon all, and to convince all that are ungodly among them of all their ungodly deeds which they have ungodly committed. (Verses 14-15)

Blake thus surrounds his own voice, or that of his prophet-speaker, in the *Prologue* with the voices of John of Patmos, Isaiah, Ezekiel, Zephaniah, Malachi, Enoch, Michael, and Milton—a formidable visionary company indeed.

Despite the clarity, or relative clarity, of the allusions I have traced, and despite Blake's assumption of the prophetic mantle he regarded as being handed down to him, problems remain in the Edward IV *Prologue*—or at least troubling ambiguities.[42] The last two lines seem straightforwardly to levy responsibility for all war on kings, nobles, and ministers. But how are we to reconcile this attribution of guilt with the speaker's charge some lines earlier that part of the carnage stems directly from the very "Throne of God" to which someone must "answer" for war's destructiveness? And even when it is "the oppressed" who "fight in the troubled air" (the "troubled sky" of war in *PL* II,534) — presumably in a truly righteous cause — the "who can stand" refrain is applied as if their warfare is no more acceptable in the eyes of the speaker than that of kings and nobles. Similarly, if in the biblical-prophetic tradition God's gathering of nations together is either for their witnessing to his omnipotence or for their receiving the divine *coup de grace* for obdurate sinfulness, Blake's God in the *Prologue* "drives" the nations together, the militant verb strongly suggesting a precipitation of the very wars His furious whirlwind of judgment is calculated to destroy. The structure of the poem unfortunately accentuates the ambiguity one would normally expect it to resolve: divine judgment and Armageddon seem buried indiscriminately in the sequence of all other "floods of death," and God's righteous cause is subverted by the allusion to Milton's Sin, Death, and the "fiends of Hell" rejoicing "upon the slain."

What seems to be a resolution of these ambiguities in the final lines is in itself ambiguous. Kings and nobles "have done it," but also Heaven's "Ministers" have done it. Although such accusations were a steady cliché in Blake's day, and though we are no doubt to understand his laying of blame as genuinely felt, the ministers do assume a prominence in the *Prologue* commensurate with the "throat of war" phrase, both urging upon us the conclusion that Blake meant firmly to anchor the frame of the *Prologue* in the ambiguities he perceived in *Paradise Lost*. The "throat of war," for Milton, unequivocally connotes earthly war. The ministers are, on the one hand, the *self-appointed* agents of God in conformance to the doctrine of divine right; on the other, they are Milton's angelic ministers, fallen as well as unfallen. For example, Satan describes God as an "angry Victor" whose "ministers of vengeance and pursuit" have driven the fallen angels to the "seat of desolation, void of light" (*PL* I,169-70, 181); but elsewhere the guardians of Eden are God's "flaming ministers" appointed to protect against Satanic incursion (IX,156). For Blake this duality (not to say duplicity) is intensified by God's delegation of his Son to wage the war to end all war. The language of that delegation was surely displeasing to Blake, whose "prophecies," even in *Poetical Sketches* as we have seen, conclude well before any battles take place. In later Blakean parlance only mental warfare can end all wars. Contrary to this principle, Milton's God urges Christ to ascend his

> chariot, guide the rapid wheels

> That shake heav'n's basis, bring forth all my war,
> My bow and thunder, my almighty arms
> Gird on, and sword upon thy puissant thigh.[43]

Furthermore, the short, terrible battle over, Christ then rides the conquering hero like any other earthly king "triumphant through mid-heav'n," "celebrated" by all before the throne of God (VI,888-89).

With all of the foregoing in mind I find it impossible to credit Blake's seeming exculpation of God and Heaven in the *Prologue* while pouring out his own righteous wrath on their ministers. Even in 1780 oppressor and oppressed were to him but two sides of the same coin. Adam says, "Death's Ministers" are not men; Blake adds, neither are they gods. *His* prophecy, then, as distinct from his speaker's, is of the potential—or perhaps only hoped-for—power of his own voice to still the troubled waters, to "drown the throat of war." *All* war, human or divine. Perhaps the point of his *Prologue*'s refrain is that no one, finally, can "stand," and no one really can (or perhaps should) "answer at the Throne of God." Answering at the throne of God is but a coming to justice at the bench and bar of the very Heaven that permits (even sanctions by its example) the sin. Angel battles angel, and man man. Paradoxically the only *true* answering resides in listening to the prophetic poet whose tongue, not sword, will silence the throat of war. Enoch did no battle, nor did Isaiah, Ezekiel, John of Patmos. Nor did Milton. Ideally Blake's Edward IV *Prologue* should assume a place parallel to Milton's "prologue" to Book VII of *Paradise Lost*, the war in heaven now over: "In darkness, and with dangers compassed round, / And solitude" he will sing the "great work of peace."[44] Milton prays that he will not suffer the fate of Orpheus, torn by a "wild rout"

> till the savage clamor drowned
> Both harp and voice; nor could the muse defend
> Her son.   (VII,34, 36-38)

Unlike the Muse, who was "an empty dream," Urania he hopes will not fail him in his task; for she is "heav'nly" (VII,39). Ultimately for Blake both the Muse and Urania are vain fictions (as were the titular characters of *To the Muses*), his faith being anchored, even if not as firmly as his poem seems to indicate, in the spirit of Revelation "which God gave unto" John:

> Blessed is he that readeth, and they that hear the words of this prophecy, and keep those things which are written therein: for the time is at hand. (1:1, 3)

The sword of carnal war is transformed in Revelation into "the sword of my mouth" (2:16), the "spirit of prophecy," what Blake will call a few years later in his first engraved works the "Poetic Genius." John imagines this figure as a warrior on a white horse, whose "name is called The Word of God" and whose sword, therefore, "out of his mouth goeth" and "with it he should smite the nations" (19:11, 13, 15). This sword heralds John's "new heaven and . . . new earth . . . the holy city, new Jerusalem, coming down from God out of heaven, prepared as a bride adorned for her husband" (21:1-2).

In *Poetical Sketches* Blake was not yet ready to tackle that eternal verity or "history," and in any case a "Dramatic Piece of King Edward the Fourth" surely would not be the appropriate vehicle for it. The play was not, as Blake may have thought in *King Edward the Third*, "the thing." Nor was mere prophetic thundering. He, and we, are still a long way from even the implied apocalypse of *The French Revolution,* that next, and necessary, step toward a capable prophetic mythology wherewith to enact the wars of intellect and imagination.

The Prologue to King John is the least interesting of the three war poems (I shall call it a poem despite its prose form). The obviousness of the allegory severely reduces the effectiveness of the even more obvious fervid rhetoric. "Justice" apparently takes Albion to task for the sins of her sons, the latter melodramatically collectivized as "crimson dy'd . . . Tyranny." But her other sons, named simply "Patriot," rise up to quell Tyranny so that Albion "may . . . smile again."[45] The full burden of the prophecy, however, rests not solely on these banalities. As in the more intricate and allusive Edward IV *Prologue* and the *War Song,* all the people, tyrant and tyrannized, suffer and die. Brothers, widows (the marriage so recent that it is unconsummated), fathers, infants, mothers, husbandmen, the court youth, aged senators, and plain old age "must work the work of death" even against "their progeny." And even if Albion's sons some day will "joy as in the morning" and "her daughters sing as to the rising year," the seasonal cycle will spin inexorably toward the winter of tyranny once more. Then, as he has done "full oft" in the past, Patriot will rise again, and all shall be as has been told. If one were to find somewhere in the *Sketches* the seeds of the "Orc cycle," I suppose one might find them here, for the King John *Prologue* is a poem of cycles: from crimson sins to "red scourge" to joy in the morning to crimson sin; from Albion's stretching "her peaceful arms" (is there a studied ambiguity in this last word?) to Tyranny's "stretch'd . . . purple arm" to peace once more; from infancy to youth to old age to death; from pride to a humbling to a resurgence of pride. The only constant is the eternal flux above which hangs the Damoclean sword of Justice ever ready "to plunge in Albion's breast." "Lingering Fate is slow," Blake's prophet intones, somewhat oddly. One might ask, as Satan asks Christ in *Paradise Regained,*

> "If I then to the worst that can be haste,
> Why move thy feet so slow to what is best,
> Happiest both to thyself and all the world." (III,223-25)

Perhaps, Satan slyly suggests, Christ "linger'st in deep thoughts detained" because of the hazard of such high enterprise (III,227-28). Christ's reply might be that of Blake's prophet in the Prologue:

> "Means I must use, thou says't, prediction else
> Will unpredict and fail me of the throne."   (III,394-95)

But his time, He says, "is not yet come" (lines 396-97). When it does, God, in his own good time,

> "by some wondrous call
> May bring them back repentant and sincere;
>
> . . . .
>
> To his due time and providence I leave them."   (Ll. 434-35, 440)

This surely must have seemed inadequate, even capricious, to Blake; but that curious slow lingering of Fate in the Prologue is hardly a worthy substitute. The certitude of prophecy seems here to be irretrievably compromised, especially when projected against the background of its triumphs, however obscure, in King Edward, the War Song, and the Edward IV Prologue. Patriot's "cause" is, it seems, the "Heaven's cause" of the war-inflamed minstrel in the War Song, and the periodic plunging of the sword of justice into Albion's breast is but a gross parody of the prophetic tongue-sword that can "drown the throat of war." No such voice is called for here; no such tongue speaks. Virtually devoid of the allusions that energized the imaginative content of the other two war poems, this one displays neither technical nor thematic advance over them. In its allegorical simplicity (as well as perhaps its prose-poem form) it appears, indeed, to be a much earlier work, perhaps Blake's first youthful venture into "prophecy."

For all its intrinsic pallidness, however, the King John Prologue does provide some interesting, perhaps even surprising, connections with Gwin, King of Norway—to the point of suggesting the latter as Blake's first non-dramatic effort to incorporate prophecy into "history" after the "failure" of his major effort in the dramatic mode, King Edward the Third. At least Gwin does seem to mediate, if uncertainly, between the submerged prophetic power of both the play and the Edward IV Prologue, and the rather routine allegorizing of history in the King John Prologue. The bardic-minstrel-like opening line of Gwin is in the accents of the Edward IV piece and, despite its radically direct form and prosody, like the Prologue the poem moves immediately out of history, indeed out of all time, into an archetypal battle in the "north" (perhaps following Gray's example).[46] Moreover the war is again both civil and internecine, the verbal echoes of the Prologue insisting on the parallel. But in Gwin the latter's elementary and ineffectual personifications become, in Ossianic and Chattertonian fashion, the battle itself (which "faints"), earth (which "groans, and shakes" as she drinks "her children's gore"), famine and death (the latter of which "is sick"), the god of war ("drunk with blood"), the heavens ("sick" from "the stench of blood"), and the "river Dorman" (which "rolls" the blood of the slain and mourns his sons). The glut of blood and slaughter diminishes to near insignificance the decisive individual combat of Gwin and the champion Gordred, which Blake relegates to a single stanza of the 29-stanza poem;[47] and though Gordred, like Patriot, triumphs, no "sons . . . joy as in the morning," no "daughters sing as to the rising year." Instead we are left with a quite un-Ossianic and un-Chattertonian vision of the bloody river overwhelming "the pleasant south country" and the eagles vying for the slain that "fill the vale of death."

Little note has been taken of *Gwin's* last stanza or its concluding bloody river, presumably because the bannered slogan of the oppressed, Liberty, seems to have been well served by its champion: Gwin is dead. But despite Gwin's being a tyrant "over the nations of the North" (an idea Blake borrowed from Chatterton's *Godred Crovan*),[48] the blood of battle flows indiscriminately over the "south country" as well as "into the northern sea." No apocalyptic vision emerges, not even a vision of an earthly interregnum of peace. Yet in the terse hurrying of the balladic lines Blake succinctly and intensively gives us a vision of cosmic (or mythologized) war and its ultimate horror, futility, and absurdity. In a sense *Gwin* may be seen as internalizing in the very texture of the "narrative" the explicitness of Chatterton's Ossianic bard in the last line of *Godred Crovan:* "May the Gods grant this war for empire be his last."

If we hear in *Gwin* echoes of the old ballads Blake had read in Percy, of Chatterton and Ossian, of the Bible and Milton, those echoes do not carry the burden of prophecy as they do in *Edward the Third* and the *War Song.* The voice now is Blake's *in propria persona;* "my song" in *Gwin's* opening line is his song, articulated by the same tongue that can "drown the throat of war." That phrase, we recall, Blake borrowed from Milton's war-mongering ministers for the Hebraic-Miltonic opening of the Edward IV prologue-prophecy, a poem that may be regarded in one sense as a summary version of *Gwin.* Blake all but quotes in the *Prologue* from *Gwin's*

> O what have Kings to answer for,
> Before that awful throne!

And the "Nobles of the Land" who "have done it" in the *Prologue* are the same "Nobles of the land" of *Gwin* who "feed / upon the hungry poor." The prevailing imagery of *Gwin* is less that of Milton or the biblical prophets, however, than it is an adaptation of Ossianic and Chattertonian formulae toward the development of a prophetic-historical imagery that Blake will employ first in *The French Revolution.* Spatially too *Gwin* anticipates *The French Revolution.* Blake thrusts us upward and outward from the earthy and affective simplicity of hungry poor, the needy, wives and children, to shaking hills, banners waving "in the clouds," armies "rolling" like "tempests black"—and thence to the heavens shuddering with "roaring war," the dust ascending the skies, and a "wild sea" of blood the shores of which are indiscernible to the eye.

By the time Gordred cleaves Gwin's skull, the social and political "meaning" of that victory has paled to insignificance—even irrelevance. "Gwin fell; the Sons of Norway fled" is all the minstrel tells us of "history." Visionary history inheres in the "vale of death" and in the "river Dorman" as the loco-descriptive symbols of the universal battle's "sea of blood" whose "trembling shore" is beyond man's ken. The whole earth faints and fails, the heavens are sick with the stench of blood, and ghosts glut the throat of hell. Only the prophet's song echoes on, albeit in a cruel wilderness, tolling eternally the death-knell of Death that is inherent in what to the world is the absurd efficacy of mental war. Or faith. If kings must "answer" for the almost random slaughter, as both *Gwin* and the Edward IV *Prologue* seem to agree, Blake makes patently clear in the former that there must be other answerers as well. "Thousand deaths for *vengeance* cry" (my italics), he says in the next breath after lashing out at kings. Patriot (or another Gordred) will rise again as "full oft" he rose, and in the "righteous cause" of Heaven even his "wives and children" will howl "like ghosts, furious as wolves / In the bleak wintry day." *Gwin* begins with "The land is desolate"; it ends with that very land in its ultimate desolation rolling in blood—the same barbarically dull round of the universe propelled and perpetuated by those who see the ratio only, the same ones who do not "listen to my song."

> The hand of Vengeance found the Bed
> To which the Purple Tyrant fled,

Blake writes later on in *The Grey Monk;*

> The iron hand crushd the Tyrants head
> And became a Tyrant in his stead.   (E481)

And then again, with greater mythological density and significance, on Plate 53 of *Jerusalem* (E199-200), where he magnifies this earlier poem into "I Saw a Monk of Charlemaine."

Frye wisely observed that Blake's "precedents for freedom consist . . . [not] in the rebellions of the chosen people against their no less chosen conquerors, but in the far more radical upheaval envisaged by the prophets. Blake's two characters, ["a protagonist fighting for liberty and an antagonist defending tyranny"] must derive from his conception of tyranny as the defense of the fallen world and of liberty as the effort of the imagination to recover the state of innocence."[49] That conception, I submit, is already well developed in his mind in the *Poetical Sketches;* and the poems I have been discussing in this chapter are essays, all of which proved to be inadequate in one way or another, in the direction of a prophetic vehicle appropriate to that cosmic-mental drama. By way of illustrating his point Frye goes on to suggest that Orc and Urizen emerge out of Blake's *To Summer* and *To Winter*. Maybe. But they clearly emerge out of nothing in the war poems—in which, if the "Deliverer" is there at all, he is there as Blake himself, prophet and "Mental Prince" (*Public Address*, E569). The seeds of Orc's later demise in favor of Los may thus already be planted. Blake had but to work out the means to expunge "revolution" from salvation.

PROPHETIC FORMS

THE COUCH OF DEATH has been called "jejune and best forgotten."[1] On the surface it seems difficult to argue with this judgment, but I should prefer to suspend mine for reasons that have less to do with literary quality than with the work's "place" in *Poetical Sketches*. Whatever else it may be, *The Couch of Death* is an evening-night poem and ought, therefore, to have some relationship to *To the Evening Star* and, more darkly, *To Winter*. Although each of those poems in its distinctive way addresses the issue of death, neither moralizes it as *The Couch of Death* openly seems to do. Indeed Blake's attitude toward death appears to be so conventional here that one critic seizes upon that as a link between *The Couch of Death* and *Fair Elenor*.[2] More judicious and perceptive is Erdman's claim that the end of the prose poem dramatizes "the recovery of individual innocence, paradise regained"—though one may want to think twice about his suggestion that the youth is "plague stricken."[3]

Although his comments on *The Couch of Death* are spare, David Wagenknecht's broader-based discussion in *Blake's Night* is richly suggestive. Among other things, as I noted in earlier chapters, he borrows Hartman's notion of "descendentalism" in *To the Evening Star* (sky to earth, angel to man to sheep) and applies that to his own analysis of the collapse of pastoralism into fact, and the supersession of the pathetic fallacy with its assurance of nature's sympathy by a countermyth of disjunctive reality. Accordingly Wagenknecht regards *To the Evening Star* as the direct progenitor of the *Night* of *Songs of Innocence*. His argument is more complex and differently aimed than would be useful to elaborate on here,[4] but the correlation he discovers between the *Poetical Sketches* poem and its later avatar in *Innocence* is instructive with respect to *The Couch of Death*. For my purposes here, the most striking of these correlations are three: (1) the presence of the evening star itself, the pervading silence, and the smilingness the evening-night assumes; (2) the pouring of blessings or protective "influence"; and (3) the wolves and lions-tygers seeking their prey. The last of these takes a particularly powerful turn in *Night:* instead of merely raging and glaring as they do in *To the Evening Star,* the wolves and tygers now "howl for prey," are patently bloodthirsty, and even "rush dreadful" upon the sheep—at which point the "protective" angels, still somehow "most heedful,"

> Receive each mild spirit,
> New worlds to inherit.

In those worlds the "lions ruddy eyes" no longer glare but "flow with tears of gold":

> And pitying the tender cries,
> And walking round the fold:
> Saying: wrath by his meekness
> And by his health, sickness,
> Is driven away,
> From our immortal day.   (E14)

No such restoration of the delicate equilibrium of the state of innocence is attained in *To the Evening Star,* as we have seen, and the playing out in *Night* of the implications of the *Evening Star's* "conclusion" thus lends an even greater ominousness retrospectively to the *Poetical Sketches* poem.[5] In *Songs of Innocence* one of Blake's prime agencies by which the "lost" are "found" is the transformational magic of tears, perhaps most vividly portrayed in *The Little Boy lost* and *The Little Boy Found.*[6] No tears flow, as they do even in *Night,* in *To the Evening Star,* unless we are to understand the "sacred dew" and the star's "influence" to be a kind of surrogate weeping. But, as we have seen, the poem's suspended inconclusiveness argues not only against such surrogateship but also against the efficacy of a departed star's influence as "protection," much less restoration.

If we turn now to *The Couch of Death,* we may find in it auguries of that tearful-joyous ever-renewed innocence developed so magnificently later by Blake, but they are auguries clouded by some of the constituent elements of *To the Evening Star.* To the former we may speak only briefly and tentatively, since it is both inapt and potentially misleading to read *Poetical Sketches* as if the *Songs* had already been written. *Innocence* (1789) is a long way off, even if three early versions surface in the 1785 *An Island in the Moon.* Yet it is tantalizing, at least, that one of these three is a draft of *The Little Boy lost,* less taut and more rhetorical than its *Songs of Innocence* version, but complete in its essentials and focus. Both the lost boy poem and *The Couch of Death,* however vastly different in other respects, deal with doubt and despair, wandering and lostness, a guiding (or misguiding) light, the efficacy of tears in innocence, the absence of an earthly father, and, finally, with being found. The only difference in this common pattern is the age of the two major characters. This difference is crucial, however, for it gives rise to the question of the relative appropriateness and efficacy of tears for boy and "youth." Furthermore, in his inability to stretch out his hand to God (a gesture prominently dramatized in the illustration to *The Little Boy lost*), the youth of *The Couch of Death* seems to anticipate directly the child's lostness. On the other hand it is now a commonplace of Blake criticism to recognize that the boy's dilemma is illusory, signaled by (despite its "mistaken" cause-and-effect reasoning) his cry, "Or else I shall be lost." His unreasoning epiphanic realization of his nonlostness is symbolized by his weeping—in perceptual terms the rescuing of his imaginative, "true" self from the mind's ratiocinative propensities and consequent perceptual error. The "result" of this epiphany in Lockean epistemology is the "flying away" of the wandering "vapour"—that is, the restoration of its imaginative nonexistence. It dis-appears. Logically the light's disappearance leaves the boy in darkness, still wet with dew, still mired in the physical world; but the visionary thrust of the poem allows us, as well as the child, illogically to reverse apparent perceptions of father, night, dew, mire, and vapor—in other words to transform them imaginatively into the eternal day-spring of innocence.[7]

In the *Songs of Innocence* companion poem, *The Little Boy Found,* the lost boy is returned to his mother who "in sorrow pale" has been seeking her child in "the lonely dale." From Blake's point of view this restoration to the maternal bosom is the familial equivalent of the epiphany in *The Little Boy lost:* God-father equals boy's tears; false light becomes true light; mother equals the state of innocence. From the point of view of the mother, however, the event appears differently, for she seems as unaware as the child of *The Little Boy lost* was that lostness is "vaporous" in innocence. In her adult mind (and world)[8] predicaments like this are "real," the protective function she herself assumes depending upon such "reality" and its concomitant logic. It is no accident, then, that *she* doesn't find the child. God, "like his father," does—which is to say the as yet unsullied imagination of the child does.[9]

In *An Island in the Moon* Blake already is beginning to investigate this difference. After Quid, who is often associated with Blake himself, sings the early version of *The Little Boy lost,* Tilly Lally interposes an excrementitious piece of doggerel that produces laughter as well as, subsequently, a song "contrary" to Quid's. It is sung, following the hilarity, by the appropriately giddy-sounding Miss Gittipin:

> Leave O leave [me] to my sorrows
> Here Ill sit & fade away
> Till Im nothing but a spirit
> And I lose this form of clay
>
> Then if chance along this forest
> Any walk in pathless ways

Thro the gloom he'll see my shadow
Hear my voice upon the Breeze.   (E454-55)

If not quite contrarious in the sense that *Songs of Experience* is to *Songs of Innocence*, this silly piece has all the earmarks of the antithetical structures I described among the "Songs" of *Poetical Sketches*. By itself it may claim descendancy from the love-melancholy lyrics of the Renaissance through the eighteenth century, the "lostness" of the speaker trivialized into fashionable indulgence and sentimental self-pity. As a kind of "commentary" on Quid's song, however, the adult perspective on losing all for love becomes a parody of the child's momentary misperception. The speaker will fade away and die to become an inverted ghostly version of the child's illusion—not a vapor now but a "shadow" and a "voice" haunting the gloom of the "pathless ways" of the forest. Or, with the later *Little Boy lost* in mind, the speaker will become an oddly parodic version of God "like his father in white" who appears to the lost child, as Blake's illustration to the song of innocence shows, deep in the "pathless ways" of the forest.[10] I cite this antithetical structuring in *An Island in the Moon* not to press the point but rather to suggest Blake's early interest in the relationship between tears of innocence and the fraudulent (later the powerfully self-debilitating) tears of those already "fallen." And though we are some distance already beyond *The Couch of Death*, bearing in mind this evolving conception will be useful in understanding what Blake was attempting there, at least in part.

Unlike the little lost boy, the youth of *The Couch of Death* is very much of and in this world, where only and ominously "the remains of a family of the tribes of Earth"[11] survive, sickness exacts its devastating toll, and a real and final lostness (death) triumphs. Like Blake's lost child he is "alone and comfortless," but there the similarity stops. The light of the youth's imagination is totally extinguished, as his lament that no "lantern" is there to "direct" his steps indicates. The inanity of "Leave O leave [me] to my sorrows" is but a farcical version of this lament. Compounding the difference between the youth and the lost child is the mother's cry, echoing David's lament for his dead son Absalom,[12] "O my son, my son," rather than the child's "Father, father"—as well as her conventional assurance that "there is a God, who made the world" if only the youth will stretch out his hand to Him. That "stretch" seems to me as misguided as the child's reaching in Blake's illustration to *The Little Boy lost;* and the error is intensified not only by the youth's extraordinary rejection of the efficacy of his own reaching but by his pleading for his sister and mother to "stretch forth" *their* hands in his stead.[13] Only in his final words does he seem to see the light: "O for a hand to pluck me forth"—though for all its biblical precedent[14] the physical nature of the locution betrays the persistence of his inner blindness. When that hand *does* appear in *The Couch of Death* it is "a visionary hand" (God like his father in white?) that does no plucking but rather, properly, wipes away his tears: "and a ray of light beamed around his head." This illumination, I suggest, is an early version of the lost child's inner illumination that is externally parodied by the ignis fatuus and the mistaken, ineffectual "help" of his mother. In similar fashion, at the end of *The Couch of Death* it is interestingly the mother and sister who are consoled by "hovering Angels" and "voices of comfort," while the youth "breathes out his soul with joy into eternity." This contrast between earthly comfort and heavenly joy Blake will exploit consistently after *Poetical Sketches*. The former is necessitated and validated by the sensory realities of affliction ("Pity would be no more, / If we did not make somebody Poor: / And Mercy no more could be, / If all were as happy as we"); the latter is a recognition of the indwelling of the divine image (mercy, pity, peace, and love).[15]

While such an interpretation of *The Couch of Death* may comfort us, secure in our perception of the youth's dawning vision of his own immortality, we must not rest so complacently on this "mature Blakean" epiphany; for it emerges rather disturbingly out of a thoroughly conventional discussion of sin and apparent grace. To understand this "discrepancy" is to understand more clearly what Blake is at least attempting, however successful or unsuccessful we may finally decide the work is. As usual Milton will help us. The source of Blake's entire conception in *The Couch of Death* seems to me to be in Book XI of *Paradise Lost*. There Michael cinematographically projects for Adam the immediate consequences of his and Eve's original sin, death—first Cain's murder of Abel, then death's other dismal shapes:

> Immediately a place
> Before his eyes appeared, sad, noisome, dark,
> A lazar-house it seemed. . . .
> . . . .
> Dire was the tossing, deep the groans; Despair
> Tended the sick, busiest from couch to couch;
> And over them triumphant Death his dart
> Shook. . . .   (Ll. 477-79, 489-92)

The cause of these "unsightly sufferings," "inhuman pains," and "deformities," Michael instructs Adam, is man himself, in whom

> "Their Maker's image . . . then
> Forsook them, when themselves they vilified
> To serve ungoverned appetite, and took
> His image whom they served, a brutish vice,
> Inductive mainly to the sin of Eve.
> Therefore so abject is their punishment,
> Disfiguring not God's likeness, but their own,
> Or if his likeness, by themselves defaced

> While they pervert pure Nature's healthful rules
> To loathsome sickness; worthily, since they
> God's image did not reverence in themselves."[16]

Whether or not we can credit completely his self-accusation as a perverting of "pure Nature's healthful rules / To loathsome sickness," Blake's youth is hardly a lost child of innocence. His sickbed is as real to him as Thel's grave plot (with its "couches of the dead") is to her, his ways "sinful" (a conception foreign to Blake's innocents), his breath loathsome and "infected." Just so Milton's Sin

> in man residing through the race,
> His thoughts, his looks, words, actions all infect,

"season[ing] him" to be Death's "last and sweetest prey" (*PL* X,607-9).

What Blake seems to be moving toward, then, is a conception of sin as self-condemnation, a nontheological ignorance of, or wilful blindness to, the self as human form divine. The concomitant and paradoxical elevation of self-consciousness to self-identification and self-assertion precipitates war with all other selves, subjection to the ravages of the fallen senses, and the ultimate brutalization, as in *Comus*, of one's divine humanness. The language of *Comus* is instructive and there is little doubt Blake remembered it. As soon as Comus's Circean potion takes effect, man's

> human count'nance
> Th' express resemblance of the gods, is changed
> Into some brutish form of wolf, or bear,
> Or ounce, or tiger, hog, or bearded goat.   (Ll. 68-71)

Herein lies an essential connection between *The Couch of Death* and *To the Evening Star*, the same star, we should recall, that presides perversely over Comus's anti-epithalamic rites of "Dark-veiled Cotytto" (lines 93-94, 129). While not "presiding" in the same fashion, Blake's evening star in its rising heralds love, but in its withdrawal it precipitates the advent not merely of Cotyttoan darkness but of wolves and lions and the urgent need for guarding the sheep against their predacity. Although the wolf-sheep trope is badly tattered by Blake's time, his application of what he learned from *Comus* and *Paradise Lost* elevates those tatters to the status of myth.

The myth emergent, however, hinges less on the traditional Christian concept of moderation than on a failure of perception. In *The Couch of Death*, if the youth's wracking sense of his own sinfulness and his un-Job-like humility seem to forecast his ultimate salvation in predictable terms, and if (as most critics assume) the mother seems to take on his sins and thereby relieve him of their poisonous effects,[17] no such humility or intercesssion is the gestative agency in the poem. Both may indeed produce "comfort" for the mother and sister, but neither is capable of producing joy. That remains to the "visionary hand"—which, in effect, transforms the youth's humility and sense of sin into a joy comparable to that occasioned by an abundant harvest. The seasonal analogy toward the end of *The Couch of Death* is more than a decorative similitude. Paralleling, without relying on, Blake's seasons poems, it is most apt. From the potentiality of "cloud tossed by the winds," to the fructifying rain and nurturing sun, to "the yellow harvest" breathing (compare the youth's earlier "infected breath"), the "cycle" (minus winter be it noted) concenters on the youth's eternal moment of joy. Blake is at some pains here to establish the simultaneity of these apparently discrete and sequential "happenings," perhaps based on the achieved temporal atemporality of Milton's structuring in the *Nativity Ode* or Spenser's in the *Epithalamion*, not to mention their ultimate stillness. Thus *The Couch of Death:* "All was still. The moon hung not out her lamp, and the stars faintly glimmered in the summer sky; the breath of night slept among the leaves of the forest . . ."; only the sounds of an angelic choir break into the silence, "riding" (the only "movement" in the scene) "upon the wings of night." Evening and night become the eternal morning of light beaming round the youth's head—or, to be more precise, the youth, no longer tossed by the winds of his own self-perturbation, now sees himself in his eternal lineaments, needing no mysterious grace to "save" him, no hand to pluck him forth, no sympathetic or empathetic intercession. As he was his own enslaver, so is he his own savior. To misappropriate (though only slightly) Milton's hymn to Light,

> . . . God is light,
> And never but in unapproachèd light
> Dwelt from eternity, dwelt then in thee,
> Bright effluence of bright essence increate.   (*PL* III,3-6)

But even as Blake's eternal morning recalls Milton's, here and elsewhere, it appears rarely without characteristic revision. For the elder poet, bereft of sight, "Seasons return; but not to me returns / Day, or the sweet approach of ev'n or morn" (III,41-42). Yet Milton knew, as Blake did, that only the irremediably fallen subscribe to such conceptions. The "human face divine" that is hidden from his corporeal sight imaginative (or spiritual) man perceives clearly in himself:

> So much the rather thou, celestial Light,
> Shine inward, and the mind through all her powers
> Irradiate, there plant eyes, all mist from thence
> Purge and disperse, that I may see and tell
> Of things invisible to mortal sight.   (III,44, 51-55)

In the silence and frozen movement of Hartman's "interlunar moment,"[18] in the moonless darkness after the mother and sister yield to their grief, the rhetorical flow of Blake's final passage clearly aspires, as I have said, to coinstantaneousness, the insistent past tense of the bulk of the work yielding to the triumphant present of "is," "ride," "lift," "are," and "breathes." That final verb, occurring for the third time and now not only free of its earlier loathsomeness and infection but incorporating the thankful harvest, iconicizes the self-transformation. To comprehend fully the otherwise odd lines of Blake's *Night* ("wrath by his meekness / And by his health, sickness, / Is driven away, / From our immortal day") we would do well to recall *The Couch of Death.*

Wagenknecht, then, may be right after all in suggesting that *The Couch of Death* contains "some of the seeds of *Thel.*"[19] As in the youth's vision, not only does "the grave" open "its mouth" for her but she sees "the couches of the dead" (E6) in a preview at least analogous to Adam's. Moreover her flight from this preview is due to (or concomitant with) her failure to achieve the kind of imaginative self-perception to which the youth finally attains.[20] Like him she seeks help from all and sundry to assuage, as well as to confirm, her self-pity, thus "escaping" finally the very possibility of her transformation. What Blake has withheld from the youth, a sign no doubt of a conception not yet completely formulated, is choice. For that an imposed and sourceless sickness is substituted. He has neither the physical ability nor the opportunity to flee back to some vales of Har; it is not "given" him "to enter, / And to return" (*Thel* 5:16-17, E6). If he has a choice at all (and I am not sure that concept is even applicable), it is between dying in groveling misery and dying Manfred-like as the man-god he is. The latter is contingent upon his capacity to deny the efficacy of the former. The catalytic agent for such a denial is unclear. In the narrative it seems to be the mother's Christ-like assumption of his sin, his "poison" entering her "marrow."[21] In fact, no such transference takes place. The direct "result" of her intercession is that, sighs succeeding sighs, the mother and sister cover their faces in weeping. In contrast the youth "lay silent," for the first time listening to the silence that now drowns out his frantic cries and theirs. Whereas his mother apparently does not, in that silence he hears the "Voice, that dwellest *in* my breast" (my emphasis). As in the antithetical repetition of the word "breath," this voice supersedes the youth's own, which is likened to one "heard from a sepulchre" (that is, already dead and buried), to "an omen" (hardly auspicious but perhaps ambiguously charged by Blake), and to that "of the Angel of Death."

The entire closing section of the poem, then, appropriately fuses the silence of the scene with the youth's silence, the former a symbolic externalization of the youth's inner state and of the epiphanic moment. The mother's seemingly self-sacrificial agency turns out to be negative. Whatever "Voice . . . dwellest in [her] breast," it imaginatively fails, for she summons it but to articulate her cries and self-pitying pleas to heaven. Consequently her "spirit is turned within [her] into confusion," the outward manifestation of which is her acceptance of the verity of her son's self-lacerating confessions of sin ("is thy breath infected? So is mine"). She may support him physically (her "arm was under his head"), but at that very moment his corporeality has been lightened to "a cloud tossed by the winds." This is surely the reason that, in the closing lines, Blake reasserts the continuing "reality" of the couch of death: the mother and sister still mourn over it, however comforted by "hovering Angels," both oblivious to the fact that the linen clothes have been folded up.

In this final tableau it is tempting to credit Blake with an allusion to Mary Magdalene's fright and sorrow at finding Christ's sepulchre empty, and to the "comfort" she received from the presiding angels at the head and foot of Christ's pallet. If indeed the allusion is there, it is a risky one, for Blake has been fairly careful not to advance his youth as a conventional "Christ-figure." Nevertheless he is the human form divine whose "crucifixion" is inherent in his self-condemnation and debilitating sense of sinfulness (indeed that may be his "sickness"), and whose "resurrection" is translated into the revivification of imaginative perception. Put this boldly, however, such a grand vision tends to freight *The Couch of Death* with a significance and prophetic power beyond its due—and, despite the clear epiphanic experience, even beyond its intrinsic claims. Blake's derivative mélange of Ossianic and biblical language and tonalities serves him less well than he apparently hoped, even with the leaven of Miltonic energy. Prophecy demands a language at the very least commensurate with the electricity and authority of its vision, a crisp yet symbolically rich enabling vehicle rather than a manner. Often submerging the notes of sureness I have indicated, particularly in the most allusive passages, is an Ossianic flaccidity, an overlay of limp similes and gasped exclamation in which the matter is sacrificed to "effects." Macpherson's bardic voice settles all too comfortably into its own accents. As McGowan suggests, Blake was drawn to the language and cadences of the hoaxer largely "because their style at best seemed Biblical or to derive from the same source of genuine inspiration"[22]—a style that seemed appropriate to "the visions of Heaven unfold[ing] their visitation." It is much to his credit that he perceived quickly how such rhetoric slides into turgidity and even silliness. Hence the periodic infusions of Milton. *Tiriel* is his last attempt to rescue Ossian's "genuineness" for his own purposes, but even there, for all its grotesquerie and hysteria, he is at least on the way to forging *his* prophetic-poetic line out of borrowed bombast.[23] The beginnings of that forging are in *The Couch of Death*.

It is not surprising that for a work dealing with sickness, sin, and death Blake painted his background in night tones—or, one might say, created an evening poem without the evening star; but it is a bit startling to find its apparent companion poem, *Contemplation,* to be a morning poem. On the other hand we have seen how in *The Couch of Death* night becomes morning once the youth perceives matters aright—although Blake is careful to effect no narrative diurnal progress in the poem. Instead he provides us the coeval moment of night-day that Milton dramatizes in *On the Morning of Christ's Nativity:*

> The stars with deep amaze
> Stand fixed in steadfast gaze,
>   Bending one way their precious influence,
> And will not take their flight
> For all the morning light,
>   Or Lucifer that often warned them thence;
> But in their glimmering orbs did glow.   (Ll. 69-75)

At the conclusion of *The Couch of Death* "stars faintly glimmered" in the same stillness evoked by stanza V of Milton's ode, and the "ray of light" that beams round the youth's head may even be Milton's "globe of circular light" that "surrounds" the sight of the awe-struck shepherds (lines 109-10). In the ode the scene is accompanied by "such music sweet"

> As never was by mortal finger strook,
> Divinely warbled voice
> Answering the stringèd noise.   (Ll. 93, 95-97)

In Blake "the voice of Angels is heard, and stringed sounds ride upon the wings of night." "If such holy song," Milton continues,

> Enwrap our fancy long,
>   Time will run back and fetch the age of gold,
> And speckled Vanity
> Will sicken soon and die,
>   And leprous Sin will melt from earthly mold,
> And hell itself will pass away,
> And leave her dolorous mansion to the peering day.   (Stanza XIV)

Blake's night and couch of sickness and death remain very much an "earthly mold," but the couch is also the deathbed of vanity and sin as well as the birthplace of eternal day and the "Prince of Light."

With this composite conception in mind we may begin to understand Blake's alteration of the conventional evening-melancholy-contemplation-wisdom trope in *Contemplation* to a morning scene. It is a shift that takes place against the background of *Il Penseroso,* properly so since Blake in his opening lines deliberately leads us to expect a poem in the penseroso vein. Milton's Melancholy comes "with even step" and "robe of darkest grain" ("staid Wisdom's hue") "flowing with majestic train," bringing with her "the Cherub Contemplation."[24] Although Blake's Contemplation comes "with unerring step . . . majestical" and is associated with the grayness of melancholy and the untrodden regions of nature, her genealogy seems to be askew, at least in relation to Milton's. His Melancholy is the daughter of Vesta and Saturn, and Contemplation seems no relative; Blake's Contemplation is explicitly the "daughter of the grey Morning." Nevertheless the opening speech of Blake's character is informed by Milton's attack on empty mirth, folly, and fond fancies:

> Hence, vain deluding Joys,
>   The brood of Folly without father bred,
> How little you bestead,
>   Or fill the fixèd mind with all your toys;
> Dwell in some idle brain,
>   And fancies fond with gaudy shapes possess.[25]

The rest of *Il Penseroso*, of course, moves in directions quite different from anything in Blake's poem. The problem seems to be "grey Morning," for while its adjective is appropriate to contemplation and melancholy, the noun contravenes that appropriateness in somewhat the same way Blake's song *When Early Morn Walks Forth in Sober Grey* quickly establishes itself as an evening poem of "pensive woe," darkened vales, black-eyed maid, and silent shades. Few, if any, of those familiar trappings cluster around *Contemplation*, but aspects of Thomas Warton's *Pleasures of Melancholy* seem to. Ingenuously basing his conception on *Il Penseroso*, Warton adds the familiar paraphernalia of the graveyard school as epitomized in Blair's *The Grave* and Hervey's *Meditations Among the Tombs*, both of which (along with Warton's *Pleasures*) Blake knew intimately. Properly "sage," Warton's Contemplation is the "Mother of musings," her "solemn glooms" and "cheerless shades" the haunts of "thoughtful Melancholy" (lines 1-20). Inspired by this gloomy but wise pair the speaker prays to be led "far remote / From Mirth's mad shouts" so that his "thought contemplative" may "explore"

> This fleeting state of things, the vain delights,
> The fruitless toils, that still our search elude,
> As thro' the wilderness of life we rove.   (Ll. 76-83)

False Folly's smile shall be unmasked,

>   that like the dazzling spells
> Of wily Comus cheat th' unweeting eye
> With blear illusion, and persuade to drink
> That charmed cup, which Reason's mintage fair
> Unmoulds, and stamps the monster on the man.   (Ll. 84-89)

Similarly Joseph Warton's *The Enthusiast* invokes "Old Midnight's sister, Contemplation sage," to lift his soul "above this little Earth, / This folly-fetter'd world" and to "purge [his] ears" of the "din of the tumultuous world" (lines 205-45). So cleansed he may walk with Philosophy, "virgin Solitude," "Virtue's self," and "Sweet Innocence"—and, "Deeply retir'd, beneath a plantane's shade," dwell with "Happiness and Quiet," with humble "Indian swains" despising

> The far-fetch'd cates of luxury, and hoards
> Of narrow-hearted avarice.   (Ll. 215-44)

This otherwise lamentable rehearsal of dreary commonplaces that defuse the power of pastoral fictions is necessary here, I think, if we are to understand why Blake rejects them—or, more accurately, stands them on their heads.

Echoing Erdman, Bloom suggests rather tentatively that Blake's *Contemplation* "seems to reject the pastoral escape offered by Contemplation."[26] Perhaps. More likely, rejection or acceptance of escape, pastoral or otherwise, has no bearing whatsoever on what happens in the poem. To be sure, what "happens" is precious little: Contemplation comes, whispers her wisdom in the speaker's ear, and the speaker "answers." If we are to understand that something further is to happen, as in *The Couch of Death* for example, the something will be whatever logically devolves from the speaker's answer, an action emerging out of the "argument." For example, Contemplation might emulate the "visionary hand" of *The Couch of Death* waving her magic wand to uncloud the mind and cleanse the grief-wracked speaker's soul; or the speaker, seeing the light, might embrace Contemplation's wisdom and, renouncing his worldly ways and the oppressions of the flesh, rise on the wings of morning to dwell (as the Wartons assure us will happen) with innocence and joy on the grassy plains or in the silent woods. After all, Contemplation herself reminds us that "like a triumph, season follows season." Can spring, then, be far behind the winter of the speaker's days? Or, in the terms Blake himself employs, morning and the sun, joying "like a hunter rouzed to the chace," inevitably succeed the night implicit in the speaker's life and lament.[27] Thomson put the case nicely and with uncharacteristic succinctness in *Autumn:*

> Then is the time
> For those whom wisdom and whom nature charm
> To steal themselves from the degenerate crowd,
> And soar above this little scene of things—
> To tread low-thoughted vice beneath their feet,
> To soothe the throbbing passions into peace,
> And woo lone Quiet in her silent walks.   (Ll. 963-71)

In fact none of these things, no such resolution, takes place in Blake's prose poem. Indeed nothing happens at all. Instead two perceptions of the way things are (both given in the present tense) clash, neither responding to the other. Some clue to the reasons behind this unresponsiveness may be found in the strange manuscript fragment beginning "then she bore Pale desire." Erdman dates the fragment very tentatively as "of the early 1780s."[28] Its allegorical excessiveness and the tumbling personifications mark it, for me, as considerably earlier, a rejected attempt perhaps at something that might well have been included in *Poetical Sketches*. In any case its relationship to that volume's prose poems is incontrovertible, lines 55-56 and 85-87 (as numbered in Erdman's edition), for example, being identical with passages in *Contemplation*. There are other, even more interesting linkages as well. In the manuscript, "Contemplation teacheth knowledge truly how to know" and even "Reinstates him on his throne once lost." The "truly how to know" seems to refer to Reason which, once "fairer than the light," became "fould in Knowledges dark Prison house. For knowledge drove sweet Innocence away." While neither Knowledge nor Reason plays a personified role in *Contemplation*, Contemplation herself obviously speaks Wisdom, writing "Wisdom's name" with "her pure quill on every flower" that blows in her pastoral dale; and the speaker just as obviously has gained the knowledge bred of sorrow that Ecclesiates speaks of, and that Blake domiciles in the same "dark Prison house" the speaker associates with his "flesh."

The "message" of *Contemplation* thus seems to be: if the speaker would but unbefoul himself of knowledge, his wisdom would shine clear; and, in his new-found humility (enabling him to see, as Ecclesiastes has it, that "All things come alike to all" and that whatever "befalleth the sons of men befalleth beasts . . . so that a man hath no preeminence above a beast") he would escape the "Clamour" and "destruction" of the city. Moreover he would find and pluck the flower with "Wisdom's name" on it and thus live for aye while "airy music fills the world with joyful sounds." "Vanity of vanities, saith the preacher; all is vanity."

Even if such conventional "wisdom" were not suspect in light of the seasons anticycle, the diurnal anti-epithalamia, and the seeming perverseness of *Mad Song* (not to mention the implicit attack on theocratic sin in *The Couch of Death*), I find it inconceivable that the eager young disciple of Milton could so denigrate the human form divine, or advance a notion of innocence regained through a humbling of self and simple transportation from city to country. That is the message of the graveyard school. In fact, as we learn from the end of the prose poem, the speaker is already humbled mightily when the poem begins—by Misery, Discontent and Sorrow. Apparently insensitive to that mood, Contemplation almost immediately bends herself to his lowly state to humble him further: "Vain foolish man, that roams on lofty rocks! where, 'cause his garments are swoln with wind, he fancies he is grown into a giant!"[29] To Blake, I think, this estimate of man could not be more inaccurate. Lest we be duped by Contemplation's "unerring step" and her conventional wisdom, the poem provides additional, more obvious clues to her values. For her, "season follows season" as if that round were a "triumph"; but more important and revealing (if more subtle) is the outworn mythology of her cosmos. "The youthful sun joys like a hunter rouzed to the chace," rushing up the sky to lay "hold on the immortal coursers of day"; and the sky in turn "glitters with the jingling trappings." These trappings, I suggest, are the "tinsel trappings" of Romance Milton rejects in the invocation to Book IX of *Paradise Lost* in favor of an "answerable style" appropriate to *true* "heroic song."[30] However "majestical," Contemplation is hardly a figure from Romance of course, but her latter-day elevation to a new poetic pantheon governing the internalizing of quest Romance was surely to Blake what tinsel trappings were to Milton. In any case it is Contemplation's sovereign power that governs her condescension to ("lowly bending"), and her denigration of, the man in whose ear she whispers her outmoded "wisdom."

On the other hand, the speaker's self-pitying thumbnail autobiography — his brotherhood with Sorrow and his life spent (perhaps with Ecclesiastes-inspired wisdom) "sitting . . . on a tomb-stone" — is scarcely the truer perception. Misery, Discontent, and Sorrow assume the same personified guises their happier counterparts do in Contemplation's speech. Each speaker thus imposes her/his "phantasy" on the other, to use the language of *The Marriage of Heaven and Hell;* and, as the Angel says to the speaker of the "Memorable Fancy," they both "oughtest to be ashamed" (Plate 20, E41). In *Contemplation,* however, there is no such wryness. Instead the work "proceeds" in an endless, inexorable round from Contemplation's appearance, to her speech, to the speaker's answer, to Contemplation's certain reapproach, and so on. The passage in *The Marriage* just cited concludes with, "It is but lost time to converse with you whose works are only Analytics." Just so. In *Contemplation* season follows season as "answer" follows "answer," *like* a triumph but without a victory. It is a dull round indeed, each speaker persistently and irrefragably seeing "the Ratio only," seeing "himself only" (*There is No Natural Religion,* E2).

The structure of *Contemplation* may be characterized in another, related way as well. The scenario would read something like this. Contemplation appears not as a "real" character but as a dramatic action in the mind of the speaker. Beaten down by misery, discontent, and sorrow, not to mention his own imprisoning mortality, he must be doing something wrong, Reason tells him; he is the "slave of each moment," a vain foolish man who fancies he is, if not a giant, the cynosure of this world. He should don the garment of Humility, therefore, and all will be right with him *and* his world. He shall be not only lord of himself but "lord of all." On the other hand, Experience (also a "character" in this mental monodrama) tells him he is not even lord of himself, much less lord of all, for powers abroad beyond his control dominate his life and being. Swollen with pride, he is paradoxically the slave of misery. Ergo, he must seriously contemplate his state to find some answer — or at least some consolation. Error gives way to self-pity, self-pity to error ("like a triumph"); for, as Blake will later tell us, error grows "in the Human Brain" in the same way the tree of "Mystery" blossoms out of the root of Humility in *The Human Abstract*.[31] To quote a much later work of Blake's that puts the case far more simply but with an aphoristic power absent entirely from the *Poetical Sketches,*

> Humility is only doubt
> And does the Sun & Moon blot out
> Rooting over with thorns & stems
> The buried Soul & all its Gems.
> This Lifes dim Windows of the Soul
> Distorts the Heavens from Pole to Pole
> And leads you to Believe a Lie
> When you see with not thro the Eye.   (*The Everlasting Gospel,* E512)

What rises in the morning of *Contemplation,* then, is not the sun but the black sun of contemplative reason;[32] for rather than being the clear windows of the morning of imagination, the speaker's "windows" are "Lifes dim Windows" through which his soul peers darkling:

> Can that which was of woman born
> In the absence of the Morn
> When the Soul fell into Sleep
> And Archangels round it weep
> Shooting out against the Light
> Fibres of a deadly night
> Reasoning upon its own dark Fiction
> In doubt which is Self Contradiction.   (Ibid.)

The speaker's need, of course, is to see (that verb and its synonyms are notably absent from his meditation), to exercise his innate capacity for imagination: as *The Everlasting Gospel* "proves" (line 75), he *is* a man, gods (and certainly goddesses) are no more. "Error or Creation," Blake writes in *A Vision of the Last Judgment,* is "Burnt up the Moment Men cease to behold it" (E555). As long as *Contemplation'*s speaker beholds only gray evening and night masquerading as morning, he will fail to arise to "Spiritual Strife" and the "Truth . . . Eternal" it yields (E511, 555). And such truth has little to do with being lord of himself or lord of all.

As is the case so often in the *Sketches, Contemplation* does not conclude. Here that seems to me the best indication we have of Blake's lack of hope for his speaker. He has adopted sorrow for his brother but, even more serious, in the symbolic geography of the poem he ends where he began: the untrodden "wilds" of nature, "dreary places," "sitting on a tomb-stone." The landscape, in other words, he fits admirably to his mind. Wagenknecht's judgment of *The Couch of Death,* "jejune and best forgotten," is a bit severe for *Contemplation,* but its fundamentally mechanical structure and unremarkable imagery, diction, and sentiment—the very elements that support its portrayal of the same dull round—do conspire to dull our sensibilities as well. If Blake did intend it as a kind of penseroso piece, he had not yet learned much from his mentor.

On the face of it, to treat *Samson,* the last of the prose poems in *Poetical Sketches,*[33] in the same context as Blake's other two efforts in the genre seems appropriate—even if *Samson's* insistent biblical and Miltonic patterns and allusions, its epyllion-like introduction, and its focused dramatic moment in a story we all know lend it an elevated tone and stylistic dignity largely absent from the Ossianized biblicism of *The Couch of Death* and the fundamentally neoclassic framework and thematic patterns of *Contemplation.* The transmutations of and departures from convention manifested in all three (and elsewhere in *Poetical Sketches*) stem from a seminal, unchanging conviction by Blake, announced rather grandly in *There Is No Natural Religion* and *All Religions Are One* but clearly gestating even earlier during his years at Basire's and at his "apprentice" writing desk. The "Poetic Genius is the true Man," according to the 1788 tractates; and without "the Poetic or Prophetic character the Philosophic & Experimental would soon be at the ratio of all things, & stand still unable to do other than repeat the same dull round over again" (E1-2). Thomson's *Seasons,* the diurnal cycle of Nature, *L'Allegro* and *Il Penseroso,* the epithalamion's fruition in time, shepherd's calendars, and shepherd's weeks all describe that basic round. They and their spate of imitations are the products of a mimetic "wisdom" derived from "natural" perception. If the personifications of Contemplation and Wisdom, as well as of their various entourages, that abound in the eighteenth century poetically function more often than not in the evening and at night, for Blake that was the apposite setting for dimness of vision, ratiocinative thinking and its resultant "ratio," and for personification itself as the symbolic mode most congruent with, as well as naturally emanative from, such an epistemology.[34] Graveyard poetry and its related celebrations of melancholy aside, the pervading melancholy of the Ossianic bard, as "genuine" as its prophetic-Hebraic mode may have seemed to Blake, was finally eloquent testimony to the fact that "if any could desire what he is incapable of possessing, despair must be his eternal lot" (*There Is No Natural Religion,* E2). The repetitive circularity of war, death, gloom, and lament, not to mention the minimally varied natural similitudes, served Blake as incontrovertible evidence of Macpherson's having none but "natural or organic thoughts" and "none but organic perceptions" (ibid., E1).

Nevertheless, unlike Collins, Gray, the Wartons, Thomson and the rest,

Macpherson and Chatterton consistently seemed to be authentic embodiments of "an universal Poetic Genius" (*All Religions Are One,* E2). As late as 1815 in his annotations to Wordsworth's *Poems,* Blake reiterates this connection, thus seeming to impugn my notion that very early he recognized their perceptual inadequacies. "I own myself," he says, "an admirer of Ossian equally with any other Poet whatever Rowley & Chatterton also" (E655). Let us examine this statement more closely. In his "Essay, Supplementary to the Preface," Wordsworth had written that "no author, in the least distinguished, has ventured formally to imitate" Macpherson's "pretended treasures of antiquity" except Chatterton. Blake's response is precisely to the point of Wordsworth's adjective "pretended": "I believe both Macpherson & Chatterton, that what they say is Ancient, Is so." He thus implicitly aligns Ossian and Rowley with the canonicity of the old balladic authors of Percy's *Reliques,* a book that Wordsworth had just cited as a contrast to the spuriousness of Macpherson's and Chatterton's efforts. From *Poetical Sketches* it is clear that Blake agreed with Wordsworth about the *Reliques,* that the poetry of "our own country . . . has been absolutely redeemed by it."[35] What his marginalia to Wordsworth's Preface to *The Excursion* assert, then, is that Macpherson's and Chatterton's turning to the "Ancient poets" was equally commendable, was indeed indicative of their perception that the "Poetic Genius which is every where call'd the Spirit of Prophecy" (*All Religions Are One,* E2) exists in these works by virtue of their very "ancientness," imitated or manufactured or not. Genuineness, for Blake, is not the issue.[36] The poet's business was not to reason and compare but to create. Ossian and Rowley did just that. Their imaginations were "the Divine Vision not of The World nor of Man nor from Man as he is a Natural Man but only as he is a Spiritual Man"—that same "Vision and . . . Faculty divine" with which Wordsworth concludes his "Essay, Supplementary to the Preface" (albeit buried in a paragraph Blake otherwise took exception to in his final marginal comment).[37]

The faculty divine was to Blake mythopoeic, epitomized in the biblical prophets and especially the Book of Revelation; its issue was not a vision of the world but a prophetic vision of eternity. His admiration of Macpherson-Ossian and Chatterton-Rowley, then, is virtually identical with his admiration of the "line of vision" extending from the bright originals of Los's halls to the Bible, Spenser, and Milton.[38] "The Jewish & Christian Testaments," he wrote in *All Religions Are One,* "are An original derivation from the Poetic Genius," a necessary *reductio* or translation because of "the confined nature of bodily sensation" (E3). *The Faerie Queene* and *Paradise Lost* are other derivatives, Chaucer and Shakespeare, Ossian and Rowley still others. All these "similars have one source. The true Man is the source he being the Poetic Genius" (E3). With some few exceptions Blake's *true* "imitations" in *Poetical Sketches* are imitations of that source, of the tenor rather than the vehicle, of achieved (or at least an informing) vision rather than of the manner or mode in which vision is poetically managed, or mismanaged. He saw acutely that in all ages all poetry, like "all sects of Philosophy," was an adaptation of the Poetic Genius "to the weaknesses of every individual" (*All Religions Are One*, E2). If "no man can think write or speak from his heart, but he must intend truth" (ibid.), the writing and speaking that clothe his intentions are the confining garments of temporality, of the age's ontology as well as its epistemology. In Blake's notorious phrase in *The Marriage of Heaven and Hell* Milton was thus "of the Devils party without knowing it" (E35), writing in the fetters of a Puritan dispensation. So too Macpherson and Chatterton who, despite their strivings for a new simplicity and their quite extraordinary imaginative reconstructions of a historical past (not to mention constructions of a fictional past), were similarly "informed," if not fettered, by the power of prevailing poetic modes. As Donald Taylor has shown, for example, for all his reliance on Percy's *Reliques* for his very being as well as his style and narrative method, Rowley was "as much of the school of Pope [particularly the translations of Homer] as of the school of Chaucer and Spenser." Indeed "Rowley is imagined" by Chatterton "as the Pope who brought 'correctness,' dramatic sophistication, and a sense of artistic selfhood to a barbarous fifteenth-century literature."[39] To credit Blake with such critical and literary-historical sophistication as early as 1769 when he first read Chatterton's poems in the *Town and Country Magazine* would be unwarranted. Yet given his own extensive familiarity with the poetry of his age, not to mention with the Bible, Shakespeare, Spenser, Milton, et al., he didn't need Thomas Tyrwhitt's appendix to his 1778 edition of Chatterton's *Miscellanies* to convince him that Rowley was a fiction, however magnificently so. More to the point, though, was Blake's reasonably quick sense of the inadequacies of Chatterton's (and Macpherson's) capacities to their visionary conceptions. Just as the use of oil by painters "became a fetter to genius,"[40] so biblical-prophetic vision was, finally, hidden behind a mannered façade that surely convinced Blake the more of the lamentable ends to which the Poetic Genius and its "wonderful originals" were being put in his time.

It is quite wrong, then, to regard the prose poems of *Poetical Sketches* as merely imitative in the conventional sense, Blake simply "trying his hand" at a currently popular mode. On the contrary, he is intent on rescuing the Poetic Genius from the trammels of derivativeness and adaptation in the same way that he will later deliver Milton's vision from the imprisoning clouds of theological dogma and familial adversity. Neither Macpherson nor Chatterton wrote "prophecy" in Blake's sense, for the imaginative worlds they created were fraught with the limitations of time and manners as well as with their fundamental ignorance of the language of prophecy. Wordsworth said that such "will always be so when words are substituted for things."[41] I doubt that Blake would have subscribed to that dictum but he would, I think, to the sentiment. Bardic and "ancient" as the language of Rowley and Ossian may have sounded, underneath its veneer of novelty it was after all but poor stuff (as Johnson saw immediately) from which to construct a vehicle appropriate to the visions of original genius that purportedly spawned it in the first place. Milton's language (and conceptions) and the Bible undiluted were another matter entirely, as the eschatology of *The Couch of Death* and the antipenserosoism of *Contemplation* testify. With those two experiments in tradition-negation behind him, Blake could now address himself positively, in *Samson,* to the undisputed heir of biblical prophets as well as to those prophets themselves.[42]

Were one to guess at the sequence of composition of the three prose poems, *Contemplation,* which does not refer to the Bible at all, seems to clear the decks, so to speak. *The Couch of Death* develops from the preceding speaker's perceptual error and implicit self-pity, assisted by corroborative biblical locutions and, by way of its Miltonic frame, amplifying the same dull round of *Contemplation* into the grounds of apocalypse. Then comes *Samson,* wholly Miltonic and biblical. Nothing is more remarkable in this conjectural sequence (which I believe is the sequence of composition) than the dimensions of the shift from the tentativeness and humble scale of *Contemplation,* to the not-quite-realized encapsulization of a paradise lost and paradise regained in *The Couch of Death,* to the prophetic intensity of Blake's "version" of *Samson Agonistes.* Comparably revealing, however, is the transformation of the main character from *Contemplation's* anonymous "I" (infant, child, youth, adult), to a dramatically self-realized man-god (Adam-Christ) in *The Couch of Death,* and thence to the mythopoeic, already realized (hence named) Deliverer of biblical fame—who is also all of the above.

Capitalizing on Lowery's pioneering analysis of the plot differences between Blake's *Samson* and the biblical and Miltonic accounts,[43] Michael Phillips advances an elaborate theory to answer the question "why Blake chose to follow Milton by writing a poem on Samson":

> Milton's life, as it was presented in the eighteenth century, offered Blake a model from which he could obtain inspiration and guidance with regard to his own sense of poetical vocation. Blake would also have been aware of the current identification of the poet with the Samson of *Samson Agonistes.* Thus the choice of subject for the one Biblical poem in his earlier volume may have been determined by two factors. First, in writing on Samson, Blake could identify himself, indirectly, with Milton. Second, the eighteenth century's biographical reading of *Samson Agonistes* would have indicated to Blake a similarity between his own position and that of the central figure of his poem.
> . . . In having Samson recall the prophecies of his birth, his father's prayer for his people's deliverance, and the corresponding visitation of the angel which concludes the poem, Blake has dramatically transformed the hour of Samson's fall into one of promise and wonder.[44]

While it is impossible to contradict the notion that in *Samson* (as well as, if less distinctly and firmly, in *The Couch of Death* and *Contemplation*) Blake was taking up the mantle of the prophetic Milton, Wittreich has shown properly that both the foundation and direction of Phillips's analysis are off the mark. Rather than a triumphant hymn of "promise and wonder," Wittreich argues, *Samson* is an attack on "carnal warfare," a work

> grimmer than usually thought ... Milton the revolutionary, from Blake's point of view, comprehended the futility of the energy embodied in Samson—an energy that precipitated a holocaust rather than an apocalypse, that instead of liberating a nation hurled it into ruins. Grasping the demonic aspect of energy, Blake dissociates both himself and Milton from Samson, insisting that the apocalypse, if it is to occur, must occur within before it can occur without.[45]

One may argue over (indeed several of Wittreich's reviewers have objected to) the severely negative value with which he invests the "holocaust" precipitated by Samson's destruction of the temple—especially if one recalls Blake's early subscription to the righteous necessity of Orc's energetic revolutionism (and the unlikelihood, therefore, of Blake's even earlier recognition in the *Poetical Sketches* of the dangers of mere energy). But it is unnecessary to accept in its entirety Wittreich's several-pronged argument —which includes his analysis of the *Albion Rose* color print and line engraving I cited in my first chapter—to sympathize with his view of *Samson* as "grimmer than usually thought" or with Tillyard's influential older view that the "settled ferocity" of the conclusion is "not very lovely."[46] If Blake had elected merely to celebrate Samson the Deliverer, his careful (even sharply restrictive) focus upon the moment before his fall into temptation[47] seems as ill-chosen as his seeming reliance on the rudimentary personification of *Contemplation* and on the youth's mother (in *The Couch of Death*) as deliverers. As they do, so does Samson fail, denying outright what was but implicit in the sin-shackled youth of *The Couch of Death* and the sorrow-fraught speaker of *Contemplation*, the ability to perceive aright that only in the self lies the power of salvation. Hence in a crucial line that echoes the speaker's "answer" to Contemplation's evocation of a conventional pastoral Eden, Samson says, "Sorrow is the lot of all of woman born: for care was I brought forth, and labour is my lot: nor matchless might, nor wisdom, nor every gift enjoyed, can from the heart of man hide sorrow" (E435). On the surface of it, as the Book of Judges and *Samson Agonistes* tell us, that sorrow is for the plight of Israel—or perhaps for Samson's own blindness and imprisonment. But as Blake's context makes clear, his Samson's sorrow is for Dalila's miserableness at Samson's unreciprocated love. Shrewdly she places herself in the position of suppliant to her God ("Thou art my God!") to whom she vainly pours her tears "for sacrifice morning and evening," all the while charging Samson with being a vengeful rather than a loving god ("thou'rt war, thou art not love!"). Death is his "servant," Destruction his father, a lioness his mother (the last an echo of Ezekiel 19:2).

Blake's transformation of Milton's (not to say the Bible's) Dalila is brilliant. Although her speeches in *Samson* are prefaced by (apparently) authorial assurances that she is treacherous, uses "woman's arts" and "wiles," is only "honest-seeming," and sheds "false tears," the fact is that her "falseness" embodies the essential truth of Samson's character as Blake evolves it. It is she who "tries his truth" and exposes him as a mocker and a liar, even a coward despite his "power . . . more than mortal." He "seemed a mountain, his brow among the clouds," Blake's speaker intones in Ossianic fashion, but just as "Philista's lords" engage in "dark council" with "black thoughts in ambush" lying, so "dark thoughts rolled to and fro" in Samson's mind, "his visage . . . troubled; his soul . . . distressed." Whereas in *Samson Agonistes* (and Judges), "shut up from outward light" (line 160), his world "dark, dark, dark" (line 80), Samson's blindness receives major emphasis (to prepare for his gradual inner illumination), Blake ignores the blindness entirely, attributing instead to "false" Dalila the "truth" of his apparent seeing: "days . . . shut up; darkened." His "repentance" and traditional "illumination," then, do not inhere in his acknowledging the reality of his being "holy unto Israel's God" in accordance with the twice-delivered prophecy, but rather in his lapse into the confessed self-defeat of a man born to sorrow (like the speaker of *Contemplation*) whose heart "shall lie at rest" only in the "ivory palace" of Dalila's breast.[48] His "matchless might," "wisdom," and "every gift enjoyed" all are sacrificed to the weakness/power of fleshly desire (his decision is made while "leaning on her bosom"), to his implicit acceptance of the "wisdom" of Ecclesiastes, to his self-abasement along the lines counseled by Blake's Contemplation, and in effect to his denial of his birthright.

Contrary to both the biblical account and Milton's precedent, Blake constructs his work to focus on this, Samson's internal fall. His epic invocation nevertheless initially leads us to expect what we already know, that the "strongest of the children of men" was "foiled" by Dalila and "brought to the gates of death." These gates of course are Milton's gates of the temple of Dagon, no mention of which is found in Blake's version (or in the Bible). And if our recall of them is inevitable given Blake's phrase, the deliverance of Israel emblemized in Samson's destruction of the temple is severely qualified by Blake's words and the passive mood of his verb. Unlike Thel later, it is not given him to enter and return. To set the stage for Samson's failure as Blake understood it, the second sentence of the invocation immediately penetrates to the "truth" of the matter—not what *was* the truth but rather what ought to have been, the event that would have turned "our earthly night to heavenly day" and led to "Sin and Death destroyed."

That neither happens in the Bible or Milton, Blake counts upon our knowing; but he heightens our awareness by portraying Samson as sinner and agent of death rather than of salvation or deliverance. The "truth" that Blake as prophet will write on "a lofty rock," then, is the truth of epitaphs: "All who pass may read"; and the familiar tombstone formula puts the reader in the position of viewing in flashback those events that led to Samson's death.[49]

In view of these inversions, it is not so curious that Blake invests in Dalila's "falseness" the "truth" and reveals the Philistines to be the oppressed, Samson the oppressor with his arts of war. "Death cloathed in flesh thou lovest," Dalila charges; not without an awareness of its unnaturalness she accuses him of having been "incircled in his [Death's] arms." Dalila thus becomes Philistia itself. Her "strength failed" and "prowess lost" she turns, paradoxically, to the mental resources Samson has abjured: "black thoughts" lie in "ambush" in her brain and she seeks to hide "her bruised head under mists of night, breeding dark plots."[50] The melodramatically sinister language Blake employs here is precisely the same vehicle by which in *The Marriage of Heaven and Hell* (and elsewhere) he inverts the "good guys" and the "bad guys" to point up the intrinsic error of all such simplistic codes, religious and secular. Accordingly the structure of the remainder of *Samson* exploits the terrible irony of Samson's birth and prophesied destiny by casting it in the commonly accepted typological guise of the birth of Christ; but most uncommonly this Christ will come not with peace and the bloodless routing of sin and death but in the guise of Samson with a "Natural Sword," not a "Spiritual" one. Blake's deliberate misappropriation of Matthew 10:34 ("I came not to send peace, but a sword") in *The Marriage of Heaven and Hell* makes the same point.[51] What will ensue from Samson's decision is an anti-apocalypse, the same bloody round of war and oppression in which the central and perennial sufferer is the "land," Israelite and Philistine alike.

> The iron hand crushd the Tyrants head
> And became a Tyrant in his stead,

Blake wrote in *The Grey Monk* (E481); and in his bitter attack on Bishop Watson's *Apology for the Bible* much of his wrath is concentrated on this very point. For example, "To Extirpate a nation by means of another nation is as wicked as to destroy an individual by means of another individual, which God considers (in the Bible) as Murder & commands that it shall not be done" (E604).

Blake's borrowed phrasings and images from both Judges and *Samson Agonistes* must be seen, then, as functioning "comfortably" in his poem, as if to "assure" us of the predictability of his story's denouement. Countering these is his telling contextualizing of these allusions in Milton's poetical canon as a whole in an attempt to reveal imaginative rather than narrational

truth. This quite sophisticated contextual modification is announced by
Blake immediately after his opening emphasis on Samson's fall and his
being "brought to the gates of death." The allusional pattern that constitutes
the next sentence is elaborate, one that in effect controls the context of the
entire work. Perhaps oddly, it is initiated by *On the Death of a Fair Infant
Dying of a Cough:*

> Or wert thou that just maid who once before
> Forsook the hated earth, O tell me sooth,
> And cam'st again to visit us once more?
> Or wert thou Mercy, that sweet smiling youth?
> Or that crowned matron, sage white-robèd Truth?
> Or any other of that heav'nly brood
> Let down in cloudy throne to do the world some good?[52]

In the first three lines of this stanza (8) Milton fancies the dead infant as
Astraea (Justice), who fled the corrupt world and now, having returned,
cuts her visit excruciatingly short once more in the face of the world's ways.
In his fourth Prolusion and elsewhere, Milton associates Astraea with Peace
and Truth as well, both of which, with Justice and Mercy, constitute not
only a familiar biblical double-pairing but *in toto* the "Four Daughters of
God." How Blake was aware of this interesting quaternary to add to his
others need not detain us here.[53] The point in Milton is that all or any of
this "heav'nly brood" would descend from heaven (Blake's "from presence
of the Almighty Father"), and visit "our darkling world with blessed feet"
"to do the world some good." For Blake, however, their prophesied earthly
incarnation, Samson, does none of these things. Least of all does he "turn
swift-rushing black perdition hence, / Or drive away the slaughtering pestilence" (*Fair Infant*, lines 67-68).

The analogy between Samson and the fair infant seems wildly askew, of
course, bold to the point of outrageousness. But it will seem less so if we
understand the infant to be typologically the infant Jesus, as Blake surely
did (even if Milton probably didn't in so early a poem); for it is against His
life and destiny that Blake projects Samson's. As Isaiah prophesies, Christ
will be Israel's Deliverer:

> For unto us a child is born, unto us a son is given: and the government shall be
> upon his shoulder: and his name shall be called Wonderful, Counseller, The
> mighty God, The everlasting Father, The Prince of Peace. (9:6)

To deepen this evolving contrast, Blake has his annunciatory angel say that
"Israel's *strength* shall be upon [Samson's] shoulders" (my italics); and, even
more striking, he reverses Isaiah by presenting his angel, not Samson, as
the one whose "name is wonderful."[54] Strength is irrelevant, counterpro-
ductive as we have been taught to say: it breeds not peace but the resurgence
of conflict we know about from the Bible and Milton. Moreover, the assump-

tion of Christ's name by the visitant angel should inspire some skepticism about the "truth" of *his* prophecy (as distinct from Blake's). We should not be surprised to hear from him no "good news of Sin and Death destroyed," no "glad tidings" like those Michael brings to Adam of Christ's pacific crushing of Satan's "strength" and his "two main arms."[55] Read even in its most optimistic light, Samson's destruction of the temple (and himself) hardly eradicates sin and death from the world, much less effecting the Philistines' defeat and the Israelites' deliverance from their yoke. As the Bible itself, particularly the two books of Samuel, abundantly makes clear, Samson's story, in the words of a respected Old Testament scholar, "does not record any deliverance of the people from Philistine oppression."[56] Perhaps this is the reason despite their being verbatim from Judges, for Blake's concluding Manoa's conversation with the angel with these ambiguous words: "When thy sayings come to pass, we may honour thee." While Manoa may be understood here as saying that he needs to know the angel's name so that when the prophecies come true Manoa may be able to honor him properly (essentially the sense of the biblical version), the construction of the passage allows for doubt on Manoa's part that the prophecies will come true. The angel's final chiding of Manoa for his mistaken thought of honoring the angel for God's work Blake leaves up in the air, so to speak, leaving us wondering whether Manoa gets the point. In any case, although, *pace* Wittreich, the conclusion of *Samson Agonistes* is less ambiguous, it certainly would not have escaped Blake's notice that Manoa characterizes his son's act as "revenge," not once but twice (lines 1591, 1711-12), and that the Chorus follows him in this: "O dearly bought revenge" (line 1660). To be sure, they are neither the most reliable judges nor the most perceptive commentators; but then Blake did not read *Samson Agonistes* as a modern Milton critic. Moreover in Judges 16:28 Samson himself prays to god that he "may be at once avenged of the Philistines for [his] two eyes."

It is to this point that Blake's repeated allusions throughout the poem to the Book of Job address themselves. The words that Job would have "graven" with *his* "iron pen and lead in the rock for ever" may also be construed as the testimony of his faith: "For I know that my redeemer liveth, and that he shall stand at the latter day upon the earth."[57] While this redeemer in Blake's context may appear to be Samson, it is the remainder of Job's speech that Blake perceived as the "real," imaginative truth of the matter: "And though after my skin worms destroy this body, yet in my flesh shall I see God. . . . Be ye afraid of the sword: for wrath bringeth the punishments of the sword, that ye may know there is a judgment" (19:26, 29). The "strength" of Israel that is upon Samson's shoulders, according to the false prophet Angel Wonderful, is clearly not Job's. The only "strength," as Isaiah says, "is to sit still" (30:7). In the words of the Chorus in *Samson Agonistes,*

> ... patience is more oft the exercise
> Of saints, the trial of their fortitude,
> Making them each his own deliverer,
> And victor over all
> That tyranny or fortune can inflict.   (Ll. 1287-91)

Blake would have liked that. False prophets, Isaiah says, "speak unto us smooth things, prophesy deceits" (30:10).

Probably too much has been made of the Christological typology of *Samson Agonistes* as well as of its main character as a "type" of Milton, but if Blake's Samson embodies typological characteristics, they prefigure not Christ or Milton but the Adam of *Paradise Lost.* Dalila is his Eve.[58] Adam, we recall, was endowed "with strength entire, and free will armed, / Complete to have discovered and repulsed / Whatever wiles of foe or seeming friend" (X,9-11). But he will "be seduced / And flattered out of all, believing lies" (X,41-42), and, as Blake's Samson says in echoing *Paradise Lost* (X,201-8), "for care was I brought forth" and "sorrow . . . the lot of all woman born." Playing her consort role to perfection Dalila embraces Samson's feet, just as Eve, "with tears that ceased not flowing / And tresses all disordered" (Blake's "neglect thy hair"), at Adam's feet

> Fell humble, and embracing them, besought
> His peace, and thus proceeded in her plaint.   (X,910-13)

Anticipating Dalila's declarations to Blake's Samson, that plaint is a protestation of her love:

> Forsake me not thus, Adam, witness Heav'n
> What love sincere and reverence in my heart
> I bear thee, and unweeting have offended,
> Unhappily deceived; thy suppliant
> I beg, and clasp thy knees; bereave me not.   (X,914-18)

Blake's Dalila "grasps his vigorous knees with her fair arms," and Samson borrows Eve's locution to style her his "beauteous suppliant." When Eve "ended weeping," her "lowly plight"

> in Adam wrought
> Commiseration; soon his heart relented
> Towards her, his life so late and sole delight,
> Now at his feet submissive in distress,
> Creature so fair his reconcilement seeking.   (X,937, 939-43)

Accordingly Blake then transforms Eve's subsequent suggestion that she and Adam commit suicide to avoid populating the world with "a woeful race," food only for death (X,979-1006), into Dalila's plea to Samson to ease her pain by killing her: "Then should I lay quiet, and have rest."[59] Blake's

point is that in his Eve-Dalila is no "something more sublime / And excellent" (*PL* X,1014-15) than thoughts of self-destruction—or, if there is,
both she and Samson discern it not. They will but endure their mutual
sorrow, abjuring strength and wisdom and "every gift enjoyed" to march
steadily toward the gates of death—with no thought of confessing "humbly
[their] faults" as Adam and Eve do. No pardon is begged,

> with tears
> Watering the ground, and with [their] sighs the air
> Frequenting, sent from hearts contrite, in sign
> Of sorrow unfeigned, and humiliation meek.   (X,1089-92)

Blake's irremediably fallen pair will brave it out, then, Samson comforting
himself with the remembrance of what we have already seen is a false
prophecy, Dalila with Samson's renewed expression of his love for her—his
self-perceived "matchless might" Blake appropriately aligning with the
"matchless might" of Sin and Death "issuing from" Satan (*PL* X,404). The
manifest lack of closure in *Samson* (even the "offering" suggested by the
angel is not made) thus constitutes Blake's structural confirmation of the
falseness of the prophecy. After Manoah makes *his* offering "unto the LORD"
in Judges 13:20, "when the flame went up toward heaven from off the altar,
. . . the angel of the LORD ascended in the flame of the altar. And Manoah
and his wife looked on it, and fell on their faces to the ground." No such
ascension (or obeisance) takes place in Blake's *Samson*. Indeed, only through
Samson's "memory" of the annunciation he never actually witnessed is the
angel presented as an angel.[60] Blake's Manoa merely assumes it, or seems to
assume it, for his greeting is, to say the least, peculiar. After hailing the
visitant as a "man of God," he asks his name and inquires of his "warfare";
but, as I have already noted, only if and "when thy sayings come to pass"
will he honor him. If an "offering unto the Lord" actually is made by any-
one, it must be Samson himself, sacrificed to a god of vengeance and war.[61]
Wittreich has proposed that this angel's "warfare" is mental, not carnal,[62]
but there is nothing in the poem to this point to support such a distinction or to suggest that Blake had it in mind. On the other hand, Blake's
entire scene here points to an ironic allusion, in Manoa's words to the angel ("thou comest from far"), to Isaiah's "the name of the LORD cometh
from far, burning with his anger, and the burden thereof is heavy: his lips
are full of indignation, and his tongue as a devouring fire" (30:27; cf. 13:
4-6). William Michael Rossetti conjectured that "warfare" is a misprint
for "wayfare."[63] Nothing could be further from Blake's intention. As Paul
says to the Corinthians, "the weapons of our warfare are not carnal, but
mighty through God to the pulling down of strong holds" (2 Corinthians
10:4). And Milton, mindful of Christ's earlier praise for his troops' "faithful
. . . warfare" (*PL* VI,803), has God revise the locution in *Paradise Regained:*

> But first I mean
> To exercise him in the wilderness;
> There he shall first lay down the rudiments
> Of his great warfare, ere I send him forth
> To conquer Sin and Death, the two grand foes,
> By humiliation and strong sufferance:
> His weakness shall o'ercome Satanic strength
> And all the world, and mass of sinful flesh.[64]

The word does not appear in either the biblical or Miltonic versions of the angel's visitation.

The true "offering unto the Lord" I should like to think is Blake's prophecy, suffusing the complementary falseness of Samson, Dalila, the Philistines, the Israelites, and the annunciatory angel with the light of Truth's "propitious beams." Only in prophecy, the vision communicated by the sword of the tongue, does "our earthly night" turn into "heavenly day." The "propitiousness" of the "fire from heav'n" that consumes Abel's sacrificial offering unto the Lord (*PL* XI,441-42) sows but the seeds of the very sin and death it was presumably dedicated to destroy. The only hero in *Samson*, then, is Blake himself. In his vision and revelation is his salvation just as surely as Samson's and Dalila's fall is in them. Lowery and others have remarked that in *Samson* "nothing is concluded,"[65] but the dissatisfaction or frustration implicit in such remarks is seriously misdirected. The "conclusion" for Blake is announced in the cyclical structure of the work—from false prophecy to false deliverer to false deliverance, an eternal, terrible round that inevitably necessitates another champion from without. To paraphrase Blake elsewhere, not entirely out of context, all deliverers are in the human breast.[66] As he says in *Samson*, earthly night is the noon-tide of the damned (the fallen) alone.[67] The self-redeemed, whose vision neither beholds seasonal and diurnal cycles nor rests complacently in the perceived ratio only, see God (not merely themselves) in seeing the infinite in all things. "Therefore God becomes as we are, that we may be as he is" (*There Is No Natural Religion*, E2). In *Samson* the poet-prophet perceives what we are and in so doing becomes as he is. For the youthful Blake, it is an extraordinary achievement. More than a mere harbinger of great prophecy to come, it is powerfully prophetic in its own right, absorbing and transforming both the Bible and Milton in the fires of intellect and redeeming from the husks of error the poetic genius ("Truth") in them so that "all who pass" this splendid "epitaph" may read. And go and do likewise. The ambitious and stunning enterprise of composite art to come will "do" much more, but the iron pen will need but little further sharpening.

EPILOGUE

EARLIER in these pages I suggested that *Poetical Sketches* might well be construed, fruitfully, as a series of essays on (not exercises in) the idea of imitation, a revealing mental fight with illustrious, and not so illustrious, predecessors out of which emerged Blake's unshakable conviction that true imitation is criticism. Indeed I was tempted to borrow that latter phrase, since it *is* Blake's, for my title. But there is a certain insufficiency in that title, just as there is in McGowan's titular assertion, for all its appropriateness and implicit compliment, "The Integrity of Blake's *Poetical Sketches.*"¹ Without my wishing to endow the volume with undue distinction, or to genuflect before its "amazing" achievement, or to revel in the discovery of gems in the dustbin of juvenilia, some genuine homage is warranted.

Poetical Sketches is, as everyone knows, Blake's only book in the conventional sense of that word. Although he essayed one more, *The French Revolution,* for which he even had a genuine publisher (Joseph Johnson), it was promptly abandoned in the midst of page proof, certainly in part because of his increased realization after 1789 of the "success" of his first major work in composite art, *Songs of Innocence.*² But if, as Spenser announced in *The Shepheardes Calender* and Milton in *L'Allegro* and *Il Penseroso,* the poet aspiring to Mount Parnassus properly makes his first flights at the lower altitudes of pastoral, and if Blake seems consciously to emulate that hallowed pattern in the "line of vision" in *Songs of Innocence, that* "book" nevertheless is not his *Prelude.* Thomas Vogler and others have argued, cogently and convincingly, that *Milton* is Blake's necessary prelude to vision (that is, to *Jerusalem*),³ as *Alastor* perhaps is to Shelley's or *Endymion* to Keats's or *Childe Harold's Pilgrimage* to Byron's. But all of these poets, indeed all great poets, wrote poetry well before they became aware of their own need for a *Prelude,* poetry that by its very nature demanded the discipline of self-sounding and reassessment such preludes afford and constitute, at least in part. And, of course, all wrote juvenilia of one sort or another, and published them, the contours of those (often) slim volumes affording us glimpses into the genesis,

however partial and even on occasion embarrassing, of genius. Nevertheless, of all the Romantic poets, perhaps oddly enough I have found the
earliest poems of Byron alone to be of abiding interest in and for themselves,
even as they technically stutter and sputter and, at their best, provide
auguries of the achievement that so took Europe by storm—and later vexed
it.

Although he had already published the unfortunate *The Fall of Robes-
pierre* in the fall of 1794, Coleridge's first volume is *Poems on Various Subjects*
(1796), about which he himself said, perceptively (even as he inclines toward
what will become a typically Coleridgean apologetic), that there is "much to
blame in them—much effeminacy of sentiment, much faulty glitter of
expression."[4] As Carl Woodring writes of Wordsworth's *An Evening Walk*
and *Descriptive Sketches*, if he had written only those poems "he would be
inglorious enough. . . . If Wordsworth [and, we can add, Coleridge] had
died at the age of Keats, we would rank him below Southey and Thomas
Campbell." For both, these early efforts afforded them "practice in shuffling
borrowed counters," counters that were, even worse, "ersatz for their own
feelings."[5] The era of sensibility was still taking its toll. Of Keats's first
volume, *Poems,* "launched amid the cheers and fond anticipations of all his
circle" as Cowden Clarke remembered it, Douglas Bush remarks that "even
the most devout modern admirer . . . would have failed to discover any
remarkable promise except in the one sonnet on Chapman's Homer."[6] If
that, in my own judgment is a bit severe, Keats *was* barely twenty-one (five
years younger than Blake was when *Poetical Sketches* appeared), undisci-
plined, unselfcritical, uncertain. This "pattern" is completed with Shelley,
even if we ignore *Original Poetry* by "Victor and Cazire" and *The Wandering
Jew* (not to mention *Zastrozzi* and *St. Irvyne, or The Rosicrucian*). *The Posthumous Fragments of Margaret Nicholson* might well be embalmed in the language
the *Poetical Register* reviewer applied to *Original Poetry:* "There is no 'original poetry' in this volume; there is nothing in it but downright scribble."[7]
Cameron was right to ignore the "art" in favor of Shelley's developing
political and ethical ideas.

Byron's early poems are another matter, as I have tried to show elsewhere.
While in many ways they represent "what is fashionable, compounded with
what all young poets write of," replete with predictable excesses of emotion
and juvenile profundity, they are also, surprisingly, structural experiments
in the manipulation of point of view, the creation of personae, and poetic
interrelationships or groupings: for example, the four poems addressed
"To Caroline," those (under varying titles) to Anne Houson, and especially
the ones circling about the figure of Byron's earliest love, Mary Chaworth.
Moreover they explore with unexpected consistency a quite extraordinary
array of fictional (and real) losses—love, dreams, youth, home, family,
friends, and assorted other "Edens"—without the suffusion of self-pity and

maudlinness that one has every right to expect of the self-confessed idler and dilettante of the Preface to *Hours of Idleness*.[8] While interesting, even revealing, relationships may be drawn between Byron's and Blake's early formalistic strategies and thematic preoccupations (relationships that may illuminate in unexpected ways the Romantic poets' habitual clusterings of reciprocally interactive poems), my point in all of this is otherwise. Nor, except incidentally, do I intend to defend my judgment of the manifold superiority of Blake's early poetry to that of his illustrious contemporary toilers in the same vineyard.

My point is this (and I think it a more important differentiation than that implicit in value judgments): Blake's *Poetical Sketches* is a "book," not merely an anthology, and as a book reflects his lifelong concern with the nature of books, most centrally with the question, "What is a book?" His artistic apprenticeship at Basire's was just that, to be sure, but it was also an education in bookmaking, not merely in "those rudimentary skills of etching and engraving that gave him a craft and trade for life."[9] Learning to be a good reproductive engraver (like Basire himself and eighteenth-century predecessors and contemporaries in book illustration) involved being a skillful copyist. Originality of any kind, in technique or content, was inapropos, for the faithfulness of his work to the original is what made a superior illustration. It is but a simple extension of this principle to say as well that the closer the book to acceptable, conventional book design, the better. A consideration of what oft was essayed but ne'er so well executed no doubt played a part in some printer-publisher endeavors, but there was that burgeoning readership out there that craved to be fed what it "liked." What the average reader-viewer saw in an illustrated book was not the creative hand or eye of the reproductive engraver but, at best, the fidelity of the copy, at worst merely its illustrative "appropriateness" to the printed text. And, of course, such a reader would read left to right, top to bottom, beginning to end. It is the way that we, perforce, read Blake's *Imitation of Spencer* or *Fair Elenor* or *Blind-Man's Buff*—and, too often, the way we read the "sequence" of poems in *Poetical Sketches,* drawing therefrom "important" critical conclusions.

My previous chapters, despite the seemingly arbitrary (though, I trust, not always arbitrary) imposition of order and arrangements of poems into more-or-less homogeneous groups, have been attempts to de-sequence the poems in the volume, to demonstrate (in other words) Blake's early efforts, within and between or among poems, to liberate them from the spatial and temporal confines of an ordinary book "that all may read" (to misappropriate a phrase from his *Introduction* to *Songs of Innocence,* to which I shall return in a moment). In the context of his discussion of the *ut pictura poesis* tradition, Hagstrum notes that "the most striking characteristic of pre-Romantic pictorialism is the painterly personification,"[10] and of course Spenser and

Milton as well as a number of their eighteenth-century disciples, raised their poems to the status of word-pictures. Still, it is also important to remember that "'literary' England was a country that traditionally hewed to the religion and world view that preferred the word to the image"[11] — that is, the verbal to the graphic image. A book (even an illustrated book) was thus a "translation" of vision into verbal equivalents when it was not merely an avowed imitation or emulation, and an illustration was a translation of the verbal equivalents into pictorial equivalents.

As Blake rapidly became aware of the visionary possibilities inherent in Gothic art (and in the "Gothicism" of Michelangelo, Raphael, Dürer, and Giulio Romano) he was immersing himself at the same time in the prophetic-visionary books of the Bible, Spenser, and Milton (the major poems of the latter two arranged into "books" within books, of course, at least in part emulative of the Bible as well as of the traditional epic). That imitations of all three of these abounded in the eighteenth century obviously did not escape Blake's notice either, and those derivatives surely constituted a kind of revelation to him of what Wittreich calls the "barriers imposed by a verbal idiom,"[12] especially when an insufficient imagination was at work with that idiom. These exemplifications of artistic degeneracy Blake's critical mind grasped as the poetic equivalents of servile reproductive engraving, books to be read, not apprehended holistically or "experienced" as those of the "line of vision" were. It is not my intent here to argue the obvious conclusion, that Blake, even at the time of *Poetical Sketches,* was already contemplating the invention of what has come to be known as his "composite art." In fact, at this point in his life, still at Basire's, the intrinsic problems of graphic art, poetic art, and the art of the book more probably were jostling discretely with each other in his mind even if he had some sense of their overlap, perhaps even their potential interpenetration.[13] Nevertheless there may be some merit in paying attention to Blake's first poetic title, *Poetical Sketches.* Aside from the fact that we do not know whether it is his title or Flaxman's or somebody else's, it is scarcely distinctive among conventional juvenilia (witness Wordsworth's *Descriptive Sketches* to cite an example ready to hand). Yet unlike those of any poet I know, Blake's title (which there is no evidence he ever tried to change) actually does reflect his dual enterprise even as an apprentice. I cannot agree with Essick that the "poetry must have been an escape from the labor of learning his profession," even if it does seem to deal "with materials less mundane than those offered by Blake's daily labors."[14] Indeed, this book is dedicated to proving that his labors at *Poetical Sketches* constituted a serious enterprise in its own right.

The word "sketches" itself, to an artist, has to do with serious beginnings, not doodling. Sketches are, at the very least (in Shelley's formulation) the initial sparks of the genuine creative imagination whether or not one agrees further with Shelley's notion of the creative mind as but a fading coal. In his

Notebook (E503) Blake wrote a scurrilous poem about an apocryphal (and therefore imaginatively true) story about Sir Joshua Reynolds's sending a self-portrait to the "birth Place of Michael Angelo," accompanied by "a dirty paper scroll" on which Reynolds wrote "Sketches by Michael Angelo." The Florentines, however, are not fooled. They said,

> Tis a Dutch English bore
> Michael Angelos Name writ on Rembrandts door
> . . . .
> Tis the trading English Venetian Cant
> To speak Michael Angelo & Act Rembrandt

—that is, a campaign by art merchants to get the Florentines to buy what to the myopic English was true art, what to Blake was nonart or at best a fraud. In the poem he calls it, obscurely, "an English Fetch"—that is, at once a trick and (perhaps, given Blake's extraordinary linguistic knowledge) an apparition or wraith as the dictionary defines its early signification. His charge against Rembrandt (as well as Titian, Rubens, and others) was consistently that he could not draw, the "Venetian Cant" of "the trading English" emanating from English connoisseurs not knowing the difference, "speak[ing] Michael Angelo & Act[ing] Rembrandt." ("Venetian" and "Flemish" were always synonymous with Blake.)

Blake's irate response to this state of affairs is: "Michael Angelo did never Sketch";

> Every line of his has Meaning
> And needs neither Suckling nor Weaning.

A "finished" sketch is thus, as applied to Michelangelo, a tautology, and the high finishings of Reynolds, the Venetians, and the Flemish were worked up "with labour / Of an hundred Journeymens" (E505).

It is no doubt too much to credit Blake in 1783 with regarding every line of his own poetical "sketches" as imbued with meaning, though it is not to be ignored that he later claimed precisely that for all his work.[15] Nevertheless, even with due allowance for the modesty implied in such a title, the working graphic artist already knew that the "sketches" of Michelangelo, Raphael, Dürer, and Giulio Romano were "finished," and in his poetry, no less than his art, he set out to emulate that conception. Similarly with the idea of a book—a book, that is, that did not merely translate or imitate and, therefore, was somehow liberated from the exigencies of machine production for conventional reader consumption. Is that why, for example, Blake himself hand-stitched the unbound printed pages of *Poetical Sketches,* the manufacture of which (as we have seen) almost certainly was not of his own choosing and, even more certainly, not under his supervision?

However that may be, it is clear from subsequent events that he was still in some doubt as to precisely how a true "antibook" might be created—or, indeed, what a booklike antibook might look like. The absence of poetic closure in *Poetical Sketches,* the militant anticyclical and antisequential structuring of individual poems as well as of groups of poems, the allusive intertextuality that raises the present artifact into the imaginative sphere of the Bible, Spenser, and Milton, and the clear thrust toward prophetic stances and forms—all these are effective deterrents to casual perusal and "normal" reader expectation.[16] Had he been less sure of the validity and rightness of his own intuitions (he was almost constitutionally incapable of doubting himself), he might very well have included in the preface to *Poetical Sketches* (which, as I have argued, he surely didn't write himself) what Wordsworth wrote in the Advertisement to *Lyrical Ballads:* "Readers accustomed to the gaudiness and inane phraseology of many modern writers, if they persist in reading this book to its conclusion, will perhaps frequently have to struggle with feelings of strangeness and awkwardness: they will look round for poetry, and will be induced to enquire by what species of courtesy these attempts can be permitted to assume that title." But had Blake deigned to write such an apologia, he surely would have been thinking the while: "I have given you what you are accustomed to but I have contrived to arouse your faculties to a perception of the fundamental imaginative errors of the customary." As he says later in his *Notebook,* "I found them blind, I taught them how to see" (E531).

Accordingly, his next nonilluminated work is in some sense an even bolder experiment, a "book" that is a kind of play, opera, burletta, narrative, *Tristram-Shandy*esque melange, with the author-speaker popping in and out of his own creation: "If I have not presented you with every character in the piece call me ass" (E442); "Then Mr. Inflammable Gass ran & shovd his head into the fire & set his hair all in a flame & ran about the room—No No he did not I was only making a fool of you" (E443); "So all the people in the book enterd into the room" (E444). Blake thought enough of this work, *An Island in the Moon,* to copy it carefully from an earlier draft (now lost), and to revise the fair copy as well. Whether or not he learned from Samuel Foote's unconventional antidramas billed as "teas,"[17] *An Island* is clearly a militant antibook. If it often flounders in its own nonsense, in it (occasionally with a certain brilliance) Blake exploits such non-sense to jolt the reader out of his ingrained habits of passive reading: "I was only making a fool of you."

The work he turned to after *An Island* is not called a book either (the *Island* fragment actually has no title at all) but rather is a series of aphorisms (as Keynes describes them); more accurately it promulgates sets of principles, embodying alternately error and truth, that lead either to "conclusions" or "applications"—all cast in the familiar language of tractates and other doctrinal formulations that emanated from the camps of his philosophical enemies. Though in prose, this book (or these books, we are not sure precisely which) is, most crucially, what Blake himself called his "Original Stereotype" (E713), that is, his first effort to transform the conventional readable page into an integrated graphic-verbal design and, therefore, to engage the reader-spectator in a more complex experience than mere reading. Moreover, it is clearly an attempt to go beyond the simpler, more direct (and often static) illustrative relationship between text and design in emblem literature.[18] In these tractates (as we have come to call them), *There Is No Natural Religion* and *All Religions Are One*, the voice is neither that of *Poetical Sketches* nor of *An Island in the Moon*, but "The Voice of one crying in the Wilderness" (E2), the voice of the prophet, one sure of his vision but acutely aware (or fearing) that he is unheard.

Leslie Tannenbaum goes so far as to argue that *All Religions Are One* identifies "the Incarnation with the process of perception and the source of all life, order, and significance." And in *There Is No Natural Religion*, echoing both Augustine and Jacob Boehme, Blake "states that man can perceive God only by appropriating godlike powers of perception through the enactment of the Incarnation within each individual."

> This Christological or incarnational rhetoric, wherein all the senses are employed to raise man to vision and thereby to a perception of the infinite through identification with the body of Christ, provides the rationale for the use of synesthesia and a combination of media in any work that purports to be divinely inspired.[19]

It is difficult, indeed well nigh impossible, to know how early in his life Blake became aware of, or read around in, the extraordinary proliferation of biblical commentary in the seventeenth and eighteenth centuries, but there is little doubt that he perceived the artistic possibilities inherent in the large number of illustrated Bibles (not to mention biblical paintings) available to him in his youth and apprenticeship days. He even contributed to such Bibles, engraving in 1780-81 for *The Protestants Family Bible,* in 1780-83 for *The Royal Universal Family Bible,* and about the same time for Edward Kimpton's *A New and Complete History of the Holy Bible*[20] — all, it should be noted, at the very time he is completing *Poetical Sketches.* In such works the intent was not merely to provide the reader visualizations of the Word to make the language of the Bible more "understandable," but to give the reader-viewer "a dramatic experience of the living Word."[21]

When, a year (or less) after the tractates, *The Book of Thel* and *Songs of Innocence* appeared virtually simultaneously, the fears of crying in the wilderness may not yet have faded, for here we have a book to be read-seen and songs to be heard-read-seen, a complementary (and contrarious) "vision" of the state of innocence. However it is interpreted, *Thel* in its very design "is a work refuting the linear conception of progression from beginning to end";[22] and the *Songs*, as we know, take on new formulations, arrangements, and "plots" with virtually each issue emanating from Blake's eye, hand, press, gathering, and binding. Blake is now, for the first time, the "Author & Printer" the title pages of these two works announce him to be. Translated, he is creator-singer-writer-artist and bookmaker. The "unity" of *Thel* and the *Songs* (particularly the latter) is synchronic, an extension in many ways of the experiments in nonlinear structures, interruptive and intertextual verbal strategies, and poetic clusterings of *Poetical Sketches*, not to mention the non-sense of *An Island in the Moon*. Indeed, retrospectively viewed, the range and even the curious mixture of genres and modes in *Poetical Sketches* take on at least a semblance of the similar mixtures habitually noted by biblical commentators in the prophets and especially in Revelation.

One need not press this point, however, to recognize that in the *Introduction to Songs of Innocence* such a creator-singer-writer-artist-bookmaker is at work: the musician-creator (piper), the singer of words, the writer and (implicitly) maker of books—but books (as the final lines indicate) that are not only to be read but heard and "seen" in the same imaginative sense that the piper initially sees a child on a cloud. "Book" has become something other (or at least more) than an artifact "out there," the reader of which is merely a Lockean perceiver and understander of object. This other-than-artifact has not only imaginatively literalized the traditional "word-picture" idea of poetry but collapsed the senses, so to speak, into a wholeness of perception by which the "reader" can emulate the perceptive-creative act of the artist himself. As Tannenbaum puts it, what is originally located in the theater of the mind of the prophet is relocated in the mind of the reader by means of the visual, dramatic, and rhetorical enactment of the Word.[23] In his preface to *Jerusalem*, entitled "To the Public," Blake writes: "I also hope the reader will be with me, wholly One in Jesus our Lord" (E144). If Wordsworth's poetry at its best is a surrogate Nature, Blake's will be a surrogate Imagination or Vision (that is, "the External nature [Blake clearly punning] & permanence of its ever Existent Images"—E544). As he says again and again, "The Nature of my Work is Visionary or Imaginative" as opposed to that Nature which is but a "Vegetable Glass."[24] Thus, in the *Introduction* to *Innocence* the conventional spatiality of up and down is annihilated as the child on a cloud vanishes from *sight* to be, obviously, internalized *in* the piper himself; and the temporality of the insistently sequential "And I," "And I," "And I," "And I" of the end of the poem turns the reader (now, Blake hopes, become the "child" of the last line) back to its beginning: "Every child may joy to hear / Piping down the valleys wild / Piping songs of pleasant glee." As Kay Easson observes, the book in this sense has an "emanative role" in that it "can adjoin one man (author) to many men (readers)"—as distinct from those books that are, in the language of *The*

Marriage of Heaven and Hell, "only Analytics," and that therefore "impose" *on* us from without.[25]

Underlying and enriching this entire conception, of course, is, as I have been suggesting, the biblical prophetic "book." If *Songs of Innocence* is, in a sense, Blake's Psalms or Canticles, *The Book of Urizen* (originally planned as *The First Book of Urizen*), *The Book of Ahania,* and *The Book of Los* are even more obviously "prophecies," constitutive of the "Bible of Hell" Blake promises us at the end of *The Marriage,* an emulation of a biblical canon by way of "combining a number of disparate books into a coherent and unified vision of human life from the Creation to the Apocalypse."[26] Even what we now refer to as *The Four Zoas* was initially entitled *The Book of Vala,* its nine "Nights" (in critical-imitation, not mimicry, of Young's *Night Thoughts*) planned as "Books." *Milton* (divided into "Books"), then, is a *Prelude* to *the* book, *Jerusalem,* now no longer needing that designation, although his first impulse was to organize this supreme antibook into "XXVIII Chapters" (E731) and he did finally settle on a four-"book" structure. For Jerusalem and *Jerusalem* are a state, a city, a woman, a "book" in which not only "Every word and every letter is studied and put into its fit place" (E144) but "every Word & Every Character" is "Human," walking "To & fro in Eternity as One Man reflecting each in each & clearly seen / And seeing" (E255). The title of the poem is *Jerusalem, The Emanation of The Giant Albion;* it/she becomes at the end "The Song of Jerusalem" (E256), that is, the Word incarnate.

We are a long way from *Poetical Sketches.* Yet in its youthful insistence upon the atemporality and aspatiality of "vision" and its quite extraordinary frustration of the ordinary act of reading ("imposition" of author upon reader as that is defined in *The Marriage*), it clearly initiates Blake's lifelong campaign against the Urizenic book—most graphically and stunningly portrayed for us on the title page of *The Book of Urizen.* Morris Eaves's splendid analysis of that plate I need not repeat here. Suffice it to say that the design is a brilliant, and even terrifying, attack on imitation and on reading imitations. Amid the crushingly oppressive (not "fearful") symmetry of the koimanic "landscape" Urizen appears, eyes tightly shut, as both writer and reader; and, as Eaves reminds us, "the only person who reads and writes at the same time is a scribe. A scribe is a professional copyist."[27] As author and printer Urizen creates a "world-book" which he then imposes on all his "sons" and "daughters" and to which he himself falls victim—the ultimate antiprophecy.

In *Poetical Sketches,* not yet ready (or perhaps even decided) to create the new kind of "world-book" only his mature composite art enabled him to do, Blake faced the problem, as Essick describes it with respect to *Tiriel,* of portraying and commenting "on fallen vision without placing his own style and point of view beyond the artistic limitations imposed by that vision."[28]

Tiriel, we tend to forget, was intended to be a letterpress book with accompanying illustrations (they are in sepia and clearly not intended for engraving or etching); and, aside from Tiriel himself, its major characters are Har and Heva, whose world, life, *and* song (Har sings "in the great cage") are governed protectively (even defensively) by a personification of memory, Mnetha. In their very conventionality, the designs not only exemplify and satirize the restrictive traditions of book illustration, but (the latest of them, at least) suggest "that Blake was attempting to move away from literal illustration and develop the Har and Heva story into a pictorial commentary on eighteenth-century aesthetics bound to the imitation of nature and to the memory of a once glorious but now decayed classical tradition."[29]

That is not too much to say of *Poetical Sketches.* It is the genesis of a kind of poetry at once conventional and radically expansive in its imaginative manipulations of conventionality. It is not only a Blake book but a genesis, the prophetic prelude not only to a *Prelude* but to that *Prelude*'s "preliminary sketchings" in the songs and early prophecies and in the abortive struggle with *The Four Zoas*—as well as to the glorious restoration of "what Eternally Exists, Really & Unchangeably" (E544). "In the aggregate" what eternally exists is the Imagination, "All Human Forms identified" (E544, 256):

And I heard the Name of their Em[a]nations they are named Jerusalem.

NOTES

CHAPTER 1

1. Michael Phillips, "William Blake and the 'Unincreasable Club': The Printing of *Poetical Sketches*," *Bulletin of The New York Public Library* 80 (1976): 6-18.

2. The earlier date is proposed by Michael Phillips in "Blake's Early Poetry," *William Blake: Essays in Honour of Sir Geoffrey Keynes*, ed. Morton D. Paley and Phillips (Oxford: Clarendon Press, 1973), p. 2; the later date by David V. Erdman, *Blake: Prophet Against Empire*, rev. ed. (Garden City, N.Y.: Doubleday, 1969), p. 17n.

3. "To My Dearest Friend, John Flaxman," in letter to Flaxman, 12 Sept. 1800, in *The Poetry and Prose of William Blake*, ed. David V. Erdman, rev. ed. (Garden City, N.Y.: Doubleday, 1970), p. 680. All Blake quotations will be from this edition, identified in text and notes as E plus the page number. Quotations from Blake's engraved works will be referred to by plate and line numbers and their locations in Erdman. In the Flaxman poem Blake also mentions reading "Paracelsus & Behmen" — apparently in "riper years" as well.

4. Ezra 5:11; cf. 1 Kings 6-7.

5. E94-95. Not entirely coincidentally, Spenser superimposes Mt. Sinai and the Mount of Olives on Parnassus in Book I of *The Faerie Queene*.

6. T. S. Eliot, "Blake," in *Selected Essays* (New York: Harcourt, Brace, 1950), p. 276; the essay originally appeared in *The Sacred Wood* (1934). Eliot's estimate of the smallness of Blake's intent is at least partly due to his conviction that Blake's "meanness of culture" led to "crankiness" and "eccentricity" of the kind that "frequently affects writers outside of the Latin tradition" — or, less charitably, due to Eliot's fundamental disagreement with Blake's ideas.

7. John Ehrstine, *William Blake's "Poetical Sketches"* (Pullman: Washington State University Press, 1967), p. 2.

8. James D. McGowan, "Rising Glories: A Study of William Blake's *Poetical Sketches*," Ph.D. dissertation, Rutgers University, 1968; Michael J. Tolley, "Blake's Songs of Spring," in *Essays in Honour of . . . Keynes*, pp. 96-128; Michael Phillips, "Blake's Early Poetry," in ibid., pp. 1-28; Erdman, *Blake: Prophet Against Empire*. McGowan has recently published "The Integrity of the *Poetical Sketches*," *Blake Studies* 8 (1979): 121-44.

9. Margaret Lowery, *Windows of the Morning: A Critical Study of William Blake's "Poetical Sketches," 1783* (New Haven: Yale University Press, 1940).

10. Tolley, "Blake's Songs of Spring," p. 98.

11. Benjamin Heath Malkin, Dedicatory epistle to his *A Father's Memoirs of his Child* (London: Longmans, Hurst, Reese, & Orme, 1806), reprinted (in part) first by Arthur Symons in his *William Blake* (London: Archibald Constable, 1907), pp. 309-29, and most recently by Gerald E. Bentley, Jr., in *Blake Records* (Oxford: Clarendon Press, 1969), pp. 421-31. Subsequent page references in my text will be to Bentley.

12. E519; Advertisement of the Exhibition, E517; *A Descriptive Catalogue of Pictures*, E520.

13. Advertisement of the Catalogue, E519.

14. David Bindman, "Blake's 'Gothicised Imagination' and the History of England," in *Essays in Honour of . . . Keynes,* p. 31.

15. Bentley, *Blake Records,* pp. 420-21, 426-27. Despite Malkin's unequivocalness I find no evidence in *Poetical Sketches* of Blake's reading of the Shakespeare and Jonson works he cites—or, if he did indeed read them, he seems sufficiently unimpressed to avoid allusions to them in his poems.

16. Bindman, "Blake's 'Gothicised Imagination,'" pp. 30, 31.

17. E. J. Rose, "The 'Gothicized Imagination' of 'Michelangelo Blake,'" in *Blake in His Time,* ed. Robert N. Essick and Donald Pearce (Bloomington: Indiana University Press, 1978), pp. 156-59. Somewhat confusingly Rose also identifies "Gothic style" as "linear and emblematic." I must believe that his use of "linear" here does not mean what mine does later in this paragraph.

18. E660. Cf. *The Laocoön:* "Christianity is Art"; "A Poet a Painter a Musician an Architect: The Man Or Woman who is not one of these is not a Christian" (E271, 272).

19. Geoffrey Keynes, *Blake Studies: Essays on His Life and Work,* 2nd ed. (Oxford: Clarendon Press, 1971), p. 28. As Robert N. Essick has noted, this later version is both technically and artistically superior to the earlier—which is nevertheless, in Essick's words, "a remarkable performance for an apprentice of only one or two years' tenure"; see his *William Blake, Printmaker* (Princeton: Princeton University Press, 1980), pp. 29-30, 185-86. My point has less to do with the work's quality than with the significance of the added legend.

20. David Bindman, "Blake's Theory and Practice of Imitation," in *Blake in His Time,* p. 95. Bindman does argue, however, that as Blake's attitude toward the classics matures, it becomes in his work more programmatic than imitative. Similarly with his use of the Gothic.

21. Ibid., pp. 96-97. Although it is not quite what he intended, another point of Bindman's is pertinent to this idea of learning the language of art: "Greek sculpture remains [for Blake] at least *primus inter pares* . . . because it is after all the best record there is of the [divine] originals"; and thus "Blake was able to argue that his work is not so much imitative of the antiques as drawn from the same sources" that *they* imitated (pp. 96-97). For a fuller discussion of this idea of imitation see Morton D. Paley's "'Wonderful Originals'—Blake and Ancient Sculpture," in *Blake in His Time,* pp. 170-97. My use of the term "formulae" here is intended to include the notion of *Pathosformeln* developed by Aby Warburg in 1914 and used by Bindman and Paley in their cited essays. See also Jenijoy LaBelle's "Blake's Visions and Re-visions of Michelangelo" in the same volume, where she helpfully cites the "pathos formulae" as forming "an important part of the language of motifs in western art" (pp. 14-15).

22. On this last point see E. J. Rose's essay, cited earlier, in *Blake in His Time,* pp. 155-56. More obscure is Rose's contention that Blake's "defense and continued admiration of Dürer is the vital link between the Gothic and Michelangelo" (p. 157).

23. Joseph A. Wittreich, *Angel of Apocalypse* (Madison: University of Wisconsin Press, 1975), p. 48.

24. Ibid., pp. 52-53.

25. Ibid., p. 54. Erdman's point is made in David V. Erdman, "The Dating of William Blake's Engravings," *Philological Quarterly* 31 (1952): 339-40.

26. Mona Wilson, *The Life of William Blake,* rev. ed. (New York: Oxford University Press, 1949), p. 12; Robert N. Essick, "Blake and the Traditions of Reproductive Engraving," *Blake Studies* 5 (1972): 63-64. The quotations are from Essick. Phillips also makes the identification in "Blake's Early Poetry," p. 13; and see Essick's *William Blake, Printmaker,* pp. 182-83.

27. Wittreich, *Angel of Apocalypse,* pp. 57, 58. Related to Wittreich's point is Stanley Fish's argument, in "The Temptation to Action in Milton," *ELH* 48 (1981): 516-31, that a characteristic, consistent pattern in Milton's poetry "when the confrontation between good and evil occurs" consists in the suspension of action or conflict. For Milton "the true form of action is not an event, but a mode of being, and it is a mode one displays not at one moment (highlighted by the

pressures of the world), but at all moments which are thus equally and indifferently its manifestations" (pp. 526-27). Although Fish does not apply this pattern to *Samson Agonistes*, clearly the implications of his argument make Samson very much a pugnacious Orc and a most unlikely Los-like "mode of being."

28. Phillips, "Blake's Early Poetry," pp. 13-16. See Chap. 7 below.

29. A. C. Swinburne, *William Blake: A Critical Essay* (1866; London: Chatto & Windus, 1906), p. 9; Vivian de Sola Pinto, *William Blake* (New York: Schocken Books, 1965), p. 9.

30. The word is Northrop Frye's in his essay on "Nature and Homer," *Fables of Identity* (New York: Harcourt, Brace & World, 1963), p. 43. In the same essay Frye argues that all "original" writers are "derivative at a deeper level" (p. 47).

31. Wittreich, *Angel of Apocalypse*, pp. xvi, 73. Alicia Ostriker, in *Vision and Verse in William Blake* (Madison: University of Wisconsin Press, 1965), could not be more wrong in saying Blake "absorbed ideas, phrases, symbols he liked, without regard to their contexts or the systems to which they belonged" (p. 31).

32. This is similar to John Beer's idea of "intensive effect" and "extensive effect" in a work caused by its alluding to a "distinctive element" in the source "which raises probability above the level where mere coincidence provides a more likely explanation" ("Influence and Independence in Blake," in *Interpreting Blake*, ed. Michael Phillips [Cambridge: At the University Press, 1978], p. 201). I cannot agree, however, with Beer's emphasis on the necessity of our knowing "the nature of the human being who effected the transformation" of his source. The section of his essay subtitled "Some Verbal Sources" (pp. 215-37) is nevertheless well worth careful reading—as is E. P. Thompson's "'London'" in the same collection, which also focuses upon what I have called significant words or allusions (pp. 5-31).

33. I quote from Beer's essay cited above, p. 236.

34. Ibid., p. 221. Beer is here talking of individual words in Blake's poetry, intensive investigations of which, including their allusive properties, may lead to the "unraveling" of the "shorthand." But, as Sigurd Burckhardt warns in his *Shakespearean Meanings* (Princeton: Princeton University Press, 1968), "there is nothing easier than to create a supporting structure for an interpretation" (p. 302). Good sense and fair play, with Blake and reader alike, one hopes, obtain.

35. A somewhat differently directed, but nevertheless admirably concise, presentation of the nature of Blake's "strivings" is Hazard Adams's "Blake and the Philosophy of Literary Symbolism," *New Literary History* 5 (1973): 135-46. Even more pertinent, however, is Joseph A. Wittreich's analysis, in *Visionary Poetics* (San Marino, Calif.: Huntington Library, 1979), of *Lycidas* in the context of *Justa Edovardo King Naufrado* where it first appeared. Borrowing some terminology from Harold Bloom's *Poetry and Repression: Revisionism from Blake to Stevens* (New Haven: Yale University Press, 1975), Wittreich characterizes Milton's elegy "as a 'psychic battleground' exemplifying the reliance of texts upon texts, as well as the fact that because texts are so often, and in such complicated ways, intervolved, 'any poem is an interpoem'" (p. 97). On the importance and ubiquity of allusion in prophecy see also pp. 87-88 (especially the reminder of the dense texture of allusion to the Old Testament in the Book of Revelation), 136, and 248 (note 28).

36. But see my "Blake and Satire," *The Wordsworth Circle* 8 (1977): 311-26, which argues, among other things, Blake's greater closeness to burlesque than to satire proper. On the distinction between Blake's "satire" and that of the Augustans see Martin Price's *To the Palace of Wisdom* (Garden City, N.Y.: Doubleday, 1965), Chap. 13 and especially pp. 431-32.

37. Bindman, "Blake's Theory and Practice of Imitation," p. 96.

38. Quoted by Wittreich, *Angel of Apocalypse*, pp. 230-31, from E. H. Gombrich, *Norm and Form*, 2nd ed. (London & New York: Phaidon, 1971), p. 122. In *The Formal Strain* (Chicago: University of Chicago Press, 1969), Howard Weinbrot puts the matter of Augustan imitation succinctly: the prevailing theory "demanded that the reader be made aware of the original

poems" (Pope, he observes, often put important words and phrases in distinctive type to arouse the reader's awareness); but the end result was often a mere changing of expression "to accommodate the new language and the new age," the "original sense" being "held sacred and inviolable" (pp. ix, 52). See, especially, the entirety of Weinbrot's first two chapters.

39. Cf. Adams's "Blake and the Philosophy of Literary Symbolism," which reminds us that to Blake "culture" is in large part "embodied in words." Los's (and Blake's) eternal act of building the "stubborn structure of the language" is thus "a struggle with a spectral or 'allegorical' system grown like a 'polypus' from his original system (original not in the historical sense but in the sense that his system represents the fundamental nature of language — its metaphorical nature)" (p. 142). In that mental and linguistic war, an author's "inner quality and tone" are irrelevant — except insofar as "by their Works ye shall know them" (*A Vision of the Last Judgment*, E553).

40. Wittreich, *Angel of Apocalypse*, p. 246.

41. My position then is something like William Empson's in his preface to the second edition of *Seven Types of Ambiguity*, where he responds to a reviewer's claim that the "first business" of the "student of poetry" is "the passing of a judgement of value"; and that Empson's "analyses do not seem to have any properly critical conclusion; they are interesting only as revelations of the poet's, or of Mr. Empson's ingenious mind." Empson's response is: "Many of the examples are only intended to show that certain techniques have been widely used. Even in the fuller examples, where I hope I have made clear what I feel about the poem as a whole, I don't try to 'make out a case' for my opinion of its value. The judgment indeed comes either earlier or later than the process I was trying to examine." I quote from the third edition (London: Chatto and Windus, 1963), pp. xi-xiii.

42. John Upton, *Spenser's Faerie Queene, A New Edition*, 2 vols. (London: J. & R. Tonson, 1758), 2: 428. The idea also appears in Upton's preface (1: xxv).

43. Burckhardt, *Shakespearean Meanings*, p. 294. Rather delightfully Burckhardt defines "explanation" as a critical procedure by which "established knowledge must be used to explain that which is not yet established" (p. 297). This entire essay in "intrinsic interpretation" has some bearing on my approach to *Poetical Sketches*, though for the most part he is not interested in allusions.

44. Leopold Damrosch, Jr., *Symbol and Truth in Blake's Myth* (Princeton: Princeton University Press, 1980), p. 358.

45. T. S. Eliot, *The Sacred Wood* (London: 1920), p. 151.

46. Phillips, "The Printing of William Blake's *Poetical Sketches*," p. 13.

47. Phillips, "Blake's Early Poetry," pp. 2ff. Geoffrey Hartman anticipates this view in "Blake and the 'Progress of Poesy,'" in *William Blake: Essays for S. Foster Damon*, ed. Alvin H. Rosenfeld (Providence: Brown University Press, 1969), pp. 57-68.

48. McGowan, "Rising Glories," p. 15. He goes even further, however, to claim that the poems are "arranged meaningfully" because of "the way the imagery progresses, is developed and modified"; and they "do fall into something roughly like the order of their composition" (pp. 40-41).

49. A position taken by a number of critics for obvious reasons, the most extreme version of it being Erdman's in *Blake: Prophet Against Empire*: a "sequence from laughing songs . . . to grim prophecies" (p. 17). Erdman's outline of the volume's progression anticipates Phillips's autobiographical "arrangement."

50. Ehrstine, *William Blake's "Poetical Sketches,"* p. 3.

CHAPTER 2

1. Margaret Lowery, *Windows of the Morning* (New Haven: Yale University Press, 1940), p. 161.

2. Albert Friedman, *The Ballad Revival* (Chicago: University of Chicago Press, 1961), cited

in Alicia Ostriker, *Vision and Verse in William Blake* (Madison: University of Wisconsin Press, 1965), p. 28.

3. Ostriker, *Vision and Verse*, p. 28.

4. Thomas Percy, *Reliques of Ancient English Poetry* (1765; Leipzig: Bernhard Tauchnitz, 1866), 1: xxi. Wordworth, we might recall, referred to Ossian in *The Prelude* as "the naked truth" (VII,567).

5. Such poverty, C. V. Deane reminds us in *Aspects of Eighteenth-Century Nature Poetry* (Oxford: Basil Blackwell, 1935), is not necessarily indicative of failed inventive power but more often than not is dictated by "set purpose," the stock language being the proved conductors to desired atmosphere or effect (p. 36).

6. Lowery, *Windows of the Morning*, p. 169.

7. Several attempts at a redemption of sorts have been made, by "grouping" (somewhat as I have done with the "Songs" in the next chapter) *Fair Elenor* with other poems: *Mad Song* (James D. McGowan, "Rising Glories," [Ph.D. dissertation, Rutgers University, 1968], p. 50), *Thel* (ibid., p. 114), *The Couch of Death* (John Ehrstine, *William Blake's "Poetical Sketches"* [Pullman: Washington State University Press, 1967], pp. 32-36).

8. S. Foster Damon, *William Blake: His Philosophy and Symbols* (1924; reprint ed., New York: Peter Smith, 1947), p. 255.

9. Mark Schorer, *William Blake: The Politics of Vision* (New York: Henry Holt, 1946), p. 415.

10. McGowan goes so far as to say that *Fair Elenor* is "an investigation of symbolic 'night'" ("Rising Glories," p. 50). For an extended discussion of this symbology (but without reference to *Fair Elenor*) see David Wagenknecht, *Blake's Night* (Cambridge: Harvard University Press, 1973).

11. "On H — —ys Friendship" (E497). McGowan cites *The Faerie Queene* I,iii,36 as sanction for the unusual transitive use of "bereave," but John Sampson long ago noted Chaucer's precedent in *The Poetical Works of William Blake* (Oxford: Clarendon Press, 1905), p. 11.

12. The most serious and elaborate analysis is Michael Phillips's in "Blake's Early Poetry," *William Blake: Essays in Honour of Sir Geoffrey Keynes*, ed. Morton D. Paley and Phillips (Oxford: Clarendon Press, 1973), pp. 4-7. His allegorizing of the dubious allusions he finds to Homer, Virgil, Ovid, and Spenser in terms of Blake's personal "progress of poesy" I find unconvincing. Interestingly the greatest to-do has been over Blake's imitation of the Spenserian stanza. Ever since his early editor, Sampson, pronounced the stanzas "all different and all wrong" there has been critical consternation at, and equally prompt defense of, Blake's "irregularity"—usually on the basis of his "impatience" at restraint and his thrust toward a new versification. Even if the variations from Spenser's pattern were not due simply to ineptness, Earl R. Wasserman in *Elizabethan Poetry in the Eighteenth Century*, Illinois Studies in Language and Literature, vol. 32, nos. 2-3 (Urbana: University of Illinois Press, 1947), has shown that such variations were commonplace in the eighteenth century (pp. 104ff.). Aside from Phillips's essay, the virtually exclusive critical focus on the stanza form rather eloquently testifies to a pervasive puzzlement about the poem's "place" in Blake's work, even in *Poetical Sketches*.

13. The liberal dose of Miltonisms (or neo-Miltonisms) in the poem seems to argue this as well, but given the widespread imitation of the diction and phraseology of both in Blake's day, firm judgments on the matter are impossible. Even "leesing" in line 13, which everybody points to as a Spenserianism, is found, in this same sense, in the Psalms (4:2, 5:16)—as well as in Chaucer (but, so far as I know, not adjectively).

14. It should also be noted that, as Wasserman points out, Hurd's emphasis in his *Letters on Chivalry and Romance* on Spenser's "air-formed visions," powerful imagination, and sense of the marvelous was "the inevitable outcome of the growing popularity of the Gothic" (p. 130). It is at least possible, given the proximity of *Fair Elenor* and the Spenser *Imitation*, that Blake made the same connections. The "tinkling rhymes, and elegances terse" presumably refer to the heroic couplet as distinct from the "Gothic" alternate rhyme of Spenser's stanza or from blank verse. In

his *Conjectures on Original Composition* (1759) Edward Young uses the phrase "tinkling sounds" in precisely this way, to characterize Pope's translation of the *Iliad;* oddly enough, though, he describes "rhyme" as "that Gothic daemon."

15. Thomas Warton used this adjective to describe Joseph Hall's *Satires* in his *Observations on the Fairy Queen of Spenser*, 2nd ed. (London: Dodsley, 1762), p. 134; and Joseph Warton used it to characterize Thomson's verse as distinct from Pope's—in *An Essay on the Genius and Writings of Pope*, 5th ed. (London, 1806), 2:327. It is also, however, a favorite word of Chatterton's.

16. I shall discuss this passage in greater detail in my analysis of *Samson* in chap. 7, but suffice it to say here that the radical translation of Mercury's feet into those of Isaiah 52:7-8 is astonishing. On the "idea" of feet see Michael J. Tolley's "Blake's Songs of Spring," in *Essays in Honour of... Keynes*, pp. 97-98.

17. See note 14 above. I cannot agree, therefore, that "Blake is following in none of the traditions of Spenser imitation" as Wasserman claims (p. 132).

18. Schorer, *The Politics of Vision*, p. 402.

19. Phillips reads Blake's "self-awakening" and his program much more positively than I in his "Blake's Early Poetry." Rather than as forecasting Blake's entire career, I find in the poem (especially the last stanza) auguries of the "prologues" of *Poetical Sketches, Contemplation, King Edward the Third* and the *War Song*, and *The Couch of Death*.

20. *The Complete Works of Thomas Chatterton*, ed. Donald S. Taylor (Oxford: Clarendon Press, 1971), 1:410. McGowan notes the reference but makes nothing of it. The suggestion is strengthened by Blake's possible echoing in his line, "The laughing jest, the love-sick tale," of Chatterton's concluding quotation from Chaucer's *Sir Thopas:*

> Doe comme, he saied, mye mynstrales,
> And jestours for to tellen Tales,
> Anon in myne armynge.
> Of Romances yatte been royals,
> Of popes and of cardinals,
> And eke of love longynge. (1: 411)

Chatterton's spelling and the last line of the quotation are inaccurate. Was Blake aware of Chaucer's burlesque intent and thus intended, in "modern" fashion, to emulate that intent here?

21, *L'Allegro*, ll. 100-103. Ostriker observes that Blake's poem is in the meter of *L'Allegro* but characterizes it as "an attempt at genre-painting" (*Vision and Verse in William Blake*, p. 34).

22. Thomas Chatterton, "Antiquity of Christmas Games," *Works*, 1: 409, 410. In light of Chatterton's inclusion in these amusements of "tales of superstition" and "terrific stories" that "make the trembling audience mutter an Ave Maria," it is not entirely inconceivable that Blake thought of his *Fair Elenor* in these terms. That Chatterton borrowed from the Thomson passage I quoted is certain.

23. The idea, of course, is as hackneyed as it can be; but cf. Pope's *Essay on Criticism*, ll. 90-91: "Nature, like liberty, is but restrain'd / By the same laws which first herself ordain'd." The classic eighteenth-century statement, though, is Thomson's *Liberty*. Blake may have recalled his early "game" (perhaps even providing us a gloss on it) when he wrote in his Notebook some thirty years later, "If you play a Game of Chance know before you begin / If you are benevolent you will never win" (E502).

24. It may be no accident that the verse form, as well as the pattern of the concluding moral, are those of Gay's *Fables*. Gay, too, mentions Blindman's-Buff in his *The Shepherd's Week* ("Monday; or the Squabble," ll. 95-98).

25. Interestingly, as Wasserman points out, "most often the neoclassic Shakespearean poem took the form of parody," a taste to which literally hundreds of parodies of Shakespeare's soliloquies and of other familiar passages pay (one hesitates to say) eloquent testimony; see Wasserman's *Elizabethan Poetry in the Eighteenth Century*, pp. 84ff.

26. Northrop Frye, "The Road of Excess," in *The Stubborn Structure* (Ithaca: Cornell University Press, 1970), p. 166.

27. Ibid., pp. 167-68.

28. E632, 635. The last phrase is actually Reynolds's, to which Blake responded "True."

29. David Bindman, "Blake's 'Gothicised Imagination' and the History of England," in *Essays in Honour of . . . Keynes*, p. 33. See also Robert N. Essick, *William Blake, Printmaker* (Princeton: Princeton University Press, 1980), pp. 3-38.

30. Geoffrey Hartman, "Blake and the 'Progress of Poesy,'" in *William Blake: Essays for S. Foster Damon*, ed. Alvin H. Rosenfeld (Providence: Brown University Press, 1969), p. 59.

31. *Milton* 37:16-17 (E136) and 1:Preface: "We do not want either Greek or Roman Models if we are but just & true to our own Imagination" (E94).

32. *Ode on the Poetical Character*, ll. 6, 19-21. The Florimel story is in *FQ* IV,v. Paul Sherwin's analysis of the Spenser-Milton tradition as it, in many ways, swamps Collins is instructive here: see his *Precious Bane: Collins and the Miltonic Legacy* (Austin: University of Texas Press, 1977), chap. 2. Also pertinent are his admirable introduction to the entire issue (pp. 3-14) and his comments on "the Progress myth" (pp. 84ff).

33. *PR* IV,254-59, 334-42.

34. Hartman, "Blake and the 'Progress of Poesy,'" pp. 63, 65. Cf. Sherwin, *Precious Bane*, pp. 17-18, 25.

35. Geoffrey Hartman, "Romantic Poetry and the Genius Loci," *Beyond Formalism: Literary Essays 1958-1970* (New Haven: Yale University Press, 1970), p. 317.

36. Ibid., p. 319. See also p. 317 (including note 11).

37. *The Passions. An Ode for Music*, ll. 95-98, 115-18. Cf. Collins's "An Epistle: Addressed to Sir Thomas Hanmer, on His Edition of Shakespeare's Works," in which the "progress" of drama ceases with Shakespeare.

38. Hartman, "Romantic Poetry and the Genius Loci," pp. 323, 325. Cf. Sherwin's succinct summary of Collins's failure at the end of the poem: "His earlier vision of Evening . . . is displaced by the bluntly abstract discourse of an adjudicative persona. Miltonic solitude gives way to Horatian retirement, as Collins offers a portrait of a Thomsonian social Beulah of the 'enlightened few' who ward off the terror of the elements with sweet reasonableness" (*Precious Bane*, p. 123).

39. The quotations here, successively, are from *To the Muses* (ll. 13-14) and *Lycidas* (ll. 15, 4, 179-80).

40. Angus Fletcher, *The Transcendental Masque* (Ithaca: Cornell University Press, 1971), p. 166.

41. Blake's statement, "Imitation is Criticism," is part of his attack on Reynolds's advocacy of imitating "models" (E632), but, as I hope I have shown in this chapter (as well as in what follows), Blake's idea goes far beyond David Simpson's gloss on the Reynolds marginal comment: "Not only is all production original in the sense that subjective perspectives will tend to appear, but even the exact re-creation of an artifact will have a new meaning in a new context and at a different time"; see his *Irony and Authority in Romantic Poetry* (Totowa, N.J.: Rowman & Littlefield, 1979), p. 171. That is, to use Blake's own marvelous coinage, a piece of "Jehoshuan" reductionism (E504).

CHAPTER 3

1. Harold Bloom, "Dialectic in *The Marriage of Heaven and Hell*," *PMLA* 73 (1958): 501-4; Northrop Frye, *Fearful Symmetry* (Princeton: Princeton University Press, 1947), p. 237. Frye, however, uses the term *satiric* rather than *dialectic*. See also Martin Price's analysis of *The Marriage*, based at least in part on Bloom's, in *To the Palace of Wisdom* (Garden City, N.Y.: Doubleday, 1964), and Geoffrey Hartman's tacit assumption of the "dialectical Blake" in "Blake and the 'Progress of Poesy,'" in *William Blake: Essays for S. Foster Damon*, ed. Alvin H. Rosenfeld

(Providence: Brown University Press, 1969). For a recent attack on this critical tradition, most specifically on "Frye and his followers" (and pointedly including "Bloom, in his Blakean phase a true disciple of Frye"), and an advocacy of a return to the "tradition" of Leavis and E. D. Hirsch (in *his* short-lived "Blakean phase"), see Zachary Leader, *Reading Blake's "Songs"* (Boston and London: Routledge & Kegan Paul, 1981). The phrases quoted appear on pp. 134, 200.

2. In his "Narrative Structure and the Antithetical Vision of *Jerusalem*," in *Blake's Visionary Forms Dramatic,* ed. David V. Erdman and John E. Grant (Princeton: Princeton University Press, 1970), pp. 391-421, Henry Lesnick rather carelessly equates contrast, antithesis, contrariety, and dichotomy in a somewhat reductive discussion. Considerably better is Stuart Curran's "The Structures of *Jerusalem*," in *Blake's Sublime Allegory,* ed. Curran and Joseph A. Wittreich (Madison: University of Wisconsin Press, 1973), pp. 329-46; in his discussion of dialectical relationships within *Jerusalem* Curran associates "contrasts" with Manicheism (although, unfortunately, he calls them "antitheses").

3. W.J.T. Mitchell, *Blake's Composite Art* (Princeton: Princeton University Press, 1978), pp. 4, 10. Mitchell acknowledges that the first use of the term "composite"—though without development of its dialectical implications—is in Jean H. Hagstrum's *William Blake: Poet and Painter* (Chicago: University of Chicago Press, 1964). See also Northrop Frye's pioneering "Poetry and Design in William Blake," *Journal of Aesthetics and Art Criticism* 10 (1951): 35-42.

4. *Milton* 38:29-32, E138. The passage is a marvelous conflation of several of Milton's, as well as a satiric attack on the corporeality of the warfare in *Paradise Lost.* See, e.g., the smitings of Michael's sword in Book VI (as contrasted, Blake surely recalled, with Satan's being "smitten" only "with amazement" in *PR* IV,562); the tabernacle-body metaphor in *Paradise Regained* IV,599 as well as in *The Passion,* l. 17; and the several uses of "greater" in *Paradise Lost* (e.g., I,4; X,515; XII,242) and *Samson Agonistes* (ll. 1644-45). I shall have more to say of this last in my analysis of Blake's *Samson* in Chap. 7.

5. Mitchell, *Blake's Composite Art,* pp. 30-34.

6. Robert F. Gleckner, "Blake's Seasons," *Studies in English Literature* 5 (1965): 533-51. See also Hartman's "Blake and the 'Progress of Poesy.'"

7. See Geoffrey Hartman, "Reflections on the Evening Star: Akenside to Coleridge," in *New Perspectives on Coleridge and Wordsworth* (Selected Papers from the English Institute), ed. Hartman (New York: Columbia University Press, 1972), pp. 83-131. See also Paul Sherwin's analysis of Collins's ode, based in part on Hartman's critical paradigm, in *Precious Bane: Collins and the Miltonic Legacy* (Austin: University of Texas Press, 1977), esp. pp. 122-23.

8. David Wagenknecht, *Blake's Night: William Blake and the Idea of Pastoral* (Cambridge: Harvard University Press, 1973), pp. 33-37.

9. Similarly in *To Spring* "we" are invited to "taste" of Spring's "morn and evening breath."

10. Annotations to Reynolds, E648. The full annotation reads: "Demonstration Similitude & Harmony are Objects of Reasoning Invention Identity & Melody are Objects of Intuition." See Blake's severely pejorative use of the term in *The Book of Urizen* 23:4 (E80).

11. *A Vision of the Last Judgment,* E544. It is perhaps not insignificant that Blake never uses the word *contrast* as verb or noun—except in his comment on Chaucer's Canterbury pilgrims where he describes the Franklin as "contrasted with the Physician, and . . . with two Citizens of London" (E526). But, as his subsequent analysis makes clear, these "visions of . . . eternal principles" are far more complexly related to each other than his own verb suggests (E527f.). In fairness it should be noted that Blake doesn't use any form of the words "antithesis" or "dialectic" either.

12. In order 1:36 (E416), 3:30-31 (E419), 3:142-45 (E421-22), 6:50-52 (E429), 3:1-5 (E418). Robert N. Essick associates this passage, or rather claims that Blake associated it, with his graphic work, *Albion Rose,* an image that he regards as exemplifying "national and revolutionary themes" even in its earliest pencil-sketch versions. Moreover, Essick connects it with the print entitled *Our End is Come,* to which Blake later (in a color-print version) added the legend, taken

from the *Prologue Intended for a Dramatic Piece of King Edward the Fourth* (in the *Poetical Sketches* volume): "When the senses are shaken / And the soul is driven to madness Page 56"—the page number referring to the poem's place in the volume. The ominousness of war (revolutionary or otherwise), its destructiveness rather than its redemptiveness, thus seems apparent in both—rather than, as Essick prefers to see, the joyousness coincident with Albion's triumph over the "mills." See Essick's entire discussion in *William Blake, Printmaker* (Princeton: Princeton University Press, 1980), pp. 70-75, as well as my earlier discussion of the *Albion Rose* "problem" in Chapter 1.

13. Michael J. Tolley, "Blake's Songs of Spring," in *William Blake: Essays in Honour of Sir Geoffrey Keynes*, ed. Morton D. Paley and Michael Phillips (Oxford: Clarendon Press, 1973), p. 105. Thirty-five years ago Mark Schorer made the nicer observation that the line "And the vale darkens at my pensive woe" at the end of the first stanza of *When Early Morn* "gives the clue to the real meaning of the imagery in the second stanza of 'Mad Song,' where a dislocation of mind results in a dislocation of nature"—*William Blake: The Politics of Vision* (New York: Henry Holt, 1946), p. 403.

14. *PL* IV,598-99. See also VII,374-75; *PR* IV,426-27; and *Lycidas*, l. 187. Perhaps this is what McGowan means in saying the poem "could be seen to derive indirectly from Milton." He gives no evidence to support his speculation, and he is surely incorrect in regarding the "influence" as deriving from "bad imitations" of Milton—James D. McGowan, "Rising Glories: A Study of William Blake's *Poetical Sketches*" (Ph.D. dissertation, Rutgers University, 1968), p. 109.

15. *King Edward the Third*, Scene 3, ll. 221-22 (E423). Given his early knowledge of Milton's poetry, and his quite extraordinary "critical essay" on *Samson Agonistes* (the prose poem *Samson*), it is possible that in the first line of the couplet quoted Blake is alluding to Samson's angry retort to Dalila's peace-making offer ("Let me approach at least, and touch thy hand"):

> Not for thy life, lest fierce remembrance wake
> My sudden rage to tear thee joint by joint. (Ll. 951-53)

In the same context the Chorus remarks on womankind's "disalliance" of qualities in part as follows: "Or was too much of self-love mixed, / Of constancy no root infixed, / That either they love nothing, or not long?" (ll. 1031-33)

16. In an unduly neglected essay that originally appeared in the *Sewanee Review* in 1971, L. C. Knights perceptively links *When Early Morn* with *Fresh from the Dewy Hill, Memory, Hither Come*, and Miss Gittipin's song, "Leave O leave [me] to my sorrows," in *An Island in the Moon* (E454). Indeed he is the only critic to my knowledge who insists that these "songs" must be "taken together . . . to see what they are doing. . . . As they stand they form a series of contrasts, all, except 'Mad Song,' explicitly dealing with sexual love"; and, later on, he defines "contrast" tellingly as "a criss-cross of mutually enlightening insights." See his entire essay, "Early Blake," in *Explorations 3* (London: Chatto & Windus, 1976), pp. 52-63 (orig. pub. in *Sewanee Review* 79 [Summer 1971]).

17. Blake's phrase "rising glories" may also derive from Milton's *Nativity Ode*, in which Truth and Justice, "orbed in a rainbow," will (with Mercy) "return to men . . . like glories." In the same passage Mercy is described as having "radiant feet" (stanza 15). See also the "holy feet" of Spring in *To Spring*, and Tolley's discussion of "the idea of 'feet'" in "Blake's Songs of Spring," pp. 97-98.

18. The second line of the poem is taken from the Attendant Spirit's first description of the Lady's voice, "a soft and solemn-breathing sound" (*Comus*, l. 555).

19. This is not to deny the validity of most modern interpretations of the two poems as a "balanced contrast between the pleasures of two ways of life" as well as "a progression . . . from common and light experience to philosophic knowledge and religious insight"; see *A Variorum Commentary on The Poems of John Milton*, vol. 2 (part 1), ed. A.S.P. Woodhouse and Douglas Bush (New York: Columbia University Press, 1972), pp. 241ff. (the above quotation is from

p. 241), esp. Rosemond Tuve's observation (from her *Images & Themes in Five Poems by Milton*) that there is no problem of reconciling opposites, only "the comprehending of things different, and not in a pattern of antithesis but in a living and experiencing mind" (*Variorum Commentary*, pp. 261-62). Others, including recently Joseph A. Wittreich in *Angel of Apocalypse* (Madison: University of Wisconsin Press, 1975), regard "Milton's two lyrics [as] based on the themes of contraries and progression"; they "trace a journey from innocence to experience that culminates in the attainment of the prophetic strain" (p. 134; see also p. 78). In Wittreich's most recent analysis, *Visionary Poetics* (San Marino, Calif.: Huntington Library, 1979), his emphasis is increasingly on Milton's "progress" through the two "states" (see, esp., pp. 81-83). Perhaps, though, the most vigorous and persuasive case for Milton's "companion poems" "needing" each other is S. K. Heninger, Jr.'s, in "Sidney and Milton: The Poet as Maker," in *Milton and the Line of Vision*, ed. Wittreich (Madison: University of Wisconsin Press, 1975), pp. 57-95. See esp. p. 80. My own sense of *Blake*'s perception of the poems in the 1770s is that he regarded them, somewhat simplistically, as contrasting, not interacting—that is, the older-fashioned critical notion of day and night poems. *Songs of Innocence and of Experience* are well over a decade away.

20. The most recent misreading of both text and design of *Laughing Song* is Zachary Leader's in *Reading Blake's "Songs,"* pp. 52-53. Leader mentions *I Love the Jocund Dance* in connection with his reading of *The Ecchoing Green* (p. 81) but does not pursue the relationship.

21. So too is *PL* V,215-19, suggested by McGowan, "Rising Glories," p. 99. However, as Douglas Bush notes in *The Complete Works of John Milton* (Boston: Houghton Mifflin, 1965), "the 'wedding' of trees and vines . . . was traditional in antiquity" (p. 303n.)—and, one might add, in the Renaissance as well. Spenser uses it, for example, in *Virgils Gnat*, ll. 217-21, which may figure otherwise as well in Blake's poem, for beneath the trees in the same passage "a silver Spring forth powring / His trickling streames, a gentle murmur sent" (ll. 227-28).

22. There is, of course, a vast literature on neoclassic ideas of imitation, and I'm aware that I have treated it somewhat simplistically. But that is the way I believe the young Blake perceived it as well. For imitation as "re-creation" in the eighteenth century see Howard Weinbrot's *The Formal Strain* (Chicago: University of Chicago Press, 1969) as well as the ample bibliography incorporated in his footnotes. A convenient summary of the neoclassic "rationale of imitation" is in Emerson R. Marks, *The Poetics of Reason* (New York: Random House, 1968), esp. chaps. 2 and 4.

23. For a dissent from this view see McGowan, "Rising Glories," p. 90; he insists that both poems are about love.

24. *The Poems of William Blake*, ed. W. H. Stevenson (London: Longman, 1971), p. 9n. The rest of his note is a refreshing departure from the usual critical complacency of identifying the poem as "Elizabethan" or "Shakespearean" and letting it go at that.

25. Harold Bloom, *Blake's Apocalypse* (Garden City, N.Y.: Doubleday, 1963), p. 10.

26. Michael Phillips, "Blake's Corrections in *Poetical Sketches,*" *Blake Newsletter* 4 (1970): 40-47. Stevenson erroneously indicates the change in only one copy (*Poems of William Blake*, p. 12n.).

27. The parodic Har and Heva in *Tiriel* are in one sense figurative of decayed pastoral as well as of imbecilic infantilism (the reverse, perhaps, of the equally mad consistency of the speaker of *Mad Song* that is as much "protection" for him as Mnetha is for Har and Heva). Cf. Robert N. Essick's revealing analysis of the *Tiriel* sepia designs in "The Altering Eye: Blake's Vision in the *Tiriel* Designs," *Essays in Honour of . . . Keynes*, pp. 50-65.

28. M. H. Abrams, *Natural Supernaturalism* (New York: W. W. Norton, 1971), p. 260.

29. S. Foster Damon, *A Blake Dictionary* (Providence: Brown University Press, 1965), p. 451.

30. The question, I'm convinced, is rhetorical.

31. Michael Phillips, "Blake's Early Poetry," in *Essays in Honour of . . . Keynes*, pp. 11-12.

32. Ibid., p. 13. James D. McGowan does something similar with the poem, but he unaccountably ignores Phillips; see his "The Integrity of the *Poetical Sketches,*" *Blake Studies* 8 (1979):

137-38. For a distressingly inept presentation of precisely the opposite point of view (that is, the speaker *does* embrace this "different light") see F. R. Duplantier's "Method in Blake's 'Mad Song,'" *Blake: An Illustrated Quarterly* 13 (1979): 102-4.

33. See especially the descent to farce of "Old Tom of Bedlam," the breezy ribaldry of "The Distracted Puritan," the fashionable love-sickness of "The Lunatic Lover," "The Lady Distracted with Love," and "The Distracted Lover." This last is by Henry Carey, whose "Second Mad Song" (not included in the *Reliques*) seems to me closer to Blake's than any of these—though even about that I am less confident than I was in my "Blake and Satire," *The Wordsworth Circle* 8 (1977): 314. Duplantier, in the essay cited in note 32, also associates the poem with Carey's second mad song—as well as with *King Lear*, Herrick's *Upon Jane and Jone*, William Basse's "Forth from my dark and dismal cell" (also cited by Lowery, *Windows of the Morning*, p. 161), *The Tempest*, and several of Percy's other mad songs.

34. *PL* I,669. The bracketed words are from IV,976. This commonplace idea and language are raised above triteness by their particular Miltonic context as well as by their relationship to the other Milton passages cited.

35. Cf. *Macbeth* I,i,25-28: "As whence the sun gins his reflection / Shipwrecking storms and direful thunders break, / So from that spring whence comfort seem'd to come / Discomfort swells."

36. Schorer says Blake attempts "to compress into two stanzas the content of Milton's companion poems, 'L'Allegro' and 'Il Penseroso'" (*The Politics of Vision*, p. 403). I don't see that myself; but if it were true it would merely underscore my point about the simplicity of the contrasts here. Damon, in *William Blake: His Philosophy and Symbols*, p. 256, cites *As You Like It* II,iv,1-5, as the "obvious" source of the opening lines, and, at first glance, there seems a certain appropriateness in Shakespeare's lines (which Blake surely *did* recall): Amiens's invitation to some congenial soul to lie with him under the greenwood becomes the summoning of Memory to tune its notes to the speaker's mood. Blake's depersonalization of the subject, however, together with his closing glance at Jaques's melancholy and his departicularization of "No enemy / But winter and rough weather" into the vague "places fit for woe," bespeak his fundamental lack of interest in engaging meaningfully with his source.

37. With a bit more chiaroscuro and a personified Memory we have dullness deepened to tragedy in the figures of Har and Heva (and Mnetha) in *Tiriel*. In my discussion of *Memory, Hither Come* I have not invoked Blake's later distinction between the Muses as Daughters of Memory and as Daughters of Imagination, since there's no evidence that Blake made that distinction this early. In fact the word *memory* does not appear again in his verse or prose until *The Four Zoas*, and there is no clear implication in *To the Muses* of their association with memory. Nevertheless one must be struck by the fact that *Mad Song* energizes the vacuity of *Memory, Hither Come* into a verbal emblem of the Lockean passiveness of memory and the imaginative unproductiveness of its "inspiration." By itself, however, the poem seems to me incapable of assuming the status of shrewd, self-destructive irony.

38. David V. Erdman, *Blake: Prophet Against Empire*, rev. ed. (Garden City, N.Y.: Doubleday, 1969), p. 17. I am being a little unfair here, for in the context of *Blake: Prophet* his point about these poems is that they seem to reflect an England at peace.

39. Bloom, *Blake's Apocalypse*, pp. 9-10. A much more elaborate version of this thesis is developed by Robert E. Simmons and Janet Warner in a somewhat strained essay, "Blake's 'How Sweet I Roam'd': From Copy to Vision," *Neohelicon* 1 (1973): 295-304.

40. Damon, *William Blake: His Philosophy and Symbols*, p. 256. He did not change his mind in *A Blake Dictionary* (see p. 64 under "cage"). Without further comment, Phillips cites the cage in Chaucer's *Manciple's Tale*, lines 160-74. Chaucer's "tale of the crowe," however, has little to do with Blake's poem despite the verbal likenesses in this particular passage. See Phillips's "William Blake and the 'Unincreasable Club,'" *Bulletin of the New York Public Library*, 80 (1976): 17n.

41. *Fearful Symmetry*, p. 178.

42. *FQ* III,vi,introd., and III,vi,42. In addition "summer's pride" is Spenserian (*Shepheardes Calender*, "December," l. 73; *Teares of the Muses*, l. 235; *FQ* I,i,7) and "in the sunny beams did glide" echoes *FQ* II,v,2 (Blake's inattention to context exemplified by the fact that Spenser's description here is of Pyrochles). For other phrases in Blake's poem see also *Amoretti* LXXVII, *FQ* III,xi,2, and *Hymne of Heauenly Beautie*, line 1. "Summer's pride" is also found in Milton, of course (*PL* VII,478), but I should hesitate to go so far as Simmons and Warner in identifying Blake's rhyme words, "pride" and "glide" as the "sin and sinuous movement of the prince of lies himself," Milton's Satan ("Blake's 'How Sweet I Roam'd,'" p. 298).

43. Mona Wilson, *The Life of William Blake*, rev. ed. (New York: Oxford University Press, 1949), p. 30.

44. From Thomas Morley's *First Book of Ballets*, quoted by Margaret Lowery in *Windows of the Morning* (New Haven: Yale University Press, 1940), p. 224, n. 47. She cites several other examples as well from the sixteenth through the eighteenth centuries. In *The Visionary Company*, rev. ed. (Ithaca: Cornell University Press, 1971), Harold Bloom prefers Sir John Davies's *A Contention Betwixt a Wife, a Widow, and a Maid* (p. 17). Indeed the very ubiquity of the trope from Chaucer to Blake's own time argues against its symbolizing marriage in *this* poem.

45. Irene Chayes, "The Presence of Cupid and Psyche," in *Visionary Forms Dramatic*, p. 233. On the widespread use of the myth in art see also Jean H. Hagstrum's "Eros and Psyche: Some Versions of Romantic Love and Delicacy," *Critical Inquiry* 3 (1977): 521-42.

46. Frye, *Fearful Symmetry*, p. 178. Bloom adjudges it "the most beautiful" of the songs in the *Sketches* and "the most profoundly deceptive" (*The Visionary Company*, p. 17).

47. *Discoveries*, in *Ben Jonson*, ed. C. H. Herford & P. and E. Simpson, 11 vols. (Oxford: Clarendon Press, 1925-52), 8: 622.

CHAPTER 4

1. Northrop Frye, *Fearful Symmetry* (Princeton: Princeton University Press, 1947), p. 182; Hazard Adams, *William Blake: A Reading of the Shorter Poems* (Seattle: University of Washington Press, 1963), pp. 223-24; Bernard Blackstone, *English Blake* (Cambridge: At the University Press, 1949), p. 9. Other critics make similar observations of course.

2. Frye, *Fearful Symmetry*, p. 177.

3. Ibid.

4. For what we do know, see Geoffrey Keynes's essay, "Blake's Library," in *Blake Studies*, 2nd ed. (Oxford: Clarendon Press, 1971), and G. E. Bentley, Jr.'s section of *Blake Books* (Oxford: Clarendon Press, 1977) entitled "Books He Owned."

5. Rosemond Tuve, *Seasons and Months: Studies in a Tradition of Middle English Poetry* (Paris: J. Gamber, 1933), p. 58.

6. See Ralph Cohen, *The Art of Discrimination: Thomson's "The Seasons" and the Language of Criticism* (Berkeley and Los Angeles: University of California Press, 1964), p. 100n. The fact that Philips's poem is therefore an imitation of an imitation, and that Mills's poem is even once more removed from its origins, has an obvious bearing on my discussion of Blake's idea of imitation—see Chap. 2 above.

7. See also Cohen's magisterial "sequel," *The Unfolding of "The Seasons"* (Baltimore: Johns Hopkins Press, 1969).

8. See, e.g., John Cunningham's *Stanzas on the Forwardness of Spring* (1761), Mark Akenside's *Ode II: For the Winter Solstice* (1745), Elijah Fenton's *An Ode on the Right Honourable John Lord Gower* (1717), Richard Blackmore's *Creation* (esp. Book II, pub. in 1712), Abraham Cowley's *The Spring* (1647), William Broome's *Ode XXXVII: The Spring* (1740), William Shenstone's *Song XV: Winter 1764* (1764), Robert Riccaltoun's *A Winter's Day* (1726; rev. by David Mallet in 1740), Swift's (or Vanessa's) *Ode to Spring* (1767), Congreve's *Imitation of Horace, Ode IX, Lib. 1* (1692), Pope's *Pastorals* (1709). See also a variety of seasonal passages by Waller, Butler, Prior, Johnson,

Cowper, Dryden, Lyttelton, Dyer, and Gay in Johnson's *English Poets*. Especially noteworthy is the fact that in all of Dodsley only five poems to the seasons appear — by Frances Fawkes, Joseph Giles, Jabez Earl, and Martha Ferrar; and in the work of the Wartons, Young, Goldsmith, Parnell, Tickell, Collins, Byrom, and John Philips there are no poems addressed to the seasons (although Warton's Ode XI is entitled "On the Approach of Summer" and Parnell has an Anacreontic beginning "When Spring came on with fresh delight"). Finally, in the *Gentleman's Magazine*, that excellent index to the popular taste of the day in reader and poet alike, Calvin D. Yost in his *The Poetry of the "Gentleman's Magazine"* (Philadelphia: University of Pennsylvania, 1936) lists some 5,200 poems published between 1731 and 1780, of which only six are nature-pastoral poems on the seasons — and two of these are the Riccaltoun-Mallet and Swift-Vanessa poems listed above (p. 137).

9. Patricia Meyer Spacks, *The Varied God: A Critical Study of Thomson's "The Seasons"* (Berkeley and Los Angeles: University of California Press, 1959), p. 1.

10. Douglas Grant, *James Thomson: Poet of "The Seasons"* (London: Cresset Press, 1951), pp. 98-99. The lack of discrimination in Grant's statement, as between direct and indirect influence, is of course part of the problem, as I have indicated.

11. Margaret Lowery, *Windows of the Morning* (New Haven: Yale University Press, 1940), p. 152.

12. Yost, *The Poetry of the "Gentleman's Magazine,"* p. 137.

13. R. F. Jones, "Eclogue Types in English Poetry," *Journal of English & Germanic Philology* 24 (1925): 39-41. According to Joseph Warton, Thomson himself said that the first hint for his *Seasons* came from Pope's *Pastorals* — though Cohen cautions us that Warton's statement is "undocumented" (see *The Art of Discrimination*, p. 59). Warton's remark is in his *Works of Alexander Pope* (London, 1797), 1: 61n.

14. Jean H. Hagstrum, *The Sister Arts* (Chicago: University of Chicago Press, 1958), pp. 256-57.

15. Geoffrey Hartman, "Romantic Poetry and the Genius Loci," *Beyond Formalism: Essays 1958-1970* (New Haven: Yale University Press, 1970), p. 319.

16. John Aiken, *An Essay on the Application of Natural History to Poetry* (London, 1777), pp. 5-6.

17. Harold Bloom, *Blake's Apocalypse* (Garden City, N.Y.: Doubleday, 1963), p. 13. To his credit, however, Bloom goes on to distinguish sharply (and valuably) between Blake's personifications and Thomson's. For fuller discussions of this important distinction see, e.g., Hagstrum's *The Sister Arts;* Adams's *William Blake: A Reading of the Shorter Poems;* W. K. Wimsatt's "The Structure of Romantic Nature Imagery," in *The Verbal Icon* (Lexington: University of Kentucky Press, 1954); Chester F. Chapin's *Personification in Eighteenth-Century English Poetry* (New York: Columbia University Press, 1955); Rachel Trickett's "The Augustan Pantheon: Mythology and Personification in Eighteenth-Century Poetry," *Essays and Studies 1953* (London, 1953); and Earl R. Wasserman's "The Inherent Values of Eighteenth-Century Personification," *PMLA* 65 (1950).

18. Lowery, *Windows of the Morning*, p. 155.

19. Irene Chayes, "Blake and the Seasons of the Poet," *Studies in Romanticism* 11 (1972): 225-40.

20. Geoffrey Hartman, "Blake and the 'Progress of Poesy,'" in *William Blake: Essays for S. Foster Damon*, ed. Alvin H. Rosenfeld (Providence: Brown University Press, 1969), pp. 57-68. The quotation appears on page 66. Jean H. Hagstrum's "hint" is on page 76 of his *William Blake: Poet and Painter* (Chicago: University of Chicago Press, 1964).

21. See Hazard Adams, "Blake and the Philosophy of Literary Symbolism," *New Literary History* 5 (1973): 135-46.

22. My quotations from Chayes are, successively, to the following pages of her "Blake and the Seasons of the Poet": 228, 229, 231, 236, 239-40. Although I do not intend to invest it with undue significance, it is perhaps worth noting here that the stanzaic patterns of the four poems tend to establish *To Spring* and *To Winter* (both four stanzas of four lines each) as the "frame"

for *To Summer* and *To Autumn* (three stanzas of six lines each)—such a patterning in itself calling into question Chayes's proposed "revision" of the sequence as it stands. In any case Chayes's analysis seems to me virtually to admit that her "sequence" is really cyclically based after all.

23. Ibid., p. 237. My earlier views on *To Winter* are in "Blake's Seasons," *Studies in English Literature* 5 (1965): 533-51.

24. Michael J. Tolley, "Blake's Songs of Spring," in *William Blake: Essays in Honour of Sir Geoffrey Keynes,* ed. Morton D. Paley and Michael Phillips (Oxford: Clarendon Press, 1973), p. 96.

25. In her *Spenser's Allegory: The Anatomy of Imagination* (Princeton: Princeton University Press, 1976), Isabel MacCaffrey, as some other critics, reads Spenser's "conclusion" to *The Faerie Queene* as his acknowledgement of "the limits of art . . . a repudiating of fictions and a confession of the human limits of imagining. . . . Imagination, in the end, is part of Nature, and participates in its relentless alterations" (pp. 431-32). In his seasons poems (his "version" of Spenser) Blake is at some pains to confute this wisdom, as Los does later, firmly keeping his "Divine Vision in time of trouble" (*Jerusalem* 44:15, 95:20, E191, 252). MacCaffrey notes that it is, for Spenser, "all *things*" that "stedfastnes doe hate," but if Spenser's appeal to "Sabaoths sight" is but a prayer for what, as mortal poet, he can but approach in his poem, Blake has no such doubts about the final efficacy and achievement of his "fictions." If "that Sabaoths sight" is, as MacCaffrey says, "a notorious crux" in Spenser studies, it is, as she also says, certainly evocative of "an ultimate vision" (p. 432). Blake's Imagination is such an ultimate.

26. Blake, *A Vision of the Last Judgment* (E544). Interestingly MacCaffrey employs this entire passage to characterize the Mutabilitie Cantos as a whole, Spenser thus bringing "us the comfort of knowing that there is a sense-making order hidden in the apparent chaos of mortality" (*Spenser's Allegory,* p. 427).

27. *Jerusalem* 12:19 (E154). MacCaffrey notes that Mutabilitie and Nature "are, in the end, versions of the same principle" (*Spenser's Allegory,* p. 429). To Blake both are, appropriately, Vala.

28. For a similar view with respect to the structure of *The Four Zoas* see James C. Evans, "The Apocalypse as Contrary Vision," *Texas Studies in Literature and Language* 14 (1972): 313-28.

29. Tuve, *Seasons and Months,* p. 14. For Spenser's use of the tradition see also Appendix III of *The Faerie Queene, Book Three,* ed. F. M. Padelford (Baltimore: Johns Hopkins Press, 1934), pp. 340-52.

30. Quoted by Tuve, *Seasons and Months,* p. 63. In the *Secreta* winter as "oon olde wyfe . . . nakyd of cloþinge" should be compared to Blake's Winter whose "hand / Unclothes the earth, and freezes up frail life."

31. Tolley, "Blake's Songs of Spring," pp. 99, 101-2, 104. Tolley acknowledges that "Bloom was the first to notice the general connection" between The Song of Solomon and Blake's *To Spring*—in Harold Bloom, *Blake's Apocalypse* (Garden City, N.Y.: Doubleday, 1963), p. 15—but that Paul Miner, in "Visions in the Darksom Air: Aspects of Blake's Biblical Symbolism," *Essays for S. Foster Damon,* pp. 259ff., first developed the connections extensively. Although I find many of Miner's parallels distant and unconvincing, Tolley's analysis remains sound.

32. A possible interesting allusion to *Comus,* l. 744, in the context of Comus's attempt to persuade the Lady not to "hoard" her beauty nor to "let slip time" lest "like a neglected rose / It withers on the stalk with languished head."

33. Song of Solomon 3:11. Cf. *Epithalamion,* ll. 157ff.

34. *Ode: Written in the Beginning of the Year 1746,* ll. 3-4. This subsuming of the Collins echo is assisted by Spenser's "calling forth out of sad Winters night, / fresh loue . . .";

> For lusty spring now in his timely howre,
>   is ready to come forth him [i.e., Love] to receiue:

and warnes the Earth with diuers colord flowre,
to deck hir selfe, and her faire mantle weave.   (*Amoretti* IV)

The decking and dighting motif is of course a major part of the *Epithalamion* ritual, but Blake may also be taking a wry look at Thomson's "Industry" whose "hardened fingers deck the gaudy Spring" (*Autumn*, 1. 146).

35. Lowery, *Windows of the Morning*, p. 151; Pierre Berger, *William Blake: Poet and Mystic,* trans. D. H. Conner (New York: E. P. Dutton, 1915), p. 259; Bloom, *Blake's Apocalypse*, p. 15; Wimsatt, *The Verbal Icon*, pp. 113-14.

36. While "steeds" does not appear in the Bible (but cf. the "fierce horses" of the Chaldeans in Habakkuk 1:8), "fierce steeds" are ubiquitous in *The Faerie Queene,* the most memorable perhaps those of III,ix,22 ("proud Encelade, whose wide nosethrils burnd / With breathed flames").

37. Vv. 5-6. "Pass through" is a common biblicism.

38. Cf. Una's "allaying" of the "scorching heat" to foster Red Crosse's recuperation in *FQ* I,xi,50. In *Comus* "the gilded car of day / His glowing axle doth allay / In the steep Atlantic stream" (11. 95-97).

39. *PL* VII,214-25. Cf. X,300-301, where the "sun / Shot down direct his fervid rays." "Fervid" does not appear in Spenser, but his Phoebus regularly rides a "fiery carre" (*FQ* I,ii,1). In the last line of *To Summer* Blake may have borrowed the phrase "sultry heat" from Collins's *Eclogue the Fourth,* 1. 39.

40. Bloom, *Blake's Apocalypse*, pp. 15-16.

41. But see Chayes's argument to the contrary ("The Seasons of the Poet," pp. 235-36). Lowery's suggestion is in *Windows of the Morning*, p. 85.

42. In this light it is interesting to note (as Chayes does in part, though she deals with it inconsistently) that the musical motif moves from "full choir" in *To Spring* to "bards" in *To Summer* and thence to a piper in *To Autumn.* This reversal of innocence to experience to apocalypse may be yet another of Blake's methods of undermining the validity of the "normal" seasonal sequence and cycle. Despite its noise *To Winter* of course is silence—or perhaps, in Orwellian terms, unmusic. Cf. Roger Murray's observation that "in Eden, sequence is illusion, and the end of Blake's art is subversively to dispel that illusion"—"Blake and the Ideal of Simplicity," *Studies in Romanticism* 13 (1974): 102.

43. Blake encourages such a reading by including in *To Autumn* Spring-Morning, Summer-Noon, Autumn-Evening as if they were now indistinguishable or, more accurately, indissolubly one.

44. My word "merely" here obviously begs an important question: Did Blake see, for example, in *The Shepheardes Calender* Spenser merely articulating the states of human life, or did he recognize that, in William Nelson's basic formulation, "when the elements are considered in terms of time and change," for Spenser "the sought-for One becomes changeless eternity, not in opposition to the mutable but comprising it and arising from it"?— *The Poetry of Edmund Spenser* (New York: Columbia University Press, 1963), p. 34. My earlier comments on the Mutabilitie Cantos are, of course, a kind of answer to this question, and Nelson's implicit evocation of those cantos in the context of his discussion of the *Calender* tends to reinforce the applicability of my earlier "answer" here. Indeed Nelson has Spenser play even further into Blake's revisionist hands by adding that the "*Calender* does not bring us from the beginning of the year to its end; it is a circle rather than a straight line" (p. 37). I can only say here, then, that I believe this is precisely the way Blake read *The Shepheardes Calender*—as a sequence rolled into a cycle, both "wrong." My book-length study of Blake and Spenser, now in progress, will explore this question (and related questions) in detail.

45. Chayes, "The Seasons of the Poet," p. 236.

46. *FQ* VII,vii,30. For Blake's phrase "blood of the grape" Miner cites Deuteronomy 32:14

("Visions in the Darksom Air," p. 260) though he acknowledges it as a cliché. Cf. Genesis 49:11.

47. *Amoretti* LXI includes "the bud of ioy, the blossome of the morne," and the blossoms that "Flourish down the bright cheek of modest eve" may suggest Petrarchan roses. In Spenser, and elsewhere (especially in the Petrarchists), love's darts regularly "thrill" hearts (rarely, if ever, "veins"), and "tune thy jolly voice" is a conflation of a number of passages in *The Shepheardes Calender.* "Clustering" is used only once by Spenser (in *FQ* II,ix,16 there is a "clustering army" of gnats), but in the context of God's Creation "Forth flourished thick the clust'ring vine" in *PL* VII,320 (indeed the language and details of Milton's entire passage on the third day of Creation are at the center of Blake's poem — fortifying the Edenic all-inclusiveness and timeless union of *To Autumn*). The strewing of flowers at the end of stanza 2 is a commonplace in epithalamia; more strikingly pertinent is the allusion in Blake's "joy, with pinions light" roving "round / The gardens" to Spenser's butterfly-joy in *Muiopotmos* (see esp. ll. 33-34, 43-44, 161-64). Interestingly Autumn's "golden load" may owe something to Pope's *Autumn* pastoral, in which "Golden Fruits on loaded Branches shine" (l. 73).

48. Hagstrum, *The Sister Arts*, p. 261; Wimsatt, *The Verbal Icon*, p. 115.

49. Cf. MacCaffrey's observation on *The Faerie Queene:* "it contains the destructiveness that periodically ruins paradises, as well as the energy that persistently restores them" (*Spenser's Allegory*, p. 426). Blake's Los rebuilds Golgonooza, the city of art, with the rising of the sun each day.

50. Adams, "Blake and the Philosophy of Literary Symbolism," pp. 142ff.

51. Hartman, "Blake and the 'Progress of Poesy,'" p. 204.

52. For other interpretations, related to, yet different from mine, see Hartman's "Blake and the 'Progress of Poesy'" and Chayes's "The Season of the Poet."

53. Some measure of Blake's distance from Thomson may be seen in the latter's simple and unsymbolic waning of a late winter storm in his *Spring:* "The Northeast spends his rage, and, now shut up / Within his iron caves, the effusive South / Warms the wide air . . ." (ll. 143-45).

54. The insistent association of Blake's Winter with war (especially in light of the several war poems included in *Poetical Sketches*, not to mention that collocation consistently in his later mythology) has often been ignored by critics.

55. Cf. Chayes's very different reading in her "Seasons of the Poet," pp. 238-39. She cites a possible source (an "indirect literary allusion") for Blake's mariner in Book I of Macpherson's *Fingal;* see *The Poems of Ossian*, ed. Malcolm Laing (Edinburgh: A. Constable, 1805; reprint ed., New York: AMS Press, 1974), 1:37. There are, however, a number of other drowning and dying mariners in Ossian. More interesting to me are Blake's apparent borrowings from Macpherson's youthful *Death: A Poem* — e.g., "High from an iron car, the gloomy king / Outstretches o'er the world his hagard eye" (ll. 22-23); "War, man destroying, on an iron car, / Death's eldest brother, scours along the world" (ll. 227-28); and a passage on Peace who will "chace the jarring monster [i.e., War] down to hell" (l. 383). Cf. Edward Young's Night who "stretches forth / Her leaden sceptre o'er a slumb'ring world" (*Night Thoughts* I,19-20). But surely Blake's "wretch" stems ultimately from Lear's speech in Act III: "Poor naked wretches, wheresoe'er you are, / That bide the pelting of this pitiless storm" and are defenseless against "seasons such as these" (iv,28-32). Lear's desire to "show the heavens more just" (l. 36) is just right for Blake's irony in *To Winter.*

56. It is possible that Blake recalled Chatterton's implicit yoking of Winter with Milton's yelling monsters in his Ossianic *Kenrick;* see *The Complete Works of Thomas Chatterton*, ed. Donald S. Taylor (Oxford: Clarendon Press, 1971), 1: 274. He would also have known Chatterton's line in the *Battle of Hastings II:* "Now rybbd in steele he rages yn the fyghte" (l. 549). If indeed this is true, that would date *To Winter* (and perhaps all the seasons poems) no earlier than 1777 when the *Battle of Hastings* was first published in *Poems, Supposed to have been written at Bristol, by Thomas Rowley, and Others, in the Fifteenth Century*, ed. Thomas Tyrwhitt. In my judgment it may also be taken as one more piece of evidence calling into doubt 1777 as the date

of the latest of the *Poetical Sketches* poems.

57. It also had its worst eruption in history in 1766. Typhon, the fierce and monsterlike son of Gaea who was set afire by Zeus and buried alive under Mt. Aetna, is also identified with the Egyptian Set, author of all evil, who murdered and butchered Osiris, the symbol of creative forces in nature and of the imperishability of life. Thomson too associates Hecla with the "grim tyrant" Winter (*Winter*, ll. 886-87, 897).

58. Chayes, "The Seasons of the Poet," p. 239; Hartman, "Blake and the 'Progress of Poesy,'" pp. 202-3.

59. *The Four Zoas*, E301. Complementing Los's surrender to time, Enitharmon "will sing a Song of Death" and "of Vala" (Nature, Mutabilitie), "In slumbers of [her] night-repose, infusing a false morning" (ibid.).

CHAPTER 5

1. Margaret Lowery, *Windows of the Morning* (New Haven: Yale University Press, 1940), chap. 4.

2. Both quoted by S. Foster Damon, *William Blake: His Philosophy and Symbols* (1924; reprint ed., New York: Peter Smith, 1947), p. 254.

3. Lowery, *Windows of the Morning*, p. 98.

4. Ibid., p. 99.

5. Michael J. Tolley, "Blake's Songs of Spring," in *William Blake: Essays in Honour of Sir Geoffrey Keynes*, ed. Morton D. Paley and Michael Phillips (Oxford: Clarendon Press, 1973), pp. 99, 96.

6. Such a "reversal" is of course not original with Blake. He could have found it near at hand, had he needed to look, in Collins's first *Persian Eclogue* (ll. 13-14), for example, or in *FQ* I,v,2.

7. *Jerusalem* 97: 1-4, E254. Tolley as well notes this repetition ("Blake's Songs of Spring," pp. 98-99).

8. Milton here borrows from Spenser's Mutabilitie Cantos where the Howres are porters at "heauens gate" (*FQ* VII,vii,45). See also *PL* VII,192-206, where Christ the Son/Sun, "with radiance crowned," issues forth from Heaven which has "opened wide / Her ever-during gates."

9. Lowery, *Windows of the Morning*, pp. 99-100. Cf. Harold Bloom's analysis of the hunting trope in *The Visionary Company*, rev. ed. (Ithaca: Cornell University Press, 1971), p. 17.

10. *The Poems of Thomas Gray, William Collins, Oliver Goldsmith* (London: Longman, 1969), p. 483n.

11. Hewlett's suggestion and Damon's comment are in S. Foster Damon, *William Blake: His Philosophy and Symbols*, p. 254.

12. Chatterton perhaps knew of Cephalus when he wrote in his earliest imitation of Ossian, *Ethelgar*, "The morn awoke the sun, who, stepping from the mountain's brow, shook his ruddy locks upon the shining dew; Ælgar arose from sleep; he seized his sword and spear, and issued to the chace"—*The Complete Works of Thomas Chatterton*, ed. Donald S. Taylor (Oxford: Clarendon Press, 1971), 1: 254. Chatterton's amalgam of Milton, the Song of Solomon, and Ossian seems just right to be at least one of Blake's "sources." If so, the fact that Ælgar is killed by a wolf in his hunt merely deepens the ominousness implicit in an epithalamion which ends in a hunt. Blake would also have been aware of the Petrarchan perversion of love to war, which clearly he read unmetaphorically; and he may even have known Drayton's *Amour 35*, with its collocation of Diana, the hunt, and the lover (fatally wounded) "wallowing in his blood" and with "stone-cold lips" kissing "the blessed shaft" that did him in.

13. Lowery provides this reference (*Windows of the Morning*, p. 100).

14. John Butt, *The Augustan Age* (1950; London: Hutchinson, 1965), p. 96.

15. It seems an unlikely "fact," but I have been able to locate no other occurrences of "radiant morn" or "radiant morning" in the eighteenth century or earlier.

16. *PL* IV,644; VI,15; II,492; III,63, 690.

17. As concerned as he is with Collins's relationship to Milton, even Paul Sherwin regards the Miltonism of the eclogue as rudimentary; see his *Precious Bane: Collins and the Miltonic Legacy* (Austin: University of Texas Press, 1977), pp. 81-82.

18. Virtually all of Milton's successors follow him in this. E.g., in Ambrose Philips, Spring is "saluted" (*Second Pastoral*) and the lark "salutes the Eastern sky" (*Occasion'd by the Early Singing of a Lark*); in Pope's *Spring* pastoral, "*Philomel* salutes the Spring," and in *The Temple of Fame* "opening Buds salute the welcome Day." Should Blake have sought an "ancient" precedent, however, he would have found it in *FQ* I,xi,51.

19. *The Complete Poetical Works of John Milton*, ed. Douglas Bush (Boston: Houghton Mifflin, 1965), p. 64.

20. Harold Bloom seems to sense something of this inconclusiveness (though he does not pursue the point) when he describes *To Morning* as that "other Spenserian fragment" — *Blake's Apocalypse* (Garden City, N.Y.: Doubleday, 1963), p. 8. The "other" fragment is of course *To the Evening Star*.

21. Cf. Wordsworth's grand conception of words in his "Essay on Epitaphs": "If words be not . . . an incarnation of the thought, but only a clothing for it, then surely will they prove an ill gift"; as incarnations they "bestow power" — *Literary Criticism of William Wordsworth*, ed. Paul M. Zall (Lincoln: University of Nebraska Press, 1966), p. 125. The last-quoted phrase appears a number of times in *The Prelude* in related contexts, but I have borrowed it from the "Essay, Supplementary to the Preface" (Zall, p. 184).

22. *A Vision of the Last Judgment*, E555. Blake's letter to Thomas Butts of 2 October 1800 contains a familiar example of such an incarnation: "The Light of the Morning" shines "In particles bright," writes Blake, and each particle "was a Man / Human formd"; then as his eyes "Continue Expanding" the "Jewels of Light / Heavenly Men beaming bright / Appeard as One Man" (E683-84).

23. Are we *really* to recall the desperation of "O Winter! bar thine adamantine doors" and hence, as Blake seems to suggest in *The Four Zoas* passage I cited earlier, the adamantine gates of Sin and Death?

24. Irene Chayes, "Blake and the Seasons of the Poet," *Studies in Romanticism* 11 (1972): 228, 240.

25. Ibid., pp. 239-40.

26. Lowery notes the Spenser phrase, but one might also cite Collins's "rich-hair'd youth of morn" (*Ode on the Poetical Character*, l. 39) and his "bright-haired sun" (*Ode to Evening*, l. 5) — both probably deriving from Milton's "bright-hair'd Vesta" (*Il Penseroso*, l. 23). Since Blake's compound adjective does not appear elsewhere in his work shifting it from morning to the evening star is all the more significant in the relationships I am examining between his two diurnal poems. "Fair" is the most frequent adjective in the Song of Solomon and is a favorite of Spenser as well, but in neither is it combined with "haired." Given what I believe to be his very recent reading in Macpherson, and given the uniqueness of Blake's use of the compound adjective here, the "fair-haired morning" of Ossian's *Berrathon* is likely his immediate source — *The Poems of Ossian*, ed. Malcolm Laing (Edinburgh, 1805; reprinted New York: AMS Press, 1974), 1: 578ff. — especially since it appears twice in the passage. Macpherson used the adjective in *Fingal* as well (*Poems*, 1: 80), but of course he may well have had Milton and Collins in mind in both cases. Blake's sun resting on the mountains may also derive from Milton: "Mountains on whose barren breast / The laboring clouds do often rest" (*L'Allegro*, ll. 73-74).

27. Both are commonplaces of course, at least from Shakespeare and Sylvester through the eighteenth century, but again both phrases here are unique in Blake's works, arguing (I think) his steady reliance on Spenser and Milton. In the *Epithalamion* there are "thousand torches flaming bright" (i.e., stars; l. 410) and in the *Prothalamion* "Radiant *Hesper*" has "golden hayre" (l. 164); but I believe Blake had at least in the back of his mind Milton's "Son . . . / . . .with ra-

diance crowned / Of majesty divine" (*PL* VII,192-94). See also IV, 763-64, and V,168. For typical eighteenth-century noncontextualized borrowings of this language from Milton and Spenser see especially Akenside's *Pleasures of Imagination,* passim; his *To the Evening Star,* while not exactly dramatizing "How wide the Gulf & Unpassable between Simplicity & Insipidity" (Blake's *Milton* 30:title design; E128), does describe the large gulf between Blake's technique of significant allusion and the more rudimentary technique of his contemporaries and immediate predecessors. See also Geoffrey Hartman's difficult but rewarding essay, "Reflections on the Evening Star: Akenside to Coleridge," in *New Perspectives on Coleridge and Wordsworth* (Selected Papers from the English Institute), ed. Hartman (New York: Columbia University Press, 1972), pp. 83-131.

28. Cf. *Prothalamion,* ll. 96-97: "And let faire *Venus,* that is Queene of loue / With her heart-quelling Sonne vpon you smile." Milton's "smiles" are usually confined to morning; see, e.g., *PL* V,124, 164-68.

29. Blake's neutral and traditional use of curtains here is an eloquent reminder of how far his later mythology is from *Poetical Sketches,* for all of his many subsequent curtains are powerfully negative in their implications—see *A Concordance to the Writings of William Blake,* ed. David V. Erdman (Ithaca: Cornell University Press, 1967), 1: 424-25.

30. Blake's participial adjective is a fine example of his ability to revivify a word numbed, if not deadened, by overuse. Spenser does not employ it but, though not unusual in Shakespeare (see, e.g., *Midsummer Night's Dream* III,ii,61, and *Cymbeline* V,iv,28-29), it is rampant in eighteenth-century poetry: Pope, Collins, Thomson, Akenside, Thomas Warton, Philips, Shenstone, Gray, Mason, and Beattie, for example, all make abundant use of it—though never, to my knowledge, with eyes and certainly not with speaking or silence. Given Arthur Sherbo's careful investigation of *English Poetic Diction from Chaucer to Wordsworth* (East Lansing: Michigan State University Press, 1975) and his conclusion that Dryden "virtually codifies poetic diction," especially in his translations (pp. 107-8), it is likely that most, if not all, of these poets borrowed the word from him. Blake did not, building instead on Milton's example (as at least some of the above poets did as well, though without reference to Milton's contexts) in *On the Morning of Christ's Nativity,* where stars "in their glimmering orbs did glow / Until their Lord himself bespake, and bid them go" (ll. 75-76) and, in the same passage, "The stars with deep amaze / Stand fixed in steadfast gaze, / Bending one way their precious influence" (ll. 69-71). Furthermore both stanzas IV and V of the *Ode,* just preceding these lines, establish the silence of the universe at Christ's advent; and again the fact that Milton's is a morning scene underscores Blake's imaginative fusing of morning and evening in his twin poems. He also surely recalled *PL* II, 1034-37: "But now at last the sacred influence / Of light appears, and from the walls of heav'n / Shoots far into the bosom of dim Night / A glimmering dawn."

31. Once again we have a word unique in Blake's works, *timely.* While Spenser's frequent use of it in the *Epithalamion* is sufficient precedent (and one directly appropriate to Blake's poem), as is so often the case Blake blends it with Milton: in *PL* IV,614-16, "the timely dew of sleep / Now falling with soft slumbrous weight inclines" on the eyelids of Adam and Eve in a mini-essay on rest and repose after labor. Cf. *PL* V,646-47 and also *FQ* I,i,33.

32. *Epithalamion,* ll. 67-70. Evening and wolves are commonly yoked in the Bible, but Blake may be alluding as well to the close of Book I of *Paradise Regained* where "Night with her sullen wing" descends and "now wild beasts came forth the woods to roam" (ll. 500-502). See also *PL* IX,134, where Satan, referring to his power, says "destruction wide may range." For my discussion of Blake's lion glaring through the dun forest, see below.

33. The flocks covered with the dew of heaven is basically a biblicism, but cf. *Lycidas,* ll. 26-31. The "influence" of the stars, of course, is badly hackneyed by Blake's time, though it is rare to find it so starkly coupled with protection, except as that is implicit in the *Paradise Lost* passage cited in note 30. More often, as in the *Epithalamion* and elsewhere in *Paradise Lost* (IV,668-72), it is a nourishing, fructifying force, so used indeed by most poets from the Bible (Job 38:31) through Shakespeare to the end of the eighteenth century. Blake's "protect" thus garners unto

itself an especially ambiguous power in *To the Evening Star*, its negative aspect here perhaps the beginning of Blake's later suspicions about the nature of stars *and* their influence. See, e.g., his letter to Richard Phillips of 14 October 1807 (E706). The "gentlest influence" of Collins's Evening is thus poetic worlds away.

34. See Kathleen Raine, *Blake and Tradition*, 2 vols. (Princeton: Princeton University Press, 1968), and my review of it in *Virginia Quarterly Review* 45 (1969): 540-44.

35. Owen Barfield's comment is pertinent here: the imitator "imitates because he must have his idiom established, acknowledged, labelled in his consciousness as 'poetic' before he can feel that he is writing poetry"; the "great poet," on the other hand, gives "meaning to language," borrowed or not—*Poetic Diction* (1928; New York: McGraw-Hill, 1964), pp. 159-60. Cf. T. S. Eliot's distinction between those poets who imitate (they are "immature") and the mature ones who "steal"—*Selected Essays* (London: Faber, 1932), p. 206.

36. Mark Schorer, *William Blake: The Politics of Vision* (New York: Henry Holt, 1946), p. 404; the "grand Bardic manner" phrase is also Schorer's (p. 405).

37. Cf. Bloom's somewhat different interpretation of these distinctions in *The Visionary Company*, p. 8.

38. A. C. Hamilton, "Our New Poet: Spenser, 'well of English undefyled,'" in *A Theatre for Spenserians*, ed. Judith M. Kennedy and James A. Reither (Toronto: University of Toronto Press, 1973), pp. 101-23. Hamilton's splendid description of *The Faerie Queene* as "an elaborate dance of meanings" would not be entirely unapt (sans invidiousness) applied to Blake's two poems. See the earlier essay on *The Faerie Queene* in which he first broached this subject, in *Critical Approaches to Six Major English Works*, ed. Robert M. Lumiansky and Herschel Baker (Philadelphia: University of Pennsylvania Press, 1968), pp. 132-66.

39. Hartman, "Reflections on the Evening Star," p. 110.

40. H. M. Margoliouth, in *William Blake* (London: Oxford University Press, 1951), notes that the line is a painterly metaphor, its language only superficially imitative (p. 49).

41. Sherbo, *English Poetic Diction from Chaucer to Wordsworth*, p. 95. Sherbo justifies his ascription by saying that "although used only once or twice" by Milton, *dun* was "sufficiently unusual to remain associated with him."

42. See, respectively, *Ode Occasioned by the Death by Mr. Thomson* (l. 34), *Spring* (l. 1027; cf. *Autumn*, l. 952, where "umbrage" is both "dusk and dun") and *Summer* (ll. 1117 and 1687), *Rural Elegance* (l. 238), *Ode Written at Vale-Royal Abbey in Cheshire* (l. 22) and *Ode Sent to a Friend* (l. 91); *Elegy Written in the Year 1758* (l. 76). Dryden and Pope each use the word once, Shakespeare twice, but it appears in neither the Bible nor Spenser. Milton's other use in the poetry is "dun air" (*PL* III,72), but "dun shadows" appears in the prose *1st Prolusion*, which is subtitled, we should recall, "Whether Day or Night is the More Excellent."

43. *PL* IV,401-2. In *Paradise Regained* "the lion and fierce tiger glared aloof," though to be sure they are "meekened" here (in Thomson's sense) by the presence of Christ in their wilderness. *Glare* is a favorite of Chatterton's (but is never coupled with lions) as *dun* is of Macpherson, especially in *Temora*. Both clearly borrowed from Milton who may have found his paradigm in Spenser's giant Disdaine, whose "fiery eies / Like two great Beacons, glared bright and wyde" and who is associated with "overweening pryde" (*FQ* VI,vii,42). Arthur, we might recall, finally overcomes Disdaine, as Christ does Satan. Joseph Warton, interestingly, has a "glaring tiger" (*Ode to a Lady on the Spring*, l. 168).

44. See *Macbeth* III,iv,95-96. The ghost in *Hamlet* also "glares" (III,iv,125); see also *King Lear* III,vi,23.

45. Cf. Thomas M. Greene's interesting comment in his "Spenser and the Epithalamic Convention," *Comparative Literature* 9 (1957): "The ominous associations of darkness are evoked again . . . in [Spenser's] last stanza. . . . Here it is not only the marriage but the whole of human experience which is menaced by the night's sad dread. Thus the threat of disaster, the irrational fear of vaguely specified suffering, hovers faintly over the poem, lending particular urgency to

the concluding prayers. It is perhaps not too fanciful to relate the wolves of the fourth stanza to this cluster of night associations" (p. 227). Schorer described the end of *To the Evening Star* as "vision" darkened "from idyllic reverie to observation of natural fact" (*The Politics of Vision*, p. 415); but see David Wagenknecht's more sophisticated (and fine) analysis of the poem in *Blake's Night: William Blake and the Idea of Pastoral* (Cambridge: Harvard University Press, 1973), pp. 33-36.

46. Bloom could not be further off the mark in describing Blake's evening star as "a pastoral deity" (*Blake's Apocalypse*, p. 8)—though, to be sure, he does find in *To Morning*, somewhat cryptically, "the classical Aurora . . . becoming the first of Blake's elusive and demonic nature goddesses, sadistic in her virginity, and mockingly cyclic in her effect on mankind" (p. 9).

47. Hartman, "Reflections on the Evening Star," pp. 91-92.

48. Ibid., p. 110.

49. Bloom, *The Visionary Company*, p. 17.

50. Wagenknecht, *Blake's Night*, p. 31.

51. Harold Fisch's reminder is apropos here: Blake's "Los is the god of history, but he is also paradoxically the god of that poetic inspiration which in a timeless moment renders all history nugatory"—"Blake's Miltonic Moment," in *William Blake: Essays for S. Foster Damon*, ed. Alvin H. Rosenfeld (Providence: Brown University Press, 1969), p. 53. History is of course sequence, some say cyclical; and, as Blake said, "The Ruins of Time builds Mansions in Eternity" (ltr. to William Hayley, 6 May 1800, E678).

52. Northrop Frye, *The Stubborn Structure* (Ithaca: Cornell University Press, 1970), pp. 167-68.

53. Millar MacLure's observation with respect to Spenser's preoccupation with the world's vanity is nicely relevant here: from the "ruins of time," he says, only new seeds of future ruins sprout; for "the vegetable creation is renewed" according to "Nature's clock," which "is circular." See his "Spenser and the Ruins of Time," in *A Theatre for Spenserians*, pp. 14-15.

CHAPTER 6

1. Alicia Ostriker, *Vision and Verse in William Blake* (Madison: University of Wisconsin Press, 1965), pp. 33, 34.

2. Northrop Frye, *Fearful Symmetry* (Princeton: Princeton University Press, 1947), pp. 182-84. Cf. Earl R. Wasserman's conclusion, in *Elizabethan Poetry in the Eighteenth Century*, Illinois Studies in Language and Literature, vol. 32, nos. 2-3 (Urbana: University of Illinois Press, 1947), that Shakespeare's blank verse was rarely imitated in the eighteenth century, and then almost always in parodies of famous soliloquies and other familiar passages (pp. 84ff.); also Bernard Groom's perception, in *The Diction of Poetry from Spenser to Bridges* (Toronto: University of Toronto Press, 1955), that the reason for Shakespeare's relatively small influence on the diction of eighteenth-century poets was its less well-defined (than Spenser's or Milton's) idiosyncracy (p. 149). As Coleridge noted, "Shakspere's poetry is characterless; that is, it does not reflect the individual Shakspere; but John Milton is in every line of 'Paradise Lost'"—*Lectures and Notes on Shakspere and Other English Poets*, ed. T. Ashe (London: George Bell, 1890), p. 532.

3. See Chap. 5 of Margaret Lowery, *Windows of the Morning* (New Haven: Yale University Press, 1940). Others have noted this general likeness as well, but have been equally unsuccessful in aligning Blake's work firmly with any one of Shakespeare's plays. My quotation is from Ostriker, *Vision and Verse in William Blake*, p. 33.

4. Frye, *Fearful Symmetry*, p. 179; David V. Erdman, *Blake: Prophet Against Empire*, rev. ed. (Garden City, N.Y.: Doubleday, 1969), p. 68.

5. *A Descriptive Catalogue*, E541. See Anthony Blunt's early "non-historical" interpretation of this painting in *The Art of William Blake* (New York: Columbia University Press, 1959), p. 9, and Erdman's corrective in *Prophet Against Empire*, p. 47. Recently Martin Butlin has argued, in "A Newly Discovered Watermark and a Visionary's Way with His Dates," *Blake: An Illustrated*

Quarterly 15 (1981), that Blake was not referring in his comment to "the small, immature example from his series of watercolors of subjects from English history . . . —that version is easily reconcilable with a date of c. 1779—but the larger, more finished and more accomplished version in the Tate Gallery that seems to date from about 1793" (p. 101). Such a judgment, however, does not invalidate the fact that the early watercolor series on British history is in itself evidence of Blake's early pondering of the relationship between history and art.

6. *A Descriptive Catalogue*, E534; ltr. to Thomas Butts, 22 Nov. 1802 (E691). Blake's model for this focus on the "spiritual agency" of history is, as he tells Butts, "Michall Angelo" (see my first chapter for further discussion of the point)—that is, *the* Artist. Supposing "Public RECORDS to be True" is "contemptible" (Annotations to Bishop Watson's *An Apology for the Bible*, E607); and, in a telling comparison, "If Homers merit was only in . . . Historical combinations" overlaid with "Moral sentiments he would be no better than Clarissa" (Annotations to Boyd's *Historical Notes* on Dante, E623). As "histories" even the Bible and Milton were suspect: thus Blake's Job series is *his* "History of Job," and the root problem of *Paradise Lost* inheres in Milton's "angelic" succumbing to history and, as a consequence, suffering the blurring, even on occasion the blotting out, of spiritual agency. The most recent discussion of Blake and history, an excellent one, is Leopold Damrosch, Jr.'s, in *Symbol and Truth in Blake's Myth* (Princeton: Princeton University Press, 1980), pp. 339-44.

7. *A Descriptive Catalogue*, E536. His watercolor of this title Blake describes as "The Horse of Intellect [i.e., Imagination] . . . leaping from the cliffs of Memory and Reasoning; it is a barren Rock: it is also called the Barren Waste of Locke and Newton" (E536). Robert N. Essick's essay, "Preludium: *Meditations on a Fiery Pegasus*," in *Blake in His Time*, ed. Essick and Donald Pearce (Bloomington: Indiana University Press, 1978), pp. 1-10, is thus doubly apropos here. Among his comments on Blake's art is this: rather than being "illusionistic," that is representational, it is, even when it seems most representational, "allusionistic," requiring "us to see as part of its form the concepts motivating its execution. Blake is always willing—indeed, eager—to violate even the most deeply rooted conventions of form, color, and space to call into question those very conventions and lead us to his own disquieting propositions about rational space and time, the ratio of the fallen senses, and Newton's world" (p. 7). I have serious doubts, however, which I shall expand on later, about Essick's interpretation of Blake's *Fiery Pegasus* design itself.

8. David Bindman, "Blake's 'Gothicised Imagination' and the History of England," *William Blake: Essays in Honour of Sir Geoffrey Keynes*, ed. Morton D. Paley and Michael Phillips (Oxford: Clarendon Press, 1973), pp. 41-42. It should be noted, however, that Blake's rather peaceful watercolor of Brutus's landing hardly prepares one for the bloodiness of that landing in *King Edward the Third*. Cf. *A Descriptive Catalogue*, E533 (paragraph 1). Professor Paley has suggested to me that Blake may have had in mind as well Colley Cibber's version of *King Lear*.

9. E534. For Blake's most extended comment on his distinctive idea of miracle in this sense, see his annotations to Watson's *Apology* (E606); also *Milton* 22:60-62 and 23:1-2 (E117).

10. Erdman, *Blake: Prophet Against Empire;* the quoted passages appear, respectively, on pp. 68, 63, 69, 74. All subsequent critics of *King Edward the Third* follow Erdman's analysis with little variation. Erdman also notes that Edward III was regularly cited in the eighteenth century "as the archetype of aggressive, frustrated 'ambition'" (p. 65); and later on Martin K. Nurmi, in *William Blake* (London: Hutchinson, 1975), reemphasizes Erdman's important citation of Blake's comment near the end of his life (with respect to his own "visionary portrait" of Edward III) about Edward's "butcheries"—a charge to which, Blake said, the king himself replied by saying that his "carnage" was merely "a trifle unworthy of notice" (p. 43; Erdman, pp. 67-68).

11. Bindman, "Blake's 'Gothicised Imagination' and the History of England," p. 44. Erdman makes abundant use of this list as well.

12. William Halloran, "*The French Revolution:* Revelation's New Form," in *Blake's Visionary Forms Dramatic*, ed. David V. Erdman and John E. Grant (Princeton: Princeton University Press, 1970), pp. 31-32. See also David Halliburton, "Blake's *French Revolution:* The *Figura* and

Yesterday's News," *Studies in Romanticism* 5 (1966): 158-68.

13. Harold Bloom, *Blake's Apocalypse* (Garden City, N.Y.: Doubleday, 1963), p. 66; Halloran, "*The French Revolution:* Revelation's New Form," p. 31n.

14. Martin Bidney, "*Cain* and *The Ghost of Abel:* Contexts for Understanding Blake's Response to Byron," *Blake Studies* 8 (1979): 145, 146.

15. E268. Much of Truman Guy Steffan's exhaustive introduction (which he entitles "Chronicle, Art, and Thought") to his variorum edition, *Lord Byron's "Cain"* (Austin: University of Texas Press, 1968), pp. 3-150, is pertinent to Bidney's and my (briefer) discussion, especially the sections on "Byron's View of His Play" (pp. 6-12), "Byron's Dramatic Theory" (pp. 18-25), "The God of This World" (pp. 26-29), and "The Re-creation of Genesis" (pp. 66-76). That *Cain* was not only biblical but Miltonic as well, that its verse was immediately (and often) attacked as mere prose poetry, and that it provoked a public furor over its unorthodoxy and blasphemy would have been more than enough to claim Blake's immediate and fascinated attention.

16. George Steiner, *The Death of Tragedy* (New York: Hill & Wang, 1961), p. 202, noted by Bidney, "*Cain* and *The Ghost of Abel*," p. 147. Along with Bidney, neither Steiner nor Steffan say much, if anything, about *Byron's* idea of a play as a "Mystery"—and, more disappointingly, Bidney is silent about the form of Blake's "play." Steffan merely calls it, alternatively, a "playlet" and a "dialogue" (*Lord Byron's "Cain,"* pp. 323-24).

17. Bidney, "*Cain* and *The Ghost of Abel*," p. 149. This "imprisonment," Blake clearly saw, was the inevitable result of Byron's being, in Bidney's words, "a seer of the world of Generation, who has revealingly set forth its fundamental polarities," but who was unable to effect, or even envision, "a restored and reorganized imaginative Eden or 'Eternity'" (p. 165).

18. This last phrase I have borrowed from Blake's account of "Fables" and "Allegories" that fall short of "The Hebrew Bible & the Gospel of Jesus," which "are not Allegory but Eternal Vision or Imagination of All that Exists" (*Vision of the Last Judgment*, E544). *Cain* thus would fall into the same category as *Pilgrim's Progress* and "the Greek Poets" (ibid.).

19. Damrosch, *Symbol and Truth in Blake's Myth*, pp. 356, 355. It is at least interesting that Byron pronounced Shakespeare as "the worst of models—though the most extraordinary of writers" (*Byron's Letters and Journals*, ed. Leslie A. Marchand, vol. 8 [Cambridge: Harvard University Press, 1978], p. 152).

20. Cf. Harold Fisch's observation that "Blake's poetry is the very antithesis of the dialogic"—"Blake's Miltonic Moment," in *William Blake: Essays for S. Foster Damon*, ed. Alvin H. Rosenfeld (Providence: Brown University Press, 1969), p. 54. Damrosch has some interesting comments on Blake's apparent preference for Macpherson's Ossianic prose poetry over Shakespeare's blank verse, in *Symbol and Truth in Blake's Myth*, pp. 356-57, 367n.

21. Rather surprisingly S. Foster Damon vigorously denies Milton's influence on the play, citing only one line (3:290) as showing "at all the influence of that poet"—*William Blake: His Philosophy and Symbols* (1924; reprint ed., New York: Peter Smith, 1947), p. 260.

22. Frye, *Fearful Symmetry*, pp. 180, 182.

23. *The Bard*, ll. 1-7. It is probably a coincidence that Gray's opening line echoes one from Nicholas Rowe's *Jane Shore*, whose "penance," we recall, Blake depicted in a circa 1779 watercolor. The echo is pointed out by Roger Lonsdale in *The Poems of Thomas Gray, William Collins, Oliver Goldsmith* (London: Longman, 1969), p. 183n. Gray's line 5 is also borrowed by Blake for lines 3-4 of Edward's first speech.

24. Erdman, *Prophet Against Empire*, p. 48.

25. Lowery, *Windows of the Morning*, p. 112. Cf. Nurmi, *William Blake*, p. 42.

26. Blake's technique of "significant allusion" is seen at its best here. At its worst it can totally compromise his intention, as in his borrowing of Milton's distinctive word *enerve*, meaning to enervate, which occurs in the context of Belial's suggestion that Satan tempt Christ by setting "women in his eye and in his walk" (*PR* II,165,153). Blake clearly intends the word to mean ennerve (*Edward the Third* 1:11).

27. *PL* II,565-69, 546ff. James D. McGowan in his 1968 Rutgers University dissertation, "Rising Glories: A Study of William Blake's *Poetical Sketches*," noted the triple-steel allusion (p. 137); aside from Erdman's his is the most elaborate analysis of *Edward the Third* we have (pp. 121-74). Chatterton also borrowed Milton's phrase but disguised it in his Rowleyan language: "In trebled armoure ys theyre courage dyghte" (*Ælla*, 1. 867).

28. *PL* VI,801-4. Cf. Raphael's characterization of that cause in VI,381-84: "For strength from truth divided and from just, / Illaudable, naught merits but dispraise / And ignominy, yet to glory aspires / Vainglorious, and through infamy seeks fame." Blake alludes again to the "Faithful . . . warfare" of Christ's army in his *Samson;* see below, Chap. 7.

29. *Edward the Third* 6:49-50; *PL* I,360-63.

30. *PL* VII,194, 196; *Edward the Third* 1:20, 24-25. Earlier Satan curses the "full-blazing sun" that sits "high in his meridian tow'r" with "surpassing glory crowned" like "the god / Of this new world" and "at whose sight all the stars / Hide their diminished heads" (*PL* IV,29-35); and we should recall that in the beginning "all the Spirits of heav'n" were "Crowned . . . with glory" equally (V, 837-39).

31. *PL* X,409; *King Edward the Third* 1:21; *PL* II,795; *Edward the Third* 1:8. As I noted earlier, Blake's Winter, "driv'n yelling to his caves" derives from the same passage on Sin and Death as does Chatterton's winter yelling "through the leafless grove" in *Kenrick*. Cf. *PR* IV,629.

32. *Edward the Third* 1:32-34; *PL* V,744-45, and III,716-18, 720. Cf. also V,470-77.

33. *PL* X,444-47, 449-53. Milton clearly alludes here to his earlier passage on "glory" as "the blaze of fame" and "the people's praise" (III,47-48).

34. Other allusions in this act are to Satan's legions, fast bound inside Hell's gates, raging "against the Highest" and "hurling defiance toward the vault of heav'n" (*PL* I,666-69; cf. Blake's 11. 19-20); and to Milton's phrase for the havoc in heaven, "grim war" (VI,236; cf. Blake's 1. 53 in which "grim war" laughs as Milton's "dogs of hell" do in Book X, lines 614, 626).

35. Erdman, *Prophet Against Empire*, p. 69.

36. Ibid., pp. 72-73.

37. *PL* VI,844-45, 862. That Blake aligned his *War Song* with Milton's ultimate conflict is further suggested by his phrase "Heaven's cause" in the last stanza. This, with the spatial reversal (Satan's fall, Blake's Englishmen rising), is in itself an effective exposing of the fundamental error of the Minstrel's prophecy.

38. Cf. Frye's speculation about Blake's choice of Edward IV as "the sign of a swing from mercantilist Whiggery to the [political] radicalism" of "the French and American revolutions" (*Fearful Symmetry*, p. 180).

39. McGowan notes that the *Prologue* is "purely the language of the Biblical prophets" and cites Nahum 1, Malachi 2:2, and Revelation 6:17 ("Rising Glories," p. 170); Erdman regards the speaker as "almost unhinged with a prophetic wrath against the 'Kings and Nobles' who have caused a sinful war" (*Prophet Against Empire*, p. 16) but cites no biblical parallels.

40. My italics. But see *PL* X,33,780. The "wrath of Jove / Speaks thunder" in *Comus*, ll. 803-4, but he, of course, is traditionally a hurler of thunderbolts, thunderclaps, and assorted other thunderings.

41. Isaiah 43:10-11. The "I, even I" locution—which is found also in Genesis (6:17), Leviticus (26:28), Deuteronomy (32:29), Judges (5:3), as well as extensively in the prophets—Blake later borrowed (and twisted) for his Urizen (see *The Book of Urizen* 4:19, E71).

42. Erdman is the only one to have noticed these ambiguities (he calls them flatly "contradictions"), which he says "will never be entirely resolved"—at least in "the inconsistent theology of the *Poetical Sketches*" (*Prophet Against Empire*, p. 29).

43. *PL* VI, 711-14. Cf. the bows and arrows of the four zoas in the apocalyptic close of *Jerusalem:* although they "flame" and "thunder," "breathe" and shine,"

the Bow is a Male & Female & the Quiver of the Arrows of Love,

Are the Children of this Bow: a Bow of Mercy & Loving-kindness: laying
Open the hidden Heart in Wars of Mutual Benevolence Wars of Love
(97:12-14, E254)

If it is indeed true, as John R. Knott, Jr., says, in *Milton's Pastoral Vision* (Chicago: University of Chicago Press, 1971), that "the tenor of Protestant commentaries of Revelation in the sixteenth and seventeenth centuries helps to explain the military aspect of Milton's heaven and the harshness of Satan's defeat" (p. 73), this or any other explanation clearly would not have satisfied Blake.

44. Ll. 27-28; Douglas Bush, ed., *The Complete Poetical Works of John Milton* (Boston: Houghton Mifflin, 1965), p. 340n.

45. One is reminded here of Heaven's smiling to drive Winter back to his subvolcanic cave in Blake's *To Winter.* See my comments on that smile above, p. 69.

46. Intent upon establishing *Gwin* as "an imaginative interpretation of the American Revolution," Erdman translates the "nations of the North" as North America (*Prophet Against Empire*, pp. 22, 20). Nurmi seems to me more nearly correct in saying that *Gwin* is "set obscurely in Norway at some mythological time" (*William Blake*, p. 42). The latter interpretation may be corroborated not only by the fact that Urizen's habitat, in Blake's later mythology, is in the north (as is Milton's Satan's) but by Blake's later redaction of the situation in *Gwin*, in *The Grey Monk* (noted by Erdman, p. 419).

47. I cannot agree with Erdman that "the insurrectionary acts of the people are subordinated to the heroic deeds of their Deliverer" (*Prophet Against Empire*, p. 28). In fact the deliverer, Gordred, *does* virtually nothing in the poem except "appear" (l. 63) and divide Gwin's head (l. 108); in between, though Gwin appears in some six lines, the entire poem is given over to the indiscriminate bloodletting.

48. Chatterton is omnipresent in the poem, as Lowery (*Windows of the Morning*, Chap. 7), Erdman, and others have shown, but despite the obvious borrowing from the *Bristowe Tragedie* (ll. 161-64) in Blake's second stanza it is Chatterton in his Ossianic, not Rowleyan, role. What Blake has done, to put it crudely, is to boil down Chatterton's *Godred Crovan* (or at least aspects thereof) into the poetic form of the *Bristowe Tragedie*. Not really interested at all, if he even knew, that *Godred* deals with "a two-day battle on the Isle of Man sometime not long after 1066" (*The Complete Works of Thomas Chatterton*, ed. Donald S. Taylor [Oxford: Clarendon Press, 1971], 2:988), Blake borrows a number of the Ossianic rhetorical and imagistic formulae Chatterton adopts (as well as the essential confusion in *Godred* as to who's fighting whom for what), severely condenses Ossian's windiness, and thus forges a rather mature critical redaction of his two bardic predecessors. In addition to these formulae and the name Godred, Blake also found in Chatterton's poem Harald the Swift (called "the wolf of Norway"), the name Egwin (from which he took his own titular character), and the phrase "sons of Norway" (cf. *Gwin*, l. 109). The "tall ghost of Barrathon" of line 53 may owe something to MacPherson's poem *Berrathon*, but I'm inclined to agree with Mark Schorer's early caution about overestimating Macpherson's role in Blake's works, even their style; see Schorer's *William Blake: The Politics of Vision* (New York: Henry Holt, 1946), pp. 405-6, as well as the implicitly similar conclusion of Roger Murray's "Blake and the Ideal of Simplicity," *Studies in Romanticism* 13 (1974): 89-104.

49. Frye, *Fearful Symmetry*, pp. 181-82. This in large measure accounts for the total absence of Spenser in those poems, as well as the constant flirting with Thomson's *Liberty* and other poems of that ilk. Macpherson's wars and Chatterton's imitations of them may indeed have implicit "causes" of one sort or another, but their overriding impact is one of wild irresponsibility and feats of derring-do for their own sakes. On the other hand, the Thomsonian wars in the name of liberty are waged under the banner of "holier than thou" (see *Jerusalem*, Plate 52, E198-99) and end with equal effectiveness in the crucifixion of Christ (see *I Saw a Monk of Charlemaine* in *Jerusalem* 52, E199-200). Only "Jerusalem is called Liberty among the Children of Albion"

(*Jerusalem* 54:5, E201). Spenser's endless conflicts, fully as gory as Ossian's and Macpherson's, in some way must have appeared to Blake, for all their moral implications, as exempla of the "Moral Law" *not* "from the Gospel rent"—a vast pageant, in other words, of mental strife in which "the fierce conflicts of earth are heard faintly as from a distance"—Ernest de Selincourt, *The Poetical Works of Spenser*, ed. J. C. Smith and de Selincourt (London: Oxford University Press, 1912), p. lxvii.

CHAPTER 7

1. David Wagenknecht, *Blake's Night: William Blake and the Idea of Pastoral* (Cambridge: Harvard University Press, 1973), p. 147. He characterizes the poem further as hanging "uneasily somewhere between Job and Ossian." Both are generally accepted judgments among Blake critics.

2. John Ehrstine, *William Blake's "Poetical Sketches"* (Pullman: Washington State University Press, 1967), p. 36.

3. David V. Erdman, *Blake: Prophet Against Empire*, rev. ed. (Garden City, N.Y.: Doubleday, 1969), p. 78. Other aspects of Erdman's analysis (pp. 77-79) seem to me in error as well.

4. See Wagenknecht, *Blake's Night*, pp. 33-51.

5. The most recent analysis of Blake's *Night*, Zachary Leader's in *Reading Blake's "Songs"* (Boston and London: Routledge & Kegan Paul, 1981), pp. 122-29, is curiously uncompelling and inconclusive (except as it regards "the earthly" to be really "divine" and "the divine earthly" in both text and design). Leader studiously ignores Wagenknecht's important reading.

6. A neglected possible "source" for Blake's conception in these two poems is Thomson's *Autumn:*

> Drear is the state of the benighted wretch
> Who then bewildered wanders through the dark
> Full of pale fancies and chimeras huge;
> Nor visited by one directive ray
> From cottage streaming or from airy hall.
> Perhaps, impatient as he stumbles on,
> Struck from the root of slimy rushes, blue
> The wild-fire scatters round, or, gathered, trails
> A length of flame deceitful o'er the moss;
> Whither decoyed by the fantastic blaze,
> Now lost and now renewed, he sinks absorbed,
> Rider and horse, amid the miry gulf—
> While still, from day to day, his pining wife
> And plaintive children his return await,
> In wild conjecture lost.   (Ll. 1145-59)

Read in the context of Blake's two *Songs* the passage is a veritable epitome of his habitual exasperation with Thomson. Note particularly Thomson's attribution of tears (presumably) only to the unlost wife and children. Cf. Wagenknecht's discussion of "the language of tears" in Blake's *Night* (pp. 65ff.) and my *The Piper and the Bard: A Study of William Blake* (Detroit: Wayne State University Press, 1959), Chap. 5. By contrast see, e.g., the tears of *The Angel*, the "blasted" tear of the infant in *London*, the hypocritical tears in *The Human Abstract*, and, most pertinent of all to Blake as well as Thomson, the tears of the father and the degeneration of infant tears to "piping loud" in *Infant Sorrow* (all *Songs of Experience*).

7. The busy to-do about whether Blake's pictured "God" in *The Little Boy Found* plate is male or female, or a masculine female or feminine male, is in this light a critical red herring. See, e.g., Sir Geoffrey Keynes, ed., *Songs of Innocence and of Experience* (London: Oxford University Press, 1970), plate 14 commentary; Thomas E. Connolly and George R. Levine,

"Pictorial and Poetic Design in Two Songs of Innocence," *PMLA* 82 (1967):257-64; John E. Grant's preciously titled "Mother of Invention, Father in Drag or Observations on the Methodology that Brought About These Deplorable Conditions and What Then Is to Be Done," *Blake Newsletter* 2 (1968): 31-32; and Zachary Leader, *Reading Blake's "Songs,"* pp. 49-50. Sanely David Bindman relegates the entire tempest to a footnote in his *Blake as an Artist* (Oxford: Phaidon Press, 1977), p. 213n.

8. This is precisely the "world" of the Thomson passage quoted in note 6 above.

9. On the controversy over the appearance of "God" in *The Little Boy Found* see note 7 above.

10. A similar retrospective parodization obtains in the relationship between *The Little Girl Lost* and *The Little Girl Found* on the one hand, and Miss Gittipin's song on the other. In the *Found* poem, e.g., the lost girl's parents, in their desperate search for her, experience a hallucinatory vision of her as a "fancied image" straying "thro' pathless ways," Miss Gittipin's "voice upon the Breeze" now become a "hollow piteous shriek." Similar relationships between *An Island in the Moon* and *Songs of Innocence and of Experience* deserve investigation.

11. While this language is commonplace in the Bible of course, it may be worth noting that Matthew employs the precise phrase "the tribes of the earth" (24:30) in a context roughly similar to Blake's—though the remains of Matthew's tribes are the "elect" gathered together to await "the sign of the Son of man in heaven . . . coming in the clouds of heaven with power and great glory" (30-31).

12. 2 Samuel 18:33. The context here is ominous, since David's lament is for the death of his favorite son, killed after rebelling against his father; and the lament itself prompts Joab's later upbraiding of David for ignoring (or at least being indifferent to) his loyal friends while loving his enemies (19:6).

13. It is perhaps not irrelevant, then, that stretching forth the hand in the Bible is more often than not a gesture of war (as is the complaint that one's hands are feeble); see, e.g., 2 Samuel 4:1, Jeremiah 6:24, 50:43. On the other hand Ezekiel prophesies that "all hands" of the iniquitous "shall be feeble" (7:17, 21:7). See also Psalm 88: "Mine eye mourneth by reason of affliction: LORD, I have called daily upon thee, I have stretched out my hands unto thee" (9); and Job 11:13.

14. See, e.g., Psalm 25:15. Most often it is transgressors who will be plucked up (see, e.g., Proverbs 2:22, Jeremiah 6:29, 12:15). Appropriately, then, the youth's loathsome breath and voiced deceit also derive from the Bible; for the former see Job 17:1 and for the latter Job 27:4, Jeremiah 9:8, and Romans 3:13.

15. I refer here to, and quote from, Blake's *The Divine Image* (*Songs of Innocence*) and *The Human Abstract* (*Songs of Experience*).

16. *PL* XI,510-13, 515-25. Cf. Joseph A. Wittreich's perceptive comment (though without reference to *The Couch of Death*) that in Blake "the death couch represents [a] state" from which characters may or may not rise—in *Angel of Apocalypse* (Madison: University of Wisconsin Press, 1975), p. 29. Beginning with *The French Revolution* (l. 2) the couch image appears extensively in *The Four Zoas, Milton,* and *Jerusalem.*

17. See, e.g., Erdman, *Prophet Against Empire,* p. 79.

18. See Geoffrey Hartman, "Reflections on the Evening Star: Akenside to Coleridge," in *New Perspectives on Coleridge and Wordsworth* (Selected Papers from the English Institute), ed. Hartman (New York: Columbia University Press, 1972), pp. 91-92. It is worth noting that Hartman's phrase derives from *Samson Agonistes* (l. 89), Milton reflecting the ancient idea that the moon retires to an "interlunar cave" when not visible.

19. Wagenknecht, *Blake's Night,* p. 147.

20. I am aware that recently an increasing number of interpretations of *The Book of Thel* argue the flight as, in one sense or another, positive. The most complex and cogent of these is Marjorie Levinson's "'The Book of Thel' by William Blake: A Critical Reading," *ELH* 47 (1980):

287-303. A convenient summary of various versions of the "negative" view is in Donald R. Pearce's "Natural Religion and the Plight of Thel," *Blake Studies* 8 (1978): 24-28. My own "version" is in *The Piper and the Bard*, pp. 161-74—recently "confirmed" by Michael Ferber, "Blake's *Thel* and the Bride of Christ," *Blake Studies* 9 (1980): 45-56.

21. It is "the arrows of the Almighty" that "are within me," Job says, "the poison whereof drinketh up my spirit" (Job 6:4).

22. James D. McGowan, "Rising Glories: A Study of William Blake's *Poetical Sketches*" (Ph.D. dissertation, Rutgers University, 1968), p. 113-14.

23. See Alicia Ostriker, *Vision and Verse in William Blake* (Madison: University of Wisconsin Press, 1965), pp. 124-25, 146-50. Recently Leopold Damrosch, Jr., suggests that although Ossian's appeal to Blake was initially due to the verse's "liberation of the reader's mind to move freely among evocative images," at his best Blake "takes Macpherson's language apart and rebuilds it," deliberately employing the "emotive words" on occasion "to shock the reader into awareness of the opacity of symbols and the potential duplicity of the language that embodies them"—*Symbol and Truth in Blake's Myth* (Princeton: Princeton University Press, 1980), pp. 356-57. I make no such case for *The Couch of Death*, nor indeed would Damrosch (whose earliest example of Blake's taking-apart of Macpherson—in this case his *Oithona*—is *Visions of the Daughters of Albion*).

24. Such details, of course, became the staple of all poets of melancholy thereafter; I cite them here not for any remarkableness of diction or image but as introductory to my discussion of Blake's (and the eighteenth century's) use of the mode. Thomas Warton, in his 1785 edition of Milton's *Poems on Several Occasions*, properly cites Dürer as the source of many of these details. One might also add the entire emblem tradition.

25. *Il Penseroso*, ll. 1-6. Cf. Gray's *Ode on the Spring* with its similar attack, there by a personified Contemplation (ll. 31-40); and Thomson's *Winter*, ll. 205-16, among a number of other passages in *The Seasons*.

26. Erdman, *Blake: Prophet Against Empire*, p. 77n.; Commentary to Erdman's *The Poetry and Prose of William Blake*, p. 889. Harold Bloom seems to have changed his mind a bit when, in *Blake's Apocalypse* (Garden City, N.Y.: Doubleday, 1963), he describes *Contemplation*, erroneously I believe, as opposing "the conviction of mortality to the comforting cycle of nature" (p. 13).

27. With this entire context in mind the relationship (whether anticipation or echo) between this conception and Blake's "conclusion" to his *To Morning* gains even greater significance and richness. See my analysis of that poem above, Chap. 4.

28. Erdman, *The Poetry and Prose of William Blake*, p. 766.

29. If the phrase "swoln with wind" derives from *Lycidas* (l. 126), the allusion would be but further evidence for dating the poem early, for it totally ignores Milton's context, however much it may "ornament" Blake's style. In the same verse paragraph Milton also refers to an "inscribed" flower, the hyacinth (l. 106), equally inappropriate to Blake's context.

30. Ll. 36, 20, 25. The phrase, appropriately, comes from Spenser's *Faerie Queene* (I,ii,13, and III,i,15), which may actually be Blake's source since Milton never uses the common Spenserian word "courser." Blake's point is made either way.

31. Similarly in *King Edward the Third*, in response to William's (Blake's) jocular description of Ambition as "a little creeping root that grows in ditches," Dagworth the warrior (clearly speaking for Blake) says: "Thou dost misunderstand me, William. It is a root that grows in every breast" (4:10-13, E425). Humility in *The Human Abstract* (and in *Contemplation*) is but the obverse of the same coin.

32. See *The Four Zoas*, VIIb (E396), and *Jerusalem* 65:11 (E214); also *The Four Zoas*, IX (E391), and the "black globe" with which the self-generating Urizen is identified in *The Book of Urizen* 5:33 (E72).

33. It is, of course, literally the last poem in the printed volume, but I tend to agree with Michael Phillips and others who regard it as probably the last written. See my discussion in

Chapter 1 of Blake's pencil sketches for his later color print and line engraving of *Albion Rose*, as well as Wittreich's analysis of those designs in *Angel of Apocalypse*.

34. See Jean H. Hagstrum's valuable discussion of personification in *The Sister Arts* (Chicago: University of Chicago Press, 1958), Chap. 4, and in *William Blake: Poet and Painter* (Chicago: University of Chicago Press, 1964), Chap. 4; also Bloom's suggestive comments in *Blake's Apocalypse*, pp. 3-4. My point here does not speak to the elevation of prosopopoeia to the status of "second creation" but rather to the "separative analogues most frequent in earlier rhetoric"— that is, "body-and-garment" and "garment-and-ornament" (I quote from M. H. Abrams, *The Mirror and the Lamp* [1953; New York: W. W. Norton, 1958], pp. 289-91). Cf. Earl R. Wasserman's "The Inherent Values of Eighteenth-Century Personification," *PMLA* 65 (1950): 435-63.

35. "Essay, Supplementary to the Preface," *The Poetical Works of Wordsworth*, ed. Thomas Hutchinson, rev. by Ernest de Selincourt (London: Oxford University Press, 1904), p. 950.

36. This may be the "message" of Chapter 7 of *An Island in the Moon* where Quid (often associated with Blake himself) reveals his *quidditas* side: "Homer is bombast & Shakespeare is too wild & Milton has no feelings they might be easily outdone Chatterton never writ those poems, a parcel of fools going to Bristol—if I was to go Id find it out in a minute. but Ive found it out already" (E446). Of course he had, just as that same "thinking" part of his mind leads him not only to pooh-pooh (and to misunderstand) the greatest of poets but to settle with militant complacency for the standard right-wing neoclassical critical description of Shakespeare. "Hang your reasoning," the Epicurean says earlier to Quid (E445); it may be "right," Blake says implicitly, but imaginatively it is the source of error.

37. In his comment Blake distinguishes between the "Divine Vision" and the imagination of a "Portrait or Landscape Painter," to whom he apocryphally ascribes Wordsworth's last paragraph and its sentiments of the "Natural Man" (E655).

38. The quoted phrase I borrow from *Milton and the Line of Vision*, ed. Joseph A. Wittreich (Madison: University of Wisconsin Press, 1975). In his preface the editor also includes in his "line" Chaucer, Sidney, "the major Romantics," and Yeats and Stevens, "as well as many other moderns" (pp. xiv-xv).

39. Donald S. Taylor, *Thomas Chatterton's Art* (Princeton: Princeton University Press, 1978), pp. 90, 9-10. It is interesting to note Taylor's conclusion that "nearly every feature of [Chatterton's] writings can be traced to a borrowed source" but that, unlike Blake, "in using these features he nearly always disregarded their original contexts" (p. 21).

40. *A Descriptive Catalogue*, E522. The second quoted phrase in this sentence is from the same source and page.

41. William Wordsworth, "Essay, Supplementary to the Preface," *Poetical Works*, p. 950. He is speaking of Macpherson's "spurious" imagery, but my point is not invalidated thereby. The word-thing (res-verba) relationship Wordsworth perceives in Ossian is quite different, of course, from the one he proposes, rather daringly, in his note to *The Thorn;* see *Poetical Works*, p. 900.

42. So intense was Blake's attention to these that Spenser, who, as Herbert Cory noted long ago, is absent from *Samson Agonistes*, is also absented from Blake's *Samson;* see Cory's "Spenser, the School of the Fletchers, and Milton," *University of California Publications in Modern Philology* 2 (1912): 371.

43. Margaret Lowery, *Windows of the Morning* (New Haven: Yale University Press, 1940), pp. 76-82.

44. Michael Phillips, "Blake's Early Poetry," in *William Blake: Essays in Honour of Sir Geoffrey Keynes*, ed. Phillips and Morton D. Paley (Oxford: Clarendon Press, 1973), p. 23. Phillips's careful analysis covers pp. 16-26.

45. Wittreich, *Angel of Apocalypse*, p. 64. At least since Samuel Johnson the critical battle over *Samson Agonistes* has continued with a vehemence unmatched by any over his other poems. Much of that battle has ebbed and flowed over precisely the point Wittreich addresses here, that is, whether the drama ends triumphantly or not (a question that gets inextricably mixed up with

whether it is a "tragedy" or not, and if so what kind of tragedy). The triumphant-Samson critics have carried the day thus far, but the battle, one fears, is far from over. Aside from Wittreich, who at least sees Samson as "at most an ambiguous figure" (*Angel of Apocalypse*, p. 51), the "negative" minority is led by Irene Samuel in a somewhat shrill essay, "*Samson Agonistes* as Tragedy," in *Calm of Mind: Tercentenary Essays on "Paradise Regained" and "Samson Agonistes" in Honor of John S. Diekhoff*, ed. Joseph A. Wittreich (Cleveland: Press of Case Western Reserve University, 1971), pp. 235-57. A middle ground is defined by William G. Madsen in *From Shadowy Types to Truth* (New Haven: Yale University Press, 1968), pp. 181-202; he argues that Samson falls far short of the ethical ideal Christ emblemizes in *Paradise Regained* but regards that shortfall as characteristic of the typological tradition. More cogently argued is John T. Shawcross's position, in "Irony as Tragic Effect," *Calm of Mind*, pp. 289-306, which allows that Samson's destructive act "would henceforth be interpreted as God's means of showing his power" but that this "does not alter the realization that for Samson his act is what Manoa and the Chorus say it is: revenge" (p. 291). Even so, Shawcross rejects William Riley Parker's conclusion that "Samson lived and died in vain, whatever heroic qualities he displayed." Parker's statement appears in his monumental *Milton: A Biography* (Oxford: Clarendon Press, 1968), 2: 908; to it he adds that he believes "readers will some day agree with him that the poem is intensely, almost unbearably pessimistic . . ." (p. 937).

46. E.M.W. Tillyard, *Milton*, rev. ed. (London: Chatto & Windus, 1966), p. 283. Some measure of the gulf between the negative and positive views of Samson's final act is suggested by Don Cameron Allen's characterizing of it as "the happy catastrophe" — *The Harmonious Vision: Studies in Milton's Poetry* (Baltimore: Johns Hopkins Press, 1954), p. 94.

47. Much of Phillips's interpretation (see note 44) hinges on his assumption that Blake calculatedly chose the hour of Samson's fall so that *Samson Agonistes*, "the next dramatic episode in Samson's life," would be considered by "his reader" as completing Blake's work, so to speak. I'm afraid that I think that idea quite wrong.

48. The allusion to the "ivory palaces" of Psalm 45:8 is marvelously and ironically apt, for the psalm, glossed as dealing with the kingdom of Christ, is "A Song of loves" that urges God's daughter to "forget also thine own people, and thy father's house" (verse 10). In their respective ways Samson and Dalila do both in Blake's poem.

49. Much has been made of Blake's "iron pens," "lofty rock" and "words of truth," I suppose properly so, as the frankest announcement anywhere in the *Sketches* of his self-imposed prophetic mission. The allusion to Job 19:23-24 is always cited, Job's wish that his words "were printed in a book" appearing particularly appropriate — to *Samson*, to *Poetical Sketches*, to Blake as emerging prophet. But the Job utterance is "prophetic" in no recognizable sense, for it is the outburst of a frustrated, puzzled, misery-ridden man, far more like Samson's and Dalila's complaints about their own conditions than like Blake's invocation to *Samson*. Equally ironic is Jeremiah's statement that "the sin of Judah is written with a pen of iron . . .: it is graven upon the table of their heart, and upon the horns of your altars" (verse 1). Perhaps Blake also recalled the Redcrosse Knight's use of the phrase at the defeat of Orgoglio and Duessa: "This dayes ensample hath this lesson deare / Deepe written in my heart with yron pen, / That blisse may not abide in state of mortall men" (*FQ* I,viii,44). Spenser's context is so apropos that one wonders whether it sustained itself somewhere in the recesses of Blake's brain and surfaced in his writing of *Samson*. The relevant stanza reads:

> Henceforth sir knight, take to you wonted strength,
> And maister these mishaps with patient might;
> Loe where your foe lyes stretcht in monstrous length,
> And loe that wicked woman in your sight,
> The roote of all your care, and wretched plight,
> Now in your powre, to let her liue, or dye.

To do her dye (quoth *Vna*) were despight,
And shame t'auenge so weake an enimy;
But spoile her of her scarlot robe, and let her fly.

Una (Truth) has guided Arthur to "redeeme her deare" (Redcrosse) who has been imprisoned in a dungeon "darke as hell" by Duessa (viii:proem, 39); thus Arthur is the "Deliverer" led by Truth, not Redcrosse-Samson who not only does not act but cannot "see": his "sad dull eyes deepe suncke in hollow pits / Could not endure th'vnwonted sunne to view" (41). If Sin and Death are not "destroyed" in Spenser's vision, the analogy to Blake's conception in *Samson* is still quite extraordinary. Spenser's only direct reference to Samson (unnamed but identified as "that mighty Iewish swaine") is in *The Faerie Queene* V,viii,2, where he is presented as a lovesick suitor who lays "his spoiles before his leman's traine."

50. The veiled reference to Satan reiterates Samson's conventional role. Bruising the serpent's head is mentioned a number of times by Milton, but the one in Book XII of *Paradise Lost* is the one Blake surely had in mind here: "thy great Deliverer, who shall bruise / The Serpent's head; whereof [says Michael to Adam] to thee anon / Plainlier shall be revealed" (ll. 148-49). Earlier in this same sentence Blake alludes to Milton's version of the Samson's jawbone victory in Judges 15:15-17 ("old warriors . . . / . . . grov'ling soiled their crested helmets in the dust"—*Samson Agonistes*, ll. 139-41).

51. *Jerusalem* 52: "To the Deists" (E198); *Marriage* 16 (E39).

52. The fourth line of this quotation, defective in its initial printing, has been filled out by Milton's editors with the word "Mercy," although "Virtue" and "Peace" have been suggested as well; see Douglas Bush, ed., *The Complete Works of John Milton* (Boston: Houghton Mifflin, 1965), p. 49n. That Blake knew the *Fair Infant* poem especially well is attested to by his quotation from it in his Notebook; see David V. Erdman, ed., *The Notebook of William Blake* (Oxford: Clarendon Press, 1973), p. N26. Wittreich notices the borrowing of Milton's phrase "white robed Truth" but makes nothing of it (*Angel of Apocalypse*, p. 63).

53. See my "Blake and the Four Daughters of God," *English Language Notes* 15 (1977): 110-15.

54. In *Samson Agonistes* Milton makes no such reference, and it is significant that Blake absorbs it into a sentence taken virtually verbatim from Judges 13:16-18 (except Blake's reference, in his previous sentence, to the angel's "warfare," absent from both Milton's poem and Judges).

55. *PL* XII,430-31. In this passage Sin and Death are destroyed by Christ's sacrifice and resurrection, and it is perfectly possible that Blake read the word "arms" as a pun. Focusing so narrowly on Samson's strength, Blake accordingly makes no mention of his shorn hair, just as he ignores his blindness, through which, paradoxically, he learns to see the truth of things (like Milton himself) in the conventional versions of the story.

56. William Lansdell Wardle, in the 1963 edition of the *Encyclopaedia Britannica*, s.v. "Samson." As he notes, it is Samuel, Saul, and David who finally subdue the Philistines (see 1 Samuel 7:13, 14:47, and 2 Samuel 8:1). Irene Samuel makes the same point ("*Samson Agonistes* as Tragedy," p. 253), as does Shawcross ("Irony as Tragic Effect," p. 296). It is a tribute to Blake's critical capacities and his concentration on *Samson* that he ignores the more general disreputableness of Samson's character in the Bible—with respect to which, as Anthony Low points out, there has been a veritable "contest to find the most apt denigrating phrase"; see Low's summary of these in *The Blaze of Noon* (New York: Columbia University Press, 1974), pp. 36-37.

57. Job 19:24-25. But see my note 49 above.

58. It would be nice to think that Blake also regarded Milton's Eden as a potential Bower of Bliss and Eve, therefore, as an incipient Acrasia, as A. Bartlett Giamatti does in *The Earthly Paradise in the Renaissance Epic* (Princeton: Princeton University Press, 1966), pp. 302-30—but I doubt it.

59. Dalila makes no such suggestion in *Samson Agonistes* of course, nor in the Bible. Some Milton critics draw the Adam-Eve Samson-Dalila parallel as well; see, e.g., Raymond B.

Waddington, "Melancholy Against Melancholy: *Samson Agonistes* as Renaissance Tragedy," in *Calm of Mind*, p. 261.

60. It is too easily forgotten that the entire final half or so of the prose poem is spoken by Samson himself, after he has been largely "discredited" by Blake.

61. Wittreich presumes that "the offering is to be one of self-sacrifice" (*Angel of Apocalypse*, p. 63). That is, of course, what it should be, and what we are led to believe from our knowledge of *Samson Agonistes* and the Book of Judges. In fact, though, Samson's "self-sacrifice" in Blake's eyes is nothing of the sort.

62. *Angel of Apocalypse*, p. 64.

63. Noted by S. Foster Damon, *William Blake: His Philosophy and Symbols* (1924; reprint ed., New York: Peter Smith, 1947), p. 263.

64. I,155-62. As Wittreich points out, after the failure of the Puritan Revolution "the true exemplar of Christian warfare . . . was not Samson but Christ; and the scene of the battle was not at the pillars but in the wilderness"—Joseph A. Wittreich, *Visionary Poetics* (San Marino, Calif.: Huntington Library, 1979), p. 198. Wittreich's gloss on his own statement is also appropriate to Blake's *Samson:* "the Lord's battle would not be fought out in history but was to be waged within every Christian." Cf. Shawcross's conclusion that "the tragedy [of *Samson Agonistes*] is that we, Samson as well as 'the people' do not realize that deliverance comes only of the individual self" ("Irony as Tragic Effect," p. 297).

65. Lowery, *Windows of the Morning*, p. 78. Phillips reads the ending as Blake's abandonment of "the anticipated" and his decision to end "his poem, not in gloom and despair over Samson's fall, but in an unexpected atmosphere of hope" ("Blake's Early Poetry," p. 19). Both seem to me equally wrong.

66. *The Marriage of Heaven and Hell*, Plate 11 (E37): "All deities reside in the human breast."

67. *Samson*, it is important to note, is entirely a night poem, whereas *Samson Agonistes* begins at daybreak and ends at noon, that time, as Albert R. Cirillo reminds us in "Time, Light, and the Phoenix: The Design of *Samson Agonistes*," which is traditionally "an image of eternity" (*Calm of Mind*, p. 225). See also his "Noon-Midnight and the Temporal Structure of *Paradise Lost*," *ELH* 29 (1962): 372-95; and also my analyses of Blake's *To Summer* and *To Morning* (above, Chaps. 4 and 5 respectively).

CHAPTER 8

1. James D. McGowan, "The Integrity of Blake's *Poetical Sketches*," *Blake Studies* 8 (1979): 121-44.

2. The full title is *The French Revolution. A Poem, in Seven Books*, and the "Advertisement" in the unnumbered page iii of the front-matter reads: "The remaining Books of this Poem are finished, and will be published in their Order" (E282). Whether Johnson was drumming up business, or Blake told him that the other six books were finished, or whether indeed Johnson already had the other six and was testing the uncertain political waters with only the first, is unknown. No other parts of the poem have surfaced. I should add that Blake may well have withdrawn the work from publication because of his increasing fear of censorship, as well as for the reason I suggested. See David V. Erdman's discussion of the matter in *Blake: Prophet Against Empire*, rev. ed. (Garden City, N.Y.: Doubleday, 1969), pp. 151-53.

3. See, e.g., Thomas A. Vogler, *Preludes to Vision: The Epic Venture in Blake, Wordsworth, Keats, and Hart Crane* (Berkeley and Los Angeles: University of California Press, 1971).

4. Letter to John Thelwall, quoted in Basil Willey, *Samuel Taylor Coleridge* (New York: Norton, 1971), p. 56.

5. Carl Woodring, *Wordsworth* (Boston: Houghton Mifflin, 1965), pp. 4-5.

6. Charles and Mary Cowden Clarke, *Recollections of Writers* (London: Low, Marston, Searle, & Rivington, 1878), p. 140; the words quoted are Walter Jackson Bate's summary of Bush's

remarks, in *John Keats* (New York: Oxford University Press, 1966; orig. pub. by Harvard University Press, 1963), p. 149.

7. Quoted by Kenneth Neill Cameron in *The Young Shelley: Genesis of a Radical* (London: Victor Gollancz, 1951), p. 34.

8. See my *Byron and the Ruins of Paradise* (Baltimore: Johns Hopkins University Press, 1967), especially the Introduction and Chapter 1. The quotation appears on p. 3.

9. Robert N. Essick, *William Blake, Printmaker* (Princeton: Princeton University Press, 1980), p. 34.

10. Jean H. Hagstrum, "Blake and the Sister-Arts Tradition," in *Blake's Visionary Forms Dramatic,* ed. David V. Erdman and John E. Grant (Princeton: Princeton University Press, 1970), p. 88. See also his *The Sister Arts* (Chicago: University of Chicago Press, 1953), passim, and W.J.T. Mitchell's important argument against Hagstrum's locating Blake on this tradition—in *Blake's Composite Art* (Princeton: Princeton University Press, 1978), esp. Chapter 2.

11. Ronald Paulson, *Emblem and Expression: Meaning in English Art of the Eighteenth Century* (Cambridge: Harvard University Press, 1975), p. 12.

12. Joseph Anthony Wittreich, "Painted Prophecies: The Tradition of Blake's Illuminated Books," in *Blake in His Time,* ed. Robert N. Essick and Donald Pearce (Bloomington: Indiana University Press, 1978), p. 108. Wittreich's entire essay is pertinent to my point, as is, more recently, Leslie Tannenbaum's fine *Biblical Tradition in Blake's Early Prophecies: The Great Code of Art* (Princeton: Princeton University Press, 1982), esp. Chapters 1-4. It is precisely these barriers that Blake's prophetic giant form Los wars against continually, laying "his words in order above the mortal brain / As cogs are formd in a wheel to turn the cogs of the adverse wheel" (*Milton* 27:9-10, E123).

13. Tannenbaum's argument (*Biblical Tradition*) implies that he did indeed have "some sense of their overlap" through his knowledge of biblical commentary—though he stops short of assigning a date to Blake's earliest acquisition of such knowledge.

14. Essick, *William Blake, Printmaker,* p. 206.

15. See *Jerusalem* 3 (E144), the paragraph Blake wrote in the autograph album of William Upcott (E674), and *A Vision of the Last Judgment* (E550).

16. These techniques are strikingly similar to those Tannenbaum identifies as characteristic of all prophetic forms, as those forms were being investigated and codified by biblical commentators and the formulators of "biblical poetics." See Chap. 2 of his *Biblical Tradition in Blake's Early Prophecies.*

17. See Martha England, "The Satiric Blake: Apprenticeship at the Haymarket?" *Bulletin of the New York Public Library* 73 (1969): 440-64, 531-50; also my "Blake and Satire," *The Wordsworth Circle* 8 (1977): 311-26.

18. See Essick's comments on Blake's general lack of success in this early effort, in *William Blake, Printmaker,* pp. 136-37, 141.

19. Tannenbaum, *Biblical Tradition in Blake's Early Prophecies,* pp. 79-80.

20. G. E. Bentley, Jr., *Blake Books* (Oxford: Clarendon Press, 1977), pp. 514-17, 589-91.

21. Tannenbaum, *Biblical Tradition in Blake's Early Prophecies,* p. 12.

22. Kay Parkhurst Easson, "Blake and the Art of the Book," in *Blake in His Time,* p. 45.

23. Tannenbaum, *Biblical Tradition in Blake's Early Prophecies,* p. 48.

24. E545. This too is a marvelous pun, for it at once refers to the doctrine of imitation (here doubly damnable since Nature itself is an imitation that is in turn imitated by artists) and to Blake's earlier statement in *There Is No Natural Religion:* "He who sees the Infinite in all things sees God. He who sees the Ratio only sees himself only" (E2).

25. Easson, "Blake and the Art of the Book," p. 35; E41.

26. Tannenbaum, *Biblical Tradition in Blake's Early Prophecies,* p. 7.

27. Morris Eaves, "The Title-Page of *The Book of Urizen,*" in *William Blake: Essays in Honour*

of Sir Geoffrey Keynes, ed. Morton D. Paley and Michael Phillips (Oxford: Clarendon Press, 1973), pp. 225-30.

28. Robert N. Essick, "The Altering Eye: Blake's Vision in the *Tiriel* Designs," in *Essays in Honour of . . . Keynes,* p. 65.

29. Ibid.

INDEX

Abel, 125, 147. *See also* Blake, William, poetic works of, *The Ghost of Abel*
Abrams, M. H., 50, 188
Adams, Hazard, 57, 60, 69, 161-62, 171
Adonis. See *Faerie Queene*, Garden of Adonis in; Venus
Aiken, John, 59-60
Akenside, Mark, 2, 81, 177; *Ode II: For the Winter Solstice*, 170; *Pleasures of the Imagination*, 177; *To the Evening Star*, 177
Allegory, 162; in Blake, 117; Blake on, 42, 181; in Spenser, 22, 63, 74; tradition of, 66. *See also* Personification
Allen, Don Cameron, 188
Allusion: contextualized, 10-12, 16, 26, 48, 56, 72, 81, 142-43, 153, 180; in prophecy, 161; "significant," 10, 12, 27, 45, 87, 90, 92, 109, 161, 177, 181; simple, 18-19, 25-26, 35, 48, 56, 81, 90, 177, 187-88
Antithetical structure, 12, 19-20, 37-56, 61, 63, 78, 109-10, 124, 128. *See also* Contrariety, Blake's idea of; Contrast, in Blake; Dialectic, in Blake
Apocalypse, 1; in Blake, 3, 19, 57, 65, 68, 74, 77-78, 94, 101, 109, 116, 118, 139-40, 142, 156, 173, 182; in Milton, 107
Apollo, 66; in Blake, 8, 20-22, 30, 34, 43; in Milton, 8, 34
Apuleius, 55
Armstrong, John, 58
Art. *See* Blake, graphic works; Classicism; Flemish art; Gothic; *names of individual artists;* Venetian art
Augustine, 154
Autumn: in Blake, 41, 67-69, 74, 94, 173; in Spenser, 58, 62, 68; in other poets, 58. See also *Poetical Sketches, To Autumn*; Thomson, James, *Autumn*
Barfield, Owen, 178

Barfield, Owen, 178
Barnes, Joshua, 98
Basire, James, 28; Blake's apprenticeship to, 1, 3-9, 136, 150-51
Basse, William, *Forth from My Dark and Dismal Cell*, 169
Bate, Walter Jackson, 190
Beattie, James, 2, 177; *Ode Written in the Year 1758*, 90
Beer, John, 161
Bentley, Gerald E., Jr., 170
Berger, Pierre, 65
Bible, 2-6, 11, 33, 37, 60, 64, 68, 81, 87, 118, 129, 138-39, 151, 153, 173, 177-78; Armageddon in, 102, 110, 112-14; Blake's illustrations to, 7, 154; commentaries on, 154-55, 183, 189, 191; Cyrus in, 2; David in, 124, 185; Enoch in, 113, 115; Mary Magdalene in, 129; prophetic books of, in general, 1, 4-6, 8, 10-11, 13, 15, 101, 110, 112, 137, 151, 155-56; Solomon in, 2, 65
— Books of: 2 Corinthians, 146; Deuteronomy, 173, 182; Ecclesiastes, 133-34, 141; Ezekiel, 112-13, 115, 141, 185; Ezra, 1-2; Genesis, 174, 182; Habakkuk, 173; Isaiah, 1, 72, 102-3, 109, 112-13, 115, 143-46, 164; Jeremiah, 185, 188; Job, 99, 126, 144, 177, 180, 184-85, 187-88; Jude, 113; Judges, 139-43, 146-47, 182, 189-90; 1 Kings, 159; Leviticus, 182; Luke, 81-82; Malachi, 112-13, 182; Matthew, 142, 185; Nahum, 112, 182; 1 Peter, 103; Proverbs, 185; Psalms, 18-19, 66, 80, 92, 108, 112, 156, 163, 185, 188; Revelation, 4, 11, 13, 68, 99-100, 103, 110-13, 115-16, 137, 155, 161, 182-83; Romans, 185; 1 Samuel, 144, 189; 2 Samuel, 124, 144, 185, 189; Song of Solomon, 18, 64-66, 77, 108, 156, 172, 175-76; Zephaniah, 112-13. *See also* Abel; Cain; Jerusalem; Mary, Virgin; Philistines

INDEX

Bible, A New and Complete History of the Holy (Edward Kimpton), 154

Bible, The Protestants Family, 154

Bible, The Royal Universal Family, 154

"Bible of Hell," Blake's, 156

Bidney, Martin, 100, 181

Bindman, David, 4-6, 11, 28, 97, 99, 160, 185

Blackmore, Richard, *Creation,* 170

Blackstone, Bernard, 57

Blair, Robert, *The Grave,* 131

Blake, William: and American Revolution, 1, 98, 182-83; apprenticeship of, 1, 3-9, 136, 150-51, 154, 160; and Beulah, idea of, 45; biblical paintings of, 7, 154; and book, idea of, 150-57; and bookmaking, 150-51, 155; on Chaucer, 97, 166; composite art of, 10, 26, 37-38, 147-48, 151, 166; on conversation, 94, 100; on copying, 27; Covering Cherub in, 3; and drama, idea of, 99-100, 109-10, 116; and energy, idea of, 38, 140; the Fall in, 54, 141; Female Will in, 3; and John Flaxman, 14, 151, 159; four zoas in, 3, 57, 182; Gilchrist's *Life* of, 23; Golgonooza in, 11, 174; and William Hayley, 20; human form divine in, 126-27, 129, 133; and humility, idea of, 126-27, 133-35, 187; and London Society of Antiquaries, 1, 6, 28; marriage of, 1, 7; and Rev. A. S. Matthew, 14; and G. M. Moser, 1; and mythopoesis, 10, 137, 139; on negation, 38, 55; nonsense in, 25, 153, 155; on Ossian, 137; at Pars's drawing school, 3-4, 7; political awareness of, 1, 3, 15, 182; prolific and devourer, idea of, in, 66; and publisher Joseph Johnson, 148, 190; reading of, 1, 4, 6, 9-10, 13, 28, 57, 170; on reason, 38, 42, 50, 123, 133-36, 166, 180; as reproductive engraver, 150-51 (*see also* Basire, James); and Henry Crabb Robinson, 50; at Royal Academy, 1; self-portraiture of, 8, 108-10; self-quotation of, 10, 93; on similitude, 38, 42, 136, 166; on sin, 126, 129, 133; taste in art of, 3-5, 11, 152; tears, idea of, in, 122-24, 184; and John Trusler, 12; Ulro in, 29. *See also* Allegory; Allusion; Antithetical structure; Apocalypse; Contrariety; Contrast; Cycles; Dialectic; Epiphany; Error; Glory; Gothic; History; Imitation; Language of art; Love; Marriage; Mental fight; Nature; Parody; Personification; Poetic closure; Poetic Genius; Satire; Sequence; Sublime; Time; Truth; War

— annotations by, to: Boyd's *Historical Notes*

on Dante, 180; Reynolds's *Discourses,* 26-27, 38, 165; Bishop Watson's *Apology for the Bible,* 142, 180; Wordsworth, 50, 137

— characters in works of (other than *Poetical Sketches*): Albion, 7-8, 31, 42, 116, 156, 167, 183; Elijah, 74; Enion, 93; Enitharmon, 73, 175; Miss Gittipin, 123, 167, 185; Los, 6, 10-11, 38, 51, 64, 73, 120, 137, 161-62, 172, 174-75, 179, 191; Noah, 74; Orc, 57, 120, 140, 161; Quid, 54, 123-24, 188; Seth, 74; Tilly Lally, 123; Urizen, 57, 64, 78, 120, 156, 182-83, 187; Vala, 63, 94, 156, 172, 175

— graphic works of: *Albion Rose,* 7, 28, 140, 166, 188; *A Cloud,* 99; illustrations for Gough's *Sepulchral Monuments,* 28; *Joseph of Arimathea Among the Rocks of Albion,* 5-6, 28; *Our End Is Come,* 167; *The Penance of Jane Shore,* 96, 179-81; *A Prospect of Liberty,* 99; Shakespeare illustrations, 97

— poetic works of (other than *Poetical Sketches,* q.v.): *America,* 3, 15, 98, 101; *The Book of Ahania,* 156; *The Book of Los,* 156; *The Book of Thel,* 50, 52, 126, 128, 141, 154-55, 163, 185-86; *The Book of Urizen,* 156, 166, 182, 187; *And Did Those Feet in Ancient Time,* 2, 43; *Europe,* 101; *The Everlasting Gospel,* 135; *The Four Zoas,* 54, 73, 78, 93-94, 156-57, 169, 172, 176, 185; *The French Revolution,* 38, 99, 101, 109, 116, 118, 148, 185, 190; *The Ghost of Abel,* 99-100; *The Grey Monk,* 120, 142, 183; *I Saw a Monk of Charlemaine,* 120, 183; *Jerusalem,* 11, 37-39, 78, 99-101, 120, 148, 156, 166, 172, 182-83, 185, 191; *Leave, Oh Leave Me to My Sorrows,* 123-24, 167, 185; *Milton,* 15, 31, 38, 148, 156, 177, 185; Notebook poems, 20, 152, 164; *Songs of Experience* (general reference), 124; *Songs of Innocence* (general reference), 1, 29, 54, 122, 124, 148, 154, 156; *Songs of Innocence and of Experience* (general reference), 4, 15, 25, 37, 39, 42, 155, 168, 185; *Tiriel,* 129, 156-57, 168-69

— prose works of: *All Religions Are One,* 7, 27-28, 136-38, 154; *A Descriptive Catalogue,* 3, 5, 12, 97-98, 166; *An Island in the Moon,* 1, 25, 54, 81, 101, 122-24, 153-55, 185; *The Laocoön,* 160; *The Marriage of Heaven and Hell,* 12-13, 37, 42, 66, 87, 134, 138, 142, 155-56, 165, 190; *Public Address,* 11, 29, 120; "Then She Bore Pale Desire," 133; *There Is No Natural Religion,* 7, 134, 136, 147, 154, 191; "To the Public" (*Jerusalem* preface), 155; *A Vision of the Last Judgment,* 61, 63, 69, 74, 135, 162, 181, 191

INDEX

Giamatti, A. Bartlett, 189

Gilchrist, Alexander, *Life of William Blake*, 23

Glory, theme of: in Blake, 98, 104-7, 109; 112; in Milton, 104-5, 107-8, 182; in Shakespeare, 98, 107

Gothic: art, 4-5, 9, 11, 26, 151, 160; Blake's idea of, 4-6, 151; conventional ideas of, 38; literature, 2, 16-19, 22, 27, 163

Gough, Richard, 28

Grant, Douglas, 59, 171

Graveyard school of poetry, 17, 131, 133, 136

Gray, Thomas, 2, 27, 57, 87, 101, 117, 136, 177; *The Bard*, 82, 102, 104, 110, 181; *Elegy Written in a Country Churchyard*, 52-53; *Ode on the Spring*, 187; *Progress of Poesy*, 29, 32. *See also* Contemplation; Melancholy; Progress of poetry theme

Greene, Thomas M., 178-79

Groom, Bernard, 179

Hagstrum, Jean H., 59-60, 150, 166, 171

Halloran, William, 99

Hamilton, A. C., 87, 178

Hartman, Geoffrey, 29, 31-32, 39, 44, 60-61, 69, 73, 84, 88, 92, 121, 127, 165-66, 177, 185

Hayley, William, 20

Hebraism: Blake's, 15, 118; Milton's, 15, 22, 33-34

Hecla, Mount: in Blake, 69, 73-74, 175; in Thomson, 175

Heemskerk, Martin van, 3

Heninger, S. K., Jr., 168

Herrick, Robert, *Upon Jane and Jone*, 169

Hervey, James, *Meditations Among the Tombs*, 131

Hewlett, H. G., 79

Hinchcliffe, William, 58

Hirsch, E. D., 166

History, Blake's idea of, 6, 28, 60-61, 96-101, 117-20, 179; in art, 28, 97, 99, 179-80

Homer, 22, 31, 59, 163, 180, 188

Hughes, John, *Ode to the Creator of the World*, 58

Hurd, Richard, *Letters on Chivalry and Romance*, 5, 20, 22, 163

Imitation: Blake's idea of, 11, 20, 26-27, 137-38, 148, 152, 156, 160, 170, 178; in Blake's poetry, 2, 12, 16-29, 98; as criticism, 26-27, 36, 148, 165; in eighteenth century, 11, 17, 23, 28, 136, 157, 161-62, 168

Influence, of stars: in Blake, 39, 42, 83, 86, 92, 94, 121-22, 177-78; in Milton, 88-89, 177; in Spenser, 40, 86, 177

Innocence, Blake's state of, 44-45, 49, 52-54, 63, 74, 119, 121-24, 126, 154, 173

Jerusalem, 2, 10, 31, 103, 111, 116, 156; as character in Blake, 63, 156-57, 183

Jesus. *See* Christ, in Blake

John of Patmos, 13, 113, 115-16. *See also* Bible, books of, Revelation

Johnson, Joseph, 148, 190

Johnson, Samuel, 139, 188; *Works of the English Poets*, 170-71

Jones, R. F., 59

Jonson, Ben, 56, 160; masques, 59; *Queene and Huntress Chaste and Fair*, 79; *Underwoods*, 4

Keats, John, 28, 87, 149; *Endymion*, 148; *Hyperion*, 98; *On First Looking into Chapman's Homer*, 27, 149; *Poems*, 149

Kent, William, 58

Keynes, Geoffrey, 6, 153, 170

Knights, L. C., 167

Knott, John R., Jr., 183

LaBelle, Jenijoy, 160

Landscape (locodescriptive) poetry, tradition of, 57-59, 64, 70. See also *Ut pictura poesis* tradition

Language of art, Blake's idea of, 6, 8, 13, 27-28, 60, 138-39, 160. *See also* Poetic diction

Leader, Zachary, 166, 168, 184

Leavis, F. R., 166

Lesnick, Henry, 166

Levinson, Marjorie, 185-86

Locke, John, 50, 123, 155, 169, 180

Lonsdale, Roger, 79, 181

Love: in Blake, 44, 47, 51, 54-55, 63-67, 93, 182-83; in Milton, 88; Petrarchan, 55; in Spenser, 62, 65. *See also* Cupid; Venus

Low, Anthony, 189

Lowery, Margaret, 2, 17, 55, 59-60, 65, 67, 76, 79, 96, 104, 139, 147

Lucretius, 64

MacCaffrey, Isabel, 172, 174

McGowan, James D., 2, 129, 148, 162-64, 167-68, 182

INDEX

Price, Martin, 161
Progress of poetry theme, 29, 31-33, 60, 73, 84, 165; in Blake, 25-26; in Collins, 31-32, 60, 165; in Gray, 29, 32; in Spenser, 29, 31
Psyche, 55, 170. *See also* Cupid

Raine, Kathleen, 87
Raphael (artist), 3-4, 6, 8, 11, 26, 151-52
Rapin de Thoyras, 98
Rembrandt, 4, 152
Reynolds, Joshua, 152; Blake's annotations to, 26-27, 38, 165
Riccaltoun, Robert, 170-71
Richardson, Samuel, *Clarissa*, 180
Robinson, Henry Crabb, 50
Romano, Giulio, 3-4, 8, 11, 151-52
Romney, George, 5
Rose, Edward J., 5, 160
Rossetti, Dante Gabriel, 23
Rossetti, William Michael, 146
Rowe, Nicholas, *Jane Shore*, 181
Rowley. *See* Chatterton, Thomas
Rubens, Peter Paul, 4, 152

Sampson, John, 163
Samson. *See* Bible, Book of Judges; *Poetical Sketches, Samson*; *Samson Agonistes*
Samson Agonistes, 99, 139-42, 144-45, 147, 161, 166-67, 185, 188-89; Chorus in, 144-45, 167, 188; critical debate over, 7-8, 187-90; Dalila in, 141, 167, 189; Manoa in, 144, 188; Samson's blindness in, 141; Temple of Dagon in, 141. *See also* Bible, Book of Judges; *Poetical Sketches, Samson*
Samuel, Irene, 188-89
Satan. See *Paradise Lost*, Satan in; *Paradise Regained*, Satan in
Satire, 23; in Blake, 11, 48-49, 61, 161, 165-66
Schorer, Mark, 19, 22, 87, 167, 169, 179, 183
Seasons: poems on (other than Blake's and Thomson's), 58, 62, 64, 170-71; tradition of, 57-59, 62, 64, 69-70, 83. *See also* Months; *entries for each season*
Seasons poems, Blake's (general reference), 2, 15, 29, 39-43, 48, 57-75, 76, 83-84, 87, 93-95, 127, 133, 172. See also *Poetical Sketches*, individual seasons poem titles
Secreta Secretorum, 64, 172

Sequence, idea of, 39, 61, 63-64, 68, 83-85, 93-94, 101, 127, 150, 153, 172-73, 179. *See also* Cycles; Time
Shakespeare, William, 1-2, 5, 15, 25-27, 96-101, 107, 137-38, 160, 165, 176-78, 181, 188; as Blake's "Fiery Pegasus," 97, 180; Blake's illustrations to, 97; eighteenth-century imitations of, 164, 179. Works: *As You Like It*, 97, 169; *Cymbeline*, 177; *Hamlet*, 97, 178; *Henry V*, 96; history plays generally, 97-98; *Julius Caesar*, 97; *King Lear*, 15, 97, 169, 174, 178; *Macbeth*, 91, 97, 169; *Midsummer-Night's Dream*, 97, 177; *The Rape of Lucrece*, 4; *Richard III*, 97; Sonnets, 4; *The Tempest*, 169; *Venus and Adonis*, 4. *See also* Glory, theme of; Melancholy; War
Shawcross, John T., 188-90
Shelley, Percy Bysshe, 151; *Alastor*, 148; *Original Poetry by "Victor and Cazire,"* 149; *Posthumous Fragments of Margaret Nicholson*, 149; *Prometheus Unbound*, 101; review of, in *Poetical Register*, 149; *St. Irvyne, or the Rosicrucian*, 149; *The Wandering Jew*, 149; *Zastrozzi*, 149
Shenstone, William, 177; *Rural Elegance*, 90; *Song XV: Winter 1764*, 170
Sherbo, Arthur, 90, 177-78
Sherwin, Paul, 165-66, 176
Silence: in Blake, 83-84, 86, 89, 121, 127-28, 173; in Milton, 88, 177; in Spenser, 40, 86, 89
Simmons, Robert E., 169-70
Simpson, David, 165
Sleep: in Blake, 44, 49-50, 86; in Milton, 88
Smart, Christopher, 87
Songs in *Poetical Sketches* (general reference), 2, 15, 19-20, 44-56, 124. See also *Poetical Sketches*, individual poem titles
Southey, Robert, 149
Spacks, Patricia Meyer, 59
Spence, Joseph, *Polymetis*, 55
Spenser, Edmund, 4-5, 12, 15, 26-27, 54, 56, 58, 60, 64-65, 68, 87, 89, 137-38, 150-51, 153, 165, 178, 188; eighteenth-century imitations of, 2, 20, 22, 27, 29, 59, 151, 163-64; Spenserian stanza of, 26-27, 163. Works (other than *The Faerie Queene*, q.v.): *Amoretti*, 65, 76-77, 170, 172-74; *Colin Clout's Come Home Againe*, 65; *Epithalamion*, 40-41, 47-48, 64, 76-80, 82, 85-86, 88, 90, 92-93, 127, 136, 173, 176-77; *Fowre Hymnes*, 21, 170; *Muiopotmos*, 174; *Prothalamion*, 76, 176-77; *The Shepheardes*

The Johns Hopkins University Press

BLAKE'S PRELUDE

This book was composed in Baskerville text and Palatino display
type by David Lorton from a design by Lisa S. Mirski. It was
printed on S. D. Warren's 50-lb. Sebago Eggshell paper and
bound in Kivar 5 by Universal Lithographers, Inc.